# Managing Information with Technology

# Managing Information with Technology

# Business Statistics

Compiled from selected chapters from the following publications:

**BUSINESS STATISTICS FOR CONTEMPORARY DECISION MAKING**
**4TH EDITION UPDATE**
Ken Black

**SPSS VERSION 13.0 FOR WINDOWS:**
**ANALYSIS WITHOUT ANGUISH**
Sheridan J Coakes, Lyndall Steed, Peta Dzidic

*A Wiley Custom Services Publication*
*Prepared for: Brunel Business School*

John Wiley & Sons, Ltd
The Atrium, Southern Gate, Chichester,
West Sussex PO19 8SQ, England
Telephone    (+44) 1243 779777

Email (for orders and customer service enquiries): cs-books@wiley.co.uk
Visit our Home Page on www.wileyeurope.com or www.wiley.com

Taken from:

*Business Statistics For Contemporary Decision Making 4th Edition Update*
by Ken Black. ISBN 0-471-70563-2
© 2006 John Wiley & Sons, Inc.

*SPSS version 13.0 for Windows: Analysis without Anguish*
by Sheridan J Coakes, Lyndall Steed, Peta Dzidic ISBN-13 978-0-470-80914-3
Copyright © John Wiley & Sons, Inc. 2003

### *Other Wiley Editorial Offices*

John Wiley & Sons Inc., 111 River Street, Hoboken, NJ 07030, USA

Jossey-Bass, 989 Market Street, San Francisco, CA 94103-1741, USA

Wiley-VCH Verlag GmbH, Boschstr. 12, D-69469 Weinheim, Germany

John Wiley & Sons Australia Ltd, 33 Park Road, Milton, Queensland 4064, Australia

John Wiley & Sons (Asia) Pte Ltd, 2 Clementi Loop #02-01, Jin Xing Distripark, Singapore 129809

John Wiley & Sons Canada Ltd, 6045 Freemont Boulevard, Mississauga, Ontario, Canada L5R 4J3

Wiley also publishes its books in a variety of electronic formats. Some content that appears in print may not be available in electronic books.

ISBN 0-470-10983-1

Printed and bound in Great Britain by Antony Rowe, Ltd. Chippenham, Wiltshire.
This book is printed on acid-free paper responsibly manufactured from sustainable forestry in which at least two trees are planted for each one used for paper production.

# Contents

## 1 INTRODUCTION TO STATISTICS

Taken from *Business Stastics for Contemporary Decision Making 4th Edition Update*
Ken Black ISBN-10 0-471-70563-2 © 2006 John Wiley & Sons, Inc.

## 2  CHARTS AND GRAPHS

**17**

Taken from *Business Stastics for Contemporary Decision Making 4th Edition Update*
Ken Black ISBN-10 0-471-70563-2 © 2006 John Wiley & Sons, Inc.

## 3  DESCRIPTIVE STATISTICS

**45**

Taken from *Business Stastics for Contemporary Decision Making 4th Edition Update*
Ken Black ISBN-10 0-471-70563-2 © 2006 John Wiley & Sons, Inc.

Taken from *Business Stastics for Contemporary Decision Making 4th Edition Update*
Ken Black ISBN-10 0-471-70563-2 © 2006 John Wiley & Sons, Inc.

## 5    PREPARATION OF DATA FIILES                                                                 159

Taken from *SPSS Version 13.0 for Windows: Analysis without Anguish*,
Sheridan J Coakes, Lyndall Steed, Peta Dzidic  ISBN-10  0-470-80914-0,
ISBN-13  978-0-470-80914-3 ©2006 Sheridan J Coakes, Lyndall Steed, Peta Dzidic.

## 6   DESCRIPTIVE STATISTICS                                                    168

Taken from *SPSS Version 13.0 for Windows: Analysis without Anguish*,
Sheridan J Coakes, Lyndall Steed, Peta Dzidic  ISBN-10  0-470-80914-0,
ISBN-13  978-0-470-80914-3  ©2006 Sheridan J Coakes, Lyndall Steed, Peta Dzidic.

## 7   CORRELATION                                                               174

Taken from *SPSS Version 13.0 for Windows: Analysis without Anguish*,
Sheridan J Coakes, Lyndall Steed, Peta Dzidic  ISBN-10  0-470-80914-0,
ISBN-13  978-0-470-80914-3  ©2006 Sheridan J Coakes, Lyndall Steed, Peta Dzidic.

## 8   T-TESTS                                                                   179

Taken from *SPSS Version 13.0 for Windows: Analysis without Anguish*,
Sheridan J Coakes, Lyndall Steed, Peta Dzidic  ISBN-10  0-470-80914-0,
ISBN-13  978-0-470-80914-3  ©2006 Sheridan J Coakes, Lyndall Steed, Peta Dzidic.

# CHAPTER 1

# Introduction to Statistics

**LEARNING OBJECTIVES**

The primary objective of Chapter 1 is to introduce you to the world of statistics, thereby enabling you to:

1. Define statistics.
2. Become aware of a wide range of applications of statistics in business.
3. Differentiate between descriptive and inferential statistics.
4. Classify numbers by level of data and understand why doing so is important.

*Business Statistics For Contemporary Decision Making 4th Edition Update,*
Ken Black . ISBN-10 0-471-70563-2 ©2006 John Wiley & Sons, Inc.

India is the second largest country in the world, with more than a billion people. Three-quarters of the people live in rural areas, yet the rural market accounts for only about one-third of total national product sales. However, because of free-market reforms in the 1990s and a strong agricultural output, India's rural market has become more open for trade in consumer goods. Although India's urban market seems to be saturated, markets in rural India are relatively untapped, offering enormous potential. Because of these factors, many U.S. firms, such as Microsoft, General Electric, Kellogg's, and others, have entered the Indian market.

Presently, rural India can be described as poor and semi-illiterate. More than 65% of the people in rural India earn less than $574 annually, and 23% earn between $574 and $1,146. Sixty-six percent of the women are illiterate, as are 38% of the men. These rates are about double those for urban Indians. Seventy-seven percent of the households in rural India use wood as the cooking fuel, 39% have electricity, 18% have piped water, and 7% have flush toilets.

Nevertheless, conditions are changing and companies are moving into this relatively untapped market. For example, by the late 1990s, Colgate-Palmolive planned to increase its rural marketing budget to five times that of 1991. Colgate-Palmolive India's goal is that more than half its revenue by the year 2003 comes from rural India, which presently accounts for only about 30% of business.

Marketing to rural India is a challenging task and requires some nontraditional approaches because the illiteracy rates are high and only about one-third of the households have a television. One such technique is the use of video vans in which half-hour infomercials are carried through the countryside. A video van cruises into a small hamlet with speakers playing a popular movie melody. As shoppers congregate to the van, a marketer opens the door and plays a video on a screen with scenarios depicting the need for a particular product. After the video is completed, free samples are distributed. Hindustan Lever Ltd., India's leading consumer-products company, estimates that the cost per contact of such marketing is about four times the cost to city dwellers. However, the rural market for personal care products is growing about three times faster than city markets, which makes such marketing efforts more viable. Other companies use direct door-to-door campaigns to promote products to rural India. In addition, the advent of satellite television to rural homes and villages in India opens up some new avenues for advertising and marketing to this population segment.

Statistics available from the first half of the 1990s shed some light on the potential market of rural India. Toothpaste consumption in rural India doubled from 8,825 metric tons in 1990 to 17,023 in 1994. The annual per capita consumption for toothpaste is still only 30 grams per person in rural India compared to 160 grams in urban India and 400 grams in the United States. Thus, the potential for much growth is there. Sales of other products have been growing rapidly in this emerging market. The sales of laundry detergent increased from 272,540 metric tons in 1990 to 422,741 metric tons in 1994. Toilet soap went from 158,919 metric tons in 1990 to 231,084 metric tons in 1994. Shampoo increased in sales nearly fourfold from 497,000 liters in 1990 to 2,116,000 liters in 1994.

Rural India is a huge untapped market for businesses. Some evidence indicates that rural Indian consumers are buying products in increasing numbers. However, annual income statistics show a limited purchasing capacity. The dilemma facing companies is whether to enter this marketplace, and if so, to what extent and how.

3

### Managerial and Statistical Questions

1. What kinds of statistics are presented in this report?
2. Are these data exact figures or estimates?
3. How would researchers go about gathering such data?
4. In measuring rural India as a marketplace, what other statistics could be gathered?
5. What levels of data measurement are represented in these data? If other statistics were gathered, what other levels of data measurement might be represented?
6. How could managers use these statistics to make better decisions about entering this marketplace?

*Source:* Adapted from Raja Ramachandran, "Understanding the Market Environment of India," *Business Horizons*, January 2000; Miriam Jordan, "In Rural India, Video Vans Sell Toothpaste and Shampoo," *Wall Street Journal*, 10 January 1996; Rinku Pegu, "Maya bazar," *The Week*, 30 May 1999, http://www.the-week.com/99may30/biz2.htm.

---

Every minute of the working day, decisions are made by businesses around the world that determine whether companies will be profitable and growing or whether they will stagnate and die. Most of these decisions are made with the assistance of information gathered about the marketplace, the economic and financial environment, the workforce, the competition, and other factors. Such information usually comes in the form of data or is accompanied by data. Business statistics provides the tool through which such data are collected, analyzed, summarized, and presented to facilitate the decision-making process. Thus, in the twenty-first century, business statistics plays an important role in the ongoing saga of decision making within the dynamic world of business.

## 1.1 STATISTICS IN BUSINESS

Virtually every area of business uses statistics in decision making. Here are examples of the use of statistics in several areas of business.

### Best Way to Market

A survey conducted by Pitney Bowes of 302 directors and vice presidents of marketing and marketing communications at midsize and large U.S. companies revealed that almost 35% said that direct mail or catalogs were the most cost-effective way to reach customers. Eleven percent felt that the Internet was most cost-effective. The study also showed that more than 25% said that the best way to increase brand identity was through direct mail or catalogs. These and other statistics gathered and summarized in this study can help decision makers solve the dilemma of finding cost-effective vehicles for their products.

### Stress on the Job

If decision makers are looking for ways to reduce healthcare expenses among their workforce, then they might do well to learn from a study of some 46,000 employees conducted by the Health Enhancement Research Organization. In it, the researchers discovered that depression and stress seem to have a greater impact on higher medical expenses than do high blood sugar, obesity, or smoking. The study showed that depressed workers had medical expenses 70% higher than nondepressed workers and that workers who said they were under constant stress had expenditures 46% higher than stress-free peers. On the other hand, the medical expenses for people who suffer from high blood pressure were just 11% higher than for those who do not. This information, along with other statistics reported in this study, can help decision makers to develop a strategy for reducing medical expenses among workers.

## Financial Decisions

In a study reported by RHI Management Resources, chief financial officers were asked which *one* of the following initiatives they would most likely put on hold in an uncertain economy: (1) expansion, (2) merger or acquisition, (3) new product or service launch, (4) technology upgrade, (5) none, and (6) other. Thirty-two percent of the respondents indicated that they would put expansion plans on hold in an uncertain economy followed by merger or acquisition (23%), technology upgrade (18%), new product or service launch (10%), none (9%), and other (8%).

## How Is the Economy Doing?

A *Wall Street Journal* report published to help investors and other decision makers track the state of the economy included such business statistics as the number of new home sales, an index of consumer confidence, the percentage increase in the gross domestic product, the number of initial jobless claims, and the unemployment rate. These statistics and others can serve as indicators of economic and financial states to come and can be used by forecasters as they attempt to predict future business climates. Figure 1.1 is an Excel-produced graph of the Consumer Price Index for all urban consumers every five years for the past 40 years. The data were published by the Federal Reserve Bank in St. Louis.

## The Impact of Technology at Work

Greenfield Online conducted an Internet survey of 1,403 respondents for the Society of Financial Service Professionals to determine whether technology users appreciate the benefits of technology more in 2001 than in 1998. Eighty-seven percent of the respondents in 2001 said that technology expands job-related knowledge compared to 54% in 1998. Eighty percent in 2001 agreed that technology increases productivity during normal work hours compared to 66% in 1998. Eighty percent in 2001 responded that technology improves communication with clients and customers compared to only 42% in 1998. Fifty-four percent in 2001 said that technology relieves job stress as compared to only 26% in 1998.

In this text we will examine several types of graphs for depicting data as we study ways to arrange or structure data into forms that are both meaningful and useful to decision makers. We will learn about techniques for sampling from a population that allow studies of the business world to be conducted more inexpensively and in a more timely manner. We will explore various ways to forecast future values and examine techniques for predicting trends. This text also includes many statistical tools for testing hypotheses and for estimating population values. These and many other exciting statistics and statistical techniques await us on this journey through business statistics. Let us begin.

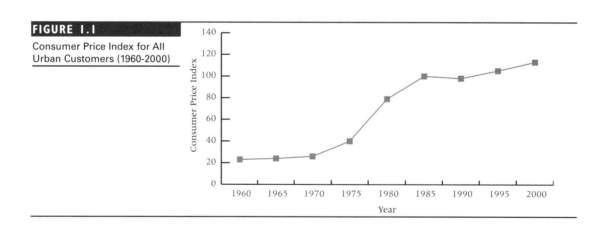

**FIGURE 1.1**

Consumer Price Index for All Urban Customers (1960-2000)

## 1.2 BASIC STATISTICAL CONCEPTS

Business statistics, like many areas of study, has its own language. It is important to begin our study with an introduction of some basic concepts in order to understand and communicate about the subject. We begin with a discussion of the word *statistics*. The word statistics has many different meanings in our culture. *Webster's Third New International Dictionary* gives a comprehensive definition of **statistics** as *a science dealing with the collection, analysis, interpretation, and presentation of numerical data.* Viewed from this perspective, statistics includes all the topics presented in this text. Statistics also is a branch of mathematics, and most of the science of statistics is based on mathematical thought and derivation. Many academic areas, including business, offer statistics courses within their own disciplines. However, statistics has become a course of study in its own right.

People often use the word *statistics* to refer to a group of data. They may say, for example, that they gathered statistics from their business operation. What they are referring to is measured facts and figures. The media and others also use the word *statistic* to refer to a death. Becoming a statistic in this sense of the word obviously is undesirable.

The word *statistics* is used in at least two other important ways. First, statistics can be descriptive measures computed from a sample and used to make determinations about a population. This usage is discussed later. Second, statistics can be the distributions used in the analysis of data. For example, a researcher using the $t$ distribution to analyze data might refer to use of the $t$ statistic in analyzing the data.

The following are some of the common uses of the word *statistics*.

1. Science of gathering, analyzing, interpreting, and presenting data
2. Branch of mathematics
3. Course of study
4. Facts and figures
5. A death
6. Measurement taken on a sample
7. Type of distribution used to analyze data

The study of statistics can be organized in a variety of ways. One of the main ways is to subdivide statistics into two branches: descriptive statistics and inferential statistics. To understand the difference between descriptive and inferential statistics, definitions of population and sample are helpful. *Webster's Third New International Dictionary* defines **population** as *a collection of persons, objects, or items of interest.* The population can be a widely defined category, such as "all automobiles," or it can be narrowly defined, such as "all Ford Mustang cars produced from 1998 to 2002." A population can be a group of people, such as "all workers presently employed by Microsoft," or it can be a set of objects, such as "all dishwashers produced on February 3, 2003, by the General Electric Company at the Louisville plant." The researcher defines the population to be whatever he or she is studying. When researchers *gather data from the whole population for a given measurement of interest,* they call it a **census.** Most people are familiar with the U.S. Census. Every 10 years, the government attempts to measure all persons living in this country. If a researcher is interested in ascertaining the Scholastic Aptitude Test (SAT) scores for all students at the University of Arizona, one way to do so is to conduct a census of all students currently enrolled at that university.

A **sample** is *a portion of the whole* and, if properly taken, is representative of the whole. For various reasons (explained in Chapter 7), researchers often prefer to work with a sample of the population instead of the entire population. For example, in conducting quality control experiments to determine the average life of lightbulbs, a lightbulb manufacturer might randomly sample only 75 lightbulbs during a production run. Because of time and money limitations, a human resources manager might take a random sample of 40 employees instead of using a census to measure company morale.

If a business analyst is *using data gathered on a group to describe or reach conclusions about that same group,* the statistics are called **descriptive statistics.** For example, if an instructor produces statistics to summarize a class's examination effort and uses those statistics to reach conclusions about that class only, the statistics are descriptive. The instructor can use these statistics to discuss class average, talk about the range of class scores, or present any other data measurements for the class based on the test.

Most athletic statistics, such as batting average, rebounds, and first downs, are descriptive statistics because they are used to describe an individual or team effort. Many of the statistical data generated by businesses are descriptive. They might include number of employees on vacation during June, average salary at the Denver office, corporate sales for 2002, average managerial satisfaction score on a company-wide census of employee attitudes, and average return on investment for the Lofton Company for the years 1988 through 2002.

Another type of statistics is called **inferential statistics.** If a researcher *gathers data from a sample and uses the statistics generated to reach conclusions about the population from which the sample was taken*, the statistics are inferential statistics. The data gathered are used to infer something about a larger group. Inferential statistics are sometimes referred to as *inductive statistics*. The use and importance of inferential statistics continue to grow.

One application of inferential statistics is in pharmaceutical research. Some new drugs are expensive to produce, and therefore tests must be limited to small samples of patients. Utilizing inferential statistics, researchers can design experiments with small randomly selected samples of patients and attempt to reach conclusions and make inferences about the population.

Market researchers use inferential statistics to study the impact of advertising on various market segments. Suppose a soft drink company creates an advertisement depicting a dispensing machine that talks to the buyer and market researchers want to measure the impact of the new advertisement on various age groups. The researcher could stratify the population into age categories ranging from young to old, randomly sample each stratum, and use inferential statistics to determine the effectiveness of the advertisement for the various age groups in the population. The advantage of using inferential statistics is that they enable the researcher to study effectively a wide range of phenomena without having to conduct a census. Most of the topics discussed in this text pertain to inferential statistics.

A *descriptive measure of the population* is called a **parameter.** Parameters are usually denoted by Greek letters. Examples of parameters are population mean ($\mu$), population variance ($\sigma^2$), and population standard deviation ($\sigma$). A *descriptive measure of a sample* is called a **statistic.** Statistics are usually denoted by Roman letters. Examples of statistics are sample mean ($\bar{x}$), sample variance ($s^2$), and sample standard deviation ($s$).

Differentiation between the terms *parameter* and *statistic* is important only in the use of inferential statistics. A business researcher often wants to estimate the value of a parameter or conduct tests about the parameter. However, the calculation of parameters is usually either impossible or infeasible because of the amount of time and money required to take a census. In such cases, the business researcher can take a random sample of the population, calculate a statistic on the sample, and infer by estimation the value of the parameter. The basis for inferential statistics, then, is the ability to make decisions about parameters without having to complete a census of the population.

For example, a manufacturer of washing machines would probably want to determine the average number of loads that a new machine can wash before it needs repairs. The parameter is the population mean or average number of washes per machine before repair. A company statistician takes a sample of machines, computes the number of washes before repair for each machine, averages the numbers, and estimates the population value or parameter by using the statistic, which in this case is the sample average. Figure 1.2 demonstrates the inferential process.

Inferences about parameters are made under uncertainty. Unless parameters are computed directly from the population, the statistician never knows with certainty whether the estimates or inferences made from samples are true. In an effort to estimate the level of confidence in the result of the process, statisticians use probability statements. Therefore, part of this text is devoted to probability (Chapter 4).

Calculate $\bar{x}$
to estimate $\mu$

Population
$\mu$
(parameter)

Sample
$\bar{x}$
(statistic)

Select a
random sample

## 1.3 DATA MEASUREMENT

Millions of numerical data are gathered in businesses every day, representing myriad items. For example, numbers represent dollar costs of items produced, geographical locations of retail outlets, weights of shipments, and rankings of subordinates at yearly reviews. All such data should not be analyzed the same way statistically because the entities represented by the numbers are different. For this reason, the business researcher needs to know the *level of data measurement* represented by the numbers being analyzed.

The disparate use of numbers can be illustrated by the numbers 40 and 80, which could represent the weights of two objects being shipped, the ratings received on a consumer test by two different products, or the football jersey numbers of a fullback and a wide receiver. Although 80 pounds is twice as much as 40 pounds, the wide receiver is probably not twice as big as the fullback! Averaging the two weights seems reasonable but averaging the football jersey numbers makes no sense. The appropriateness of the data analysis depends on the level of measurement of the data gathered. The phenomenon represented by the numbers determines the level of data measurement. Four common levels of data measurement follow.

1. Nominal
2. Ordinal
3. Interval
4. Ratio

### Nominal Level

The *lowest level of data measurement* is the **nominal level.** Numbers representing nominal-level data (the word *level* often is omitted) can be *used only to classify or categorize.* Employee identification numbers are an example of nominal data. The numbers are used only to differentiate employees and not to make a value statement about them. Many demographic questions in surveys result in data that are nominal because the questions are used for classification only. The following is an example of such a question that would result in nominal data:

Which of the following employment classifications best describes your area of work?

a. Educator
b. Construction worker
c. Manufacturing worker
d. Lawyer
e. Doctor
f. Other

Suppose that, for computing purposes, an educator is assigned a 1, a construction worker is assigned a 2, a manufacturing worker is assigned a 3, and so on. These numbers should be used only to classify respondents. The number 1 does not denote the top classification. It is used only to differentiate an educator (1) from a lawyer (4).

Some other types of variables that often produce nominal-level data are gender, religion, ethnicity, geographic location, and place of birth. Social security numbers, telephone numbers, employee ID numbers, and ZIP code numbers are further examples of nominal data. Statistical techniques that are appropriate for analyzing nominal data are limited. However, some of the more widely used statistics, such as the chi-square statistic, can be applied to nominal data, often producing useful information.

## Ordinal Level

**Ordinal-level data** measurement is higher than the nominal level. In addition to the nominal-level capabilities, ordinal-level measurement can be used to rank or order objects. For example, using ordinal data, a supervisor can evaluate three employees by ranking their productivity with the numbers 1 through 3. The supervisor could identify one employee as the most productive, one as the least productive, and one as somewhere between by using ordinal data. However, the supervisor could not use ordinal data to establish that the intervals between the employees ranked 1 and 2 and between the employees ranked 2 and 3 are equal; that is, she could not say that the differences in the amount of productivity between workers ranked 1, 2, and 3 are necessarily the same. With ordinal data, the distances or spacing represented by consecutive numbers are not always equal.

Some questionnaire Likert-type scales are considered by many researchers to be ordinal in level. The following is an example of one such scale:

| This computer tutorial is | ___ | ___ | ___ | ___ | ___ |
|---|---|---|---|---|---|
| | not helpful | somewhat helpful | moderately helpful | very helpful | extremely helpful |
| | 1 | 2 | 3 | 4 | 5 |

When this survey question is coded for the computer, only the numbers 1 through 5 will remain, not the adjectives. Virtually everyone would agree that a 5 is higher than a 4 on this scale and that ranking responses is possible. However, most respondents would not consider the differences between not helpful, somewhat helpful, moderately helpful, very helpful, and extremely helpful to be equal.

Mutual funds as investments are sometimes rated in terms of risk by using measures of default risk, currency risk, and interest rate risk. These three measures are applied to investments by rating them as having high, medium, and low risk. Suppose high risk is assigned a 3, medium risk a 2, and low risk a 1. If a fund is awarded a 3 rather than a 2, it carries more risk, and so on. However, the differences in risk between categories 1, 2, and 3 are not necessarily equal. Thus, these measurements of risk are only ordinal-level measurements. Another example of the use of ordinal numbers in business is the ranking of the top 50 most admired companies in *Fortune* magazine. The numbers ranking the companies are only ordinal in measurement. Certain statistical techniques are specifically suited to ordinal data, but many other techniques are not appropriate for use on ordinal data.

Because nominal and ordinal data are often derived from imprecise measurements such as demographic questions, the categorization of people or objects, or the ranking of items, *nominal and ordinal data* are **nonmetric data** and are sometimes referred to as *qualitative data.*

## Interval Level

**Interval-level data** measurement is the *next to the highest level of data in which the distances between consecutive numbers have meaning and the data are always numerical.* The distances represented by the differences between consecutive numbers are equal; that is, interval data have equal intervals. An example of interval measurement is Fahrenheit temperature. With Fahrenheit temperature numbers, the temperatures can be ranked, and the amounts of heat between consecutive readings, such as 20°, 21°, and 22°, are the same.

In addition, with interval-level data, the zero point is a matter of convention or convenience and not a natural or fixed zero point. Zero is just another point on the scale and does not mean the absence of the phenomenon. For example, zero degrees Fahrenheit is not the lowest possible temperature. Some other examples of interval level data are the percentage change in employment, the percentage return on a stock, and the dollar change in stock price.

With interval level data, converting the units from one measurement to another involves multiplying by some factor, $a$, and adding another factor, $b$, such that $y = b + ax$. As an example, converting from centigrade temperature to Fahrenheit temperature involves the relationship.

$$\text{Fahrenheit} = 32 + \frac{9}{5}\text{centigrade}$$

## Ratio Level

**Ratio-level data** measurement is *the highest level of data measurement*. Ratio data *have the same properties as interval data,* but ratio data have an *absolute zero* and *the ratio of two numbers is meaningful*. The notion of absolute zero means that zero is fixed, and *the zero value in the data represents the absence of the characteristic being studied.* The value of zero cannot be arbitrarily assigned because it represents a fixed point. This definition enables the statistician to create *ratios* with the data.

Examples of ratio data are height, weight, time, volume, and Kelvin temperature. With ratio data, a researcher can state that 180 pounds of weight is twice as much as 90 pounds or, in other words, make a ratio of 180:90. Many of the data gathered by machines in industry are ratio data.

Other examples in the business world that are ratio level in measurement are production cycle time, work measurement time, passenger miles, number of trucks sold, complaints per 10,000 fliers, and number of employees. With ratio-level data, no $b$ factor is required in converting units from one measurement to another, that is, $y = ax$. As an example, in converting height from yards to feet: feet = 3 · yards.

Because interval- and ratio-level data are usually gathered by precise instruments often used in production and engineering processes, in national standardized testing, or in standardized accounting procedures, they are called **metric data** and are sometimes referred to as *quantitative* data.

## Comparison of the Four Levels of Data

Figure 1.3 shows the relationships of the usage potential among the four levels of data measurement. The concentric squares denote that each higher level of data can be analyzed by any of the techniques used on lower levels of data but, in addition, can be used in other statistical techniques. Therefore, ratio data can be analyzed by any statistical technique applicable to the other three levels of data plus some others.

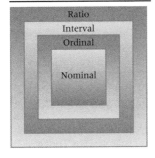

**FIGURE 1.3**

Usage Potential of Various Levels of Data

Ratio
Interval
Ordinal
Nominal

Nominal data are the most limited data in terms of the types of statistical analysis that can be used with them. Ordinal data allow the researcher to perform any analysis that can be done with nominal data and some additional analyses. With ratio data, a statistician can make ratio comparisons and appropriately do any analysis that can be performed on nominal, ordinal, or interval data. Some statistical techniques require ratio data and cannot be used to analyze other levels of data.

Statistical techniques can be separated into two categories: parametric statistics and nonparametric statistics. **Parametric statistics** require that data be interval or ratio. If the data are nominal or ordinal, **nonparametric statistics** must be used. Nonparametric statistics can also be used to analyze interval or ratio data. This text focuses largely on parametric statistics, with the exception of Chapter 12 and Chapter 17, which contain nonparametric techniques. Thus much of the material in this text requires that data be interval or ratio data.

| DEMONSTRATION PROBLEM 1.1 |
|---|

Many changes continue to occur in the healthcare industry. Because of increased competition for patients among providers and the need to determine how providers can better serve their clientele, hospital administrators sometimes mail a quality satisfaction survey to their patients after the patient is released. The following types of questions are sometimes asked on such a survey. These questions will result in what level of data measurement?

1. How long ago were you released from the hospital?
2. Which type of unit were you in for most of your stay?
   ___ Coronary care
   ___ Intensive care
   ___ Maternity care
   ___ Medical unit
   ___ Pediatric/children's unit
   ___ Surgical unit
3. In choosing a hospital, how important was the hospital's location?

   (circle one)

   | Very Important | Somewhat Important | Not Very Important | Not at All Important |
   |---|---|---|---|

4. How serious was your condition when you were first admitted to the hospital?
   ___Critical    ___Serious    ___Moderate    ___Minor
5. Rate the skill of your doctor:
   ___Excellent    ___Very Good    ___Good    ___Fair    ___Poor
6. On the following scale from one to seven, rate the nursing care:
   Poor   1   2   3   4   5   6   7   Excellent

*Solution*

Question 1 is a time measurement with an absolute zero and is therefore ratio-level measurement. A person who has been out of the hospital for two weeks has been out twice as long as someone who has been out of the hospital for one week.

Question 2 yields nominal data because the patient is asked only to categorize the type of unit he or she was in. This question does not require a hierarchy or ranking of the type of unit. Questions 3, 4, and 5 are likely to result in ordinal-level data. Suppose a number is assigned the descriptors in each of these three questions. For question 3, "very important" might be assigned a 4, "somewhat important" a 3, "not very important" a 2, and "not at all important" a 1. Certainly, the higher the number, the more important is the hospital's location. Thus, these responses can be ranked by selection. However, the increases in importance from 1 to 2 to 3 to 4 are not necessarily equal. This same logic applies to the numeric values assigned in questions 4 and 5.

Question 6 displays seven numeric choices with equal distances between the numbers shown on the scale and no adjective descriptors assigned to the numbers. Many researchers would declare this to be interval-level measurement because of the equal distance between numbers and the absence of a true zero on this scale. Some researchers might argue that because of the imprecision of the scale and the vagueness of selecting values between "poor" and "excellent" the measurement is only ordinal in level.

## Statistical Analysis Using the Computer: Excel and MINITAB

The advent of the modern computer opened many new opportunities for statistical analysis. The computer allows for storage, retrieval, and transfer of large data sets. Furthermore, computer software has been developed to analyze data by means of sophisticated statistical techniques. Some widely used statistical techniques, such as multiple regression, are so tedious and cumbersome to compute manually that they were of little practical use to researchers before computers were developed.

Business statisticians use many popular statistical software packages, including MINITAB, SAS, and SPSS. Many computer spreadsheet software packages also have the capability of analyzing data statistically. In this text, the computer statistical output presented is from both the MINITAB and the Microsoft Excel software.

## Statistics Describe the State of Business in India's Countryside

In the Decision Dilemma, many statistics were reported about rural India, its potential as a market, and its sales. Total sales figures are given for both 1990 and 1994 for four different products. The average annual consumption of toothpaste per person is reported. Percentages describing demographic characteristics of rural India are given including illiteracy rates and possession of household conveniences. The authors of the sources from which the Decision Dilemma is drawn never state whether the figures are actual figures drawn from a census of rural Indians or estimates taken from a sample of such people. If the figures come from a census, then the totals, averages, and percentages presented in the Decision Dilemma are parameters. Because governments sometimes conduct censuses, these data could be parameters. However, more often than not, data are gathered from samples of people or things. In many countries, researchers are capable of gathering relatively accurate, useful data by taking a well-planned sample that is representative of the population. The resulting data are analyzed producing statistics that, in turn, can be used to estimate population parameters. This process is an inferential process. A variety of reasons would make the use of an inferential process preferable to conducting a census. In Chapter 7, we will explore the use of sampling in greater detail.

In this particular situation, whether to market to rural India, researchers could be sent to representative areas of rural India and consumers could be surveyed about their economic state, their ownership of possessions, their personal and family characteristics, their consumer usage of products, and their willingness to expand their purchasing. A wide variety of statistics could be gathered representing several levels of data. For example, ratio-level measurements on such things as income, number of children, age of household

## STATISTICS IN BUSINESS TODAY

### U.S. Wireless Usage Grows

According to a Cellular Telecommunications & Internet Association's semiannual wireless industry survey, more than 110 million customers in the United States used wireless in the year 2001. This figure represented a growth of almost 28% from the end of 1999. Not only were more people using wireless devices, they were using them more often. The average length of a call by 2001 was 3 minutes compared to 2 minutes and 38 seconds at the end of 1999. The average monthly bill for wireless usage, reflecting this increase in usage, went from $41.24 to $45.27 over the same one-year period.

Total revenues for U.S. wireless operators topped $50 billion for the year 2000. Roaming revenues were down reflecting continued network expansion. As carriers expand their covered territories, roaming revenues decrease because users are in the network more often.

What will happen to wireless usage in the future? As the market becomes more mature, will usage level off? Will factors such as public safety concerns, driving laws, personal safety, or etiquette debates curb the usage of wireless devices? These and other questions can be addressed through the gathering and analysis of business statistics.

*Source:* Adapted from "No Slump in U.S. Wireless Usage," *allNetDevices*, 27 April 2001, http://www.allnetdevices.com/wireless/news/2001/04/27/no_slump.html

## ETHICAL CONSIDERATIONS

With the abundance and proliferation of statistical data, potential misuse of statistics in business dealings is a concern. It is, in effect, unethical business behavior to use statistics out of context. Unethical business people might use only selective data from studies to underscore their point, omitting statistics from the same studies that argue against their case. The results of statistical studies can be misstated or overstated to gain favor.

This chapter noted that if data are nominal or ordinal, then only nonparametric statistics are appropriate for analysis. The use of parametric statistics to analyze nominal and/or ordinal data is wrong and could be considered under some circumstances to be unethical.

In this text, each chapter contains a section on ethics that discusses how businesses can misuse the techniques presented in the chapter in an unethical manner. As both users and producers, business students need to be aware of the potential ethical pitfalls that can occur with statistics.

heads, number of livestock, value of house/land, and grams of toothpaste consumed per year might be obtained. In some instances, Likert scales (1-to-5 measurements) are used to gather responses about interests and likes, thus producing an ordinal-level of measurement. For privacy reasons, some question topics such as age or income are stated in class ranges also resulting in an ordinal level of measurement. In addition, rural Indians may be asked to rank a variety of products in terms of which they would be most likely to purchase, yielding ordinal data. Other variables such as geographic location, political party affiliation, occupation, and religion result in nominal data.

The decision to enter the rural India market is not just a marketing decision. It involves production capacity and schedule issues, transportation challenges, financial commitments, managerial growth or reassignment, accounting issues (accounting for rural India may differ from techniques used in traditional markets), information systems, and other related areas. With so much on the line, company decision makers need as much relevant information available as possible. In this Decision Dilemma, it is obvious to the decision maker that rural India is still quite poor and illiterate. Its capacity as a market is great. The statistics on the increasing sales of a few personal-care products look promising. What are the future forecasts for the earning power of people in rural India? Will major cultural issues block the adoption of the types of products that companies want to sell there? The answers to these and many other interesting and useful questions can be obtained by the appropriate use of statistics. The 750 million people living in rural India represent the second largest group of people in the world. It certainly is a market segment worth studying further.

## SUMMARY

Statistics is an important decision-making tool in business and is used in virtually every area of business. The word *statistics* has many different connotations. Among the more common meanings of the word are (1) the science of gathering, analyzing, interpreting, and presenting data, (2) a branch of mathematics, (3) a course of study, (4) facts and figures, (5) a death, (6) sample measurement, and (7) type of distribution used to analyze data. Statistics are broadly used in business, including the disciplines of accounting, decision sciences, economics, finance, management, management information systems, marketing, and production.

The study of statistics can be subdivided into two main areas: *descriptive statistics* and *inferential statistics*.

Descriptive statistics result from gathering data from a body, group, or population and reaching conclusions only about that group. Inferential statistics are generated from the process of gathering sample data from a group, body, or population and reaching conclusions about the larger group from which the sample was drawn.

The appropriate type of statistical analysis depends on the level of data measurement, which can be (1) *nominal,* (2) *ordinal,* (3) *interval,* or (4) *ratio.* Nominal is the lowest level, representing classification of only such data as geographic location, gender, or social security number. The next level is ordinal, which provides rank ordering measurements in which the intervals between consecutive numbers do not necessarily represent equal distances. Interval is the next to highest level of data measurement in which the distances represented by consecutive numbers are equal. The highest level of data measurement is ratio, which has all the qualities of interval measurement, but ratio data contain an absolute zero and ratios between numbers are meaningful. Interval and ratio data sometimes are called *metric* or *quantitative* data. Nominal and ordinal data sometimes are called *nonmetric* or *qualitative* data.

The two major types of inferential statistics are (1) *parametric statistics* and (2) *nonparametric statistics.* Use of parametric statistics requires interval or ratio data and certain assumptions about the distribution of the data. The techniques presented in this text are largely parametric. If data are only nominal or ordinal in level, nonparametric statistics must be used.

## KEY TERMS

| | | | |
|---|---|---|---|
| census | metric data | ordinal-level data | ratio-level data |
| descriptive statistics | nominal-level data | parameter | sample |
| inferential statistics | nonmetric data | parametric statistics | statistic |
| interval-level data | nonparametric statistics | population | statistics |

## SUPPLEMENTARY PROBLEMS

1.1   Give a specific example of data that might be gathered from each of the following business disciplines: accounting, finance, human resources, marketing, information systems, production, and management. An example in the marketing area might be "number of sales per month by each salesperson."

1.2   State examples of data that can be gathered for decision-making purposes from each of the following industries: manufacturing, insurance, travel, retailing, communications, computing, agriculture, banking, and healthcare. An example in the travel industry might be the cost of business travel per day in various European cities.

1.3   Give an example of *descriptive* statistics in the recorded music industry. Give an example of how *inferential* statistics could be used in the recorded music industry. Compare the two examples. What makes them different?

1.4   Suppose you are an operations manager for a plant that manufactures batteries. Give an example of how you could use *descriptive* statistics to make better managerial decisions. Give an example of how you could use *inferential* statistics to make better managerial decisions.

1.5   Classify each of the following as nominal, ordinal, interval, or ratio data.

   a. The time required to produce each tire on an assembly line

   b. The number of quarts of milk a family drinks in a month

   c. The ranking of four machines in your plant after they have been designated as excellent, good, satisfactory, and poor

   d. The telephone area code of clients in the United States

   e. The age of each of your employees

   f. The dollar sales at the local pizza house each month

   g. An employee's ID number

   h. The response time of an emergency unit

1.6   Classify each of the following as nominal, ordinal, interval, or ratio data.

   a. The ranking of a company by *Fortune* 500

   b. The number of tickets sold at a movie theater on any given night

   c. The identification number on a questionnaire

   d. Per capita income

   e. The trade balance in dollars

   f. Socioeconomic class (low, middle, upper)

   g. Profit/loss in dollars

   h. A company's tax ID

   i. The Standard & Poor's bond ratings of cities based on the following scales.

| Rating | Grade |
|---|---|
| Highest quality | AAA |
| High quality | AA |
| Upper medium quality | A |
| Medium quality | BBB |
| Somewhat speculative | BB |
| Low quality, speculative | B |
| Low grade, default possible | CCC |
| Low grade, partial recovery possible | CC |
| Default, recovery unlikely | C |

1.7   The Rathburn Manufacturing Company makes electric wiring, which it sells to contractors in the construction industry. Approximately 900 electric contractors purchase wire from Rathburn annually. Rathburn's director of marketing wants to determine electric contractors' satisfaction with Rathburn's wire. He developed a questionnaire that yields a satisfaction score between 10 and 50 for participant responses. A random sample of 35 of the 900 contractors is asked to complete a satisfaction

survey. The satisfaction scores for the 35 participants are averaged to produce a mean satisfaction score.

a. What is the population for this study?
b. What is the sample for this study?
c. What is the statistic for this study?
d. What would be a parameter for this study?

## ANALYZING THE DATABASES

*see* **www.wiley.com/college/black**

Seven major databases constructed for this text can be used for applying the techniques presented in this course. These databases are found on the CD-ROM that accompanies this text, and each of these databases is available in either MINITAB or Excel format for your convenience. These seven databases represent a wide variety of business areas, such as the stock market, manufacturing, international labor, finance, energy, healthcare, and agribusiness. Altogether, these databases contain 56 variables and 8,350 observations. The data are gathered from such reliable sources as the U.S. government's Bureau of Labor, the New York Stock Exchange, the U.S. Department of Agriculture, *Moody's Handbook of Common Stocks,* the American Hospital Association, and the U.S. Census Bureau. Four of the seven databases contain time-series data that can be especially useful in forecasting and regression analysis. Here is a description of each database along with information that may help you to interpret outcomes.

### Stock Market Database

The stock market database contains eight variables on the New York Stock Exchange. Three observations per month for nine years yields a total of 324 observations per variable. The variables include Composite Index, Industrial Index, Transportation Index, Utility Index, Stock Volume, Reported Trades, Dollar Value, and Warrants Volume. Dollar value is reported in units of millions of dollars. Recognizing that time of the month may make a difference in the value of an observation, each variable contains an observation from on or near to the tenth of the month denoted in the database as 1 under the variable Part of the Month, an observation from on or near to the twentieth of the month denoted as 2, and an observation from on or near to the thirtieth of the month denoted as 3. This database was constructed from data displayed on the Internet by the New York Stock Exchange. The original data can be accessed at the Data Library at http://www.nyse.com/marketinfo/marketinfo.html under the title "NYSE Statistics Archive."

### Manufacturing Database

This database contains eight variables taken from 20 industries and 140 subindustries in the United States. The source of the database is the *1996 Annual Survey of Manufactures,* which is published by the Census Bureau of the U.S. Department of Commerce. Some of the industries are food

products, textile mill products, furniture, chemicals, rubber products, primary metals, industrial machinery, and transportation equipment. The eight variables are Number of Employees, Number of Production Workers, Value Added by Manufacture, Cost of Materials, Value of Industry Shipments, New Capital Expenditures, End-of-Year Inventories, and Industry Group. Two variables, Number of Employees and Number of Production Workers, are in units of 1,000. Four variables, Value Added by Manufacture, Cost of Materials, New Capital Expenditures, and End-of-Year Inventories, are in million-dollar units. The Industry Group variable consists of numbers from 1 to 20 to denote the industry group to which the particular subindustry belongs. Value of Industry Shipments has been recoded to the following 1-to-4 scale.

1 = $0 to $4.9 billion
2 = $5 billion to $13.9 billion
3 = $14 billion to $28.9 billion
4 = $29 billion or more

### International Labor Database

This time-series database contains the civilian unemployment rates in percent from seven countries presented yearly from 1959 through 1998. The data are published by the Bureau of Labor Statistics of the U.S. Department of Labor. The countries are the United States, Canada, Australia, Japan, France, Germany, and Italy.

### Financial Database

The financial database contains observations on eight variables for 100 companies. The variables are Type of Industry, Total Revenues ($ millions), Total Assets ($ millions), Return on Equity (%), Earnings per Share ($), Average Yield (%), Dividends per Share ($), and Average Price per Earnings (P/E) ratio. The data were gathered from *Moody's Handbook of Common Stocks* (Summer 1998). The companies represent seven different types of industries. The variable "Type" displays a company's industry type as:

1 = apparel
2 = chemical
3 = electric power
4 = grocery

5 = healthcare products

6 = insurance

7 = petroleum

**Energy Database**

The energy database consists of data on seven energy variables over a period of 26 years. The database is adopted from *Monthly Energy Review*, February 1999 (Office of Energy Markets and End Use, Energy Information Administration, U.S. Department of Energy). The seven variables are World Crude Oil Production (million barrels per day), U.S. Energy Consumption (quadrillion BTUs per year), U.S. Nuclear Electricity Gross Generation (billion kilowatt-hours), U.S. Coal Production (million short tons), U.S. Total Dry Gas Production (million cubic feet), U.S. Fuel Rate for Automobiles (miles per gallon), and Cost of Unleaded (regular) Gasoline (U.S. city average).

**Hospital Database**

This database contains observations for 11 variables on U.S. hospitals. These variables include Geographic Region, Control, Service, Number of Beds, Number of Admissions, Census, Number of Outpatients, Number of Births, Total Expenditures, Payroll Expenditures, and Personnel. Information for these databases is taken from the *American Hospital Association Guide to the Health-Care Field*, 1998–99 edition, published in Chicago, Illinois.

The region variable is coded from 1 to 7, and the numbers represent the following regions.

1 = South

2 = Northeast

3 = Midwest

4 = Southwest

5 = Rocky Mountain

6 = California

7 = Northwest

Control is a type of ownership. Four categories of control are included in the database:

1 = government, nonfederal

2 = nongovernment, not-for-profit

3 = for-profit

4 = federal government

Service is the type of hospital. The two types of hospitals used in this database are:

1 = general medical

2 = psychiatric

The total expenditures and payroll variables are in units of $1,000.

**Agribusiness Time-Series Database**

The agribusiness time-series database contains the monthly weight (in 1,000 lbs.) of cold storage holdings for six different vegetables and for total frozen vegetables over a 14-year period. Each of the seven variables represents 168 months of data from 1984 to 1997. The six vegetables are green beans, broccoli, carrots, sweet corn, onions, and green peas. The data are published by the National Agricultural Statistics Service of the U.S. Department of Agriculture.

Use the databases to answer the following questions.

1. In the manufacturing database, what is the level of data for each of the following variables?
   a. Number of production workers
   b. Cost of materials
   c. Value of industry shipments
   d. Industry group

2. In the hospital database, what is the level of data for each of the following variables?
   a. Region
   b. Control
   c. Number of beds
   d. Personnel

3. In the financial database, what is the level of data for each of the following variables?
   a. Type of industry
   b. Total assets
   c. P/E ratio

## CASE: DIGIORNO PIZZA: INTRODUCING A FROZEN PIZZA TO COMPETE WITH CARRY-OUT

In 1996, Kraft's DiGiorno Pizza hit the market. DiGiorno Pizza was a booming success with sales of $120 million the first year followed by $200 million the next year. It was neither luck nor coincidence that DiGiorno Pizza was an instant success. Kraft conducted extensive research about the product and the marketplace before introducing this product to the public. Many questions had to be answered before Kraft began production. For example, why do people eat pizza? When do they eat pizza? Do consumers believe that carry-out pizza is always more tasty?

SMI-Alcott conducted a research study for Kraft in which they sent out 1,000 surveys to pizza lovers. The results indicated that people ate pizza during fun social occasions or at home when no one wanted to cook. People used frozen pizza mostly for convenience but selected carry-out pizza for a variety of other reasons, including quality and the avoidance of cooking. The Loran Marketing Group conducted focus groups for Kraft with women ages 25 to 54. Their findings showed that consumers used frozen pizza for convenience but wanted carry-out pizza taste. To satisfy these seemingly divergent goals (convenience and taste), Kraft developed DiGiorno Pizza, which rises in the oven as it cooks. This impressed focus group members, and in a series of blind taste tests conducted by Product Dynamics, DiGiorno Pizza beat out all frozen pizzas and finished second overall behind one carry-out brand.

Through advertising Kraft was able to overcome two concerns that were raised by marketing research: people had trouble pronouncing "DiGiorno" and people needed to be convinced that the frozen pizza actually tasted good. Kraft had the name DiGiorno repeated several times in advertisements to make certain that consumers could pronounce the name. As a by-product, the ads also generated strong brand identification. In addition, the ads emphasized "fresh-baked taste" and the rising dough aspect of the product, which helped convince people of DiGiorno's higher quality of taste.

DiGiorno Pizza now has a 13% market share of the U.S. $2.3 billion frozen pizza category. It is the fastest Kraft product ever to break the $200 million barrier.

### Discussion

Think about the market research that was conducted by Kraft and the fact that they used several companies. If you were in charge of conducting this research to help launch such a new product, what decisions would you make about whom to survey, where and when to survey, and what to measure?

1.  What are some of the populations that Kraft might have been interested in measuring for these studies? Did Kraft actually attempt to contact entire populations? What samples were taken? In light of these two questions, how was the inferential process used by Kraft in their market research? Can you think of any descriptive statistics that might have been used by Kraft in their decision-making process?

2.  In the various market research efforts made by Kraft for DiGiorno, some of the possible measurements appear in the following list. Categorize these by level of data. Think of some other measurements that Kraft researchers might have made to help them in this research effort and categorize them by level of data.

    a. Number of pizzas consumed per week per household

    b. Age of pizza purchaser

    c. Zip code of the survey respondent

    d. Dollars spent per month on pizza per person

    e. Time in between purchases of pizza

    f. Rating of taste of a given pizza brand on a scale from 1 to 10, where 1 is very poor tasting and 10 is excellent taste

    g. Ranking of the taste of four pizza brands on a taste test

    h. Number representing the geographic location of the survey respondent

    i. Quality rating of a pizza brand as excellent, good, average, below average, poor

    j. Number representing the pizza brand being evaluated.

    k. Gender of survey respondent

*Source:* Adapted from "Upper Crust," *American Demographics,* March 1999, p. 58; *Marketwatch—News That Matters* Web sites, "What's in a Name? Brand Extension Potential" and "DiGiorno Rising Crust Delivers $200 Million," formerly at http://www.foodexplorer.com/BUSINESS/Products/MarketAnalysis/PF02896b.htm, last accessed in 1999.

CHAPTER **2**

# Charts and Graphs

### LEARNING OBJECTIVES

The overall objective of Chapter 2 is for you to master several techniques for summarizing and depicting data, thereby enabling you to:

1. Recognize the difference between grouped and ungrouped data.
2. Construct a frequency distribution.
3. Construct a histogram, a frequency polygon, an ogive, a pie chart, a stem and leaf plot, a Pareto chart, and a scatter plot.

18

## State of Auto Manufacturing

According to data released by the Automotive News Data Center, General Motors Corporation is number one in the world in total vehicle sales of cars and light trucks. Ford Motor Company is number two followed by Toyota Motor Corporation and Volkswagen, respectively. Between 1999 and 2000, while General Motors maintained its number one position, it sold nearly 200,000 fewer cars worldwide. During this same period, Ford Motor increased sales by more than 200,000. The greatest percentage growth from 1999 to 2000 was for PSA Peugeot-Citroen, which increased sales by 14.2%. The global sales figures for the top 10 auto manufacturers of cars and light trucks for both 1999 and 2000 follow.

| Company | 1999 | 2000 | % Change |
|---|---|---|---|
| General Motors | 8,786,000 | 8,591,327 | -2.2 |
| Ford Motor | 7,148,000 | 7,350,495 | 2.8 |
| Toyota Motor | 5,359,000 | 5,703,446 | 6.4 |
| Volkswagen | 4,860,203 | 5,161,188 | 6.2 |
| DaimlerChrysler | 4,864,500 | 4,749,000 | -2.4 |
| PSA Peugeot-Citroen | 2,519,600 | 2,877,900 | 14.2 |
| Fiat | 2,521,000 | 2,646,500 | 5.0 |
| Hyundai Motor | 2,600,862 | 2,634,530 | 1.3 |
| Nissan Motor | 2,567,878 | 2,629,044 | 2.4 |
| Honda Motor | 2,395,000 | 2,540,000 | 6.1 |

### Managerial and Statistical Questions

Suppose you are a business analyst for one of these companies. Your manager asks you to prepare a brief report showing the state of car and light truck sales in the world. You are to compare your company's position with other firms.

1. What is the best way to convey the sales data in a report? Is the raw data enough? Can you effectively display the data graphically?

2. Suppose DaimlerChrysler randomly samples 40 dealerships and discovers that the following data tell how many car and light trucks were sold at these dealerships last month. How can you summarize these data in a report?

   34 58 40 49 49 57 44 57 69 45 64 31 47 30 44 44 51 65 60 65
   61 62 68 43 66 63 44 34 57 44 67 61 47 67 52 34 58 59 45 33

3. How might you graphically depict the 1999 data against the 2000 data?

*Source:* Adapted from Automotive News Data Center, "Top 10 Auto Manufacturers," *Ad Age Almanac*, 31 December 2001, p. 23.

20 CHAPTER 2 CHARTS AND GRAPHS

## TABLE 2.1

Unemployment Rates for
France Over 40 Years
(Ungrouped Data)

| | | | | |
|---|---|---|---|---|
| 1.6 | 2.1 | 4.2 | 8.6 | 9.6 |
| 1.5 | 2.7 | 4.6 | 10.0 | 10.4 |
| 1.2 | 2.3 | 5.2 | 10.5 | 11.8 |
| 1.4 | 2.5 | 5.4 | 10.6 | 12.3 |
| 1.6 | 2.8 | 6.1 | 10.8 | 11.8 |
| 1.2 | 2.9 | 6.5 | 10.3 | 12.5 |
| 1.6 | 2.8 | 7.6 | 9.6 | 12.4 |
| 1.6 | 2.9 | 8.3 | 9.1 | 11.8 |

In Chapters 2 and 3 many techniques are presented for reformatting or reducing data so that the data are more manageable and can be used to assist decision makers more effectively. Two techniques for grouping data are the frequency distribution and the stem and leaf plot presented in this chapter. In addition, Chapter 2 discusses and displays several graphical tools for summarizing and presenting data, including histogram, frequency polygon, ogive, pie chart, and Pareto chart for one-variable data; and the scatter plot for two-variable numerical data. By using these and other techniques, decision makers can begin to "get a handle" on information contained in data and begin to use the data to enhance the decision-making process.

*Raw data, or data that have not been summarized in any way,* are sometimes referred to as **ungrouped data.** Table 2.1 contains raw data of the unemployment rates for France over 40 years. *Data that have been organized into a frequency distribution* are called **grouped data.** Table 2.2 presents a frequency distribution for the data displayed in Table 2.1. The distinction between ungrouped and grouped data is important because the calculation of statistics differs between the two types of data. This chapter focuses on organizing ungrouped data into grouped data and displaying them graphically.

## 2.1 FREQUENCY DISTRIBUTIONS

One particularly useful tool for grouping data is the **frequency distribution,** which is *a summary of data presented in the form of class intervals and frequencies.* How is a frequency distribution constructed from raw data? That is, how are frequency distributions like the one displayed in Table 2.2 constructed from raw data like those presented in Table 2.1? Frequency distributions are relatively easy to construct. Although some guidelines and rules of thumb help in their construction, frequency distributions vary in final shape and design, even when the original raw data are identical. In a sense, frequency distributions are constructed according to individual business researchers' taste.

When constructing a frequency distribution, the business researcher should first determine the range of the raw data. The **range** often is defined as *the difference between the largest and smallest numbers.* The range for the data in Table 2.1 is 11.3 (12.5 − 1.2).

The second step in constructing a frequency distribution is to determine how many classes it will contain. One rule of thumb is to select between *5 and 15 classes.* If the frequency distribution contains too few classes, the data summary may be too general to be useful. Too many classes may result in a frequency distribution that does not aggregate the data enough to be helpful. The final number of classes is arbitrary. The business researcher arrives at a number by examining the range and determining a number of classes that will span the range adequately and also be meaningful to the user. The data in Table 2.1 were grouped into six classes for Table 2.2.

After selecting the number of classes, the business researcher must determine the width of the class interval. An approximation of the class width can be calculated by dividing the range by the number of classes. For the data in Table 2.1, this approximation would be 11.3/6, or 1.9. Normally, the number is rounded up to the next whole number, which in this case is 2. The frequency distribution must start at a value equal to or lower than the lowest number of the ungrouped data and end at a value equal to or higher than the highest number. The lowest unemployment rate is 1.2 and the highest is 12.5, so the business researcher starts the frequency distribution at 1 and ends it at 13. Table 2.2 contains the completed frequency distribution for the data in Table 2.1. Class endpoints are selected so that no value of the data can fit into more than one class. The class interval expression, "under," in the distribution of Table 2.2 avoids such a problem.

### Class Midpoint

The *midpoint of each class interval* is called the **class midpoint** and is sometimes referred to as the **class mark.** It is *the value halfway across the class interval* and can be calculated as *the*

## TABLE 2.2

Frequency Distribution of the
Unemployment Rates of
France (Grouped Data)

| Class Interval | Frequency |
|---|---|
| 1–under 3 | 16 |
| 3–under 5 | 2 |
| 5–under 7 | 4 |
| 7–under 9 | 3 |
| 9–under 11 | 9 |
| 11–under 13 | 6 |

Managing Information with Technology   19

*average of the two class endpoints.* For example, in the distribution of Table 2.2, the midpoint of the class interval 3–under 5 is 4, or (3+5)/2. A second way to obtain the class midpoint is to calculate one-half the distance across the class interval (half the class width) and add it to the class beginning point, as for the unemployment rates distribution:

$$Class\ Beginning\ Point = 3$$
$$Class\ Width = 2$$
$$Class\ Midpoint = 3 + \frac{1}{2}(2) = 4$$

The class midpoint is important, because it becomes the representative value for each class in most group statistics calculations. The third column in Table 2.3 contains the class midpoints for all classes of the data from Table 2.2.

## Relative Frequency

**Relative frequency** is *the proportion of the total frequency that is in any given class interval in a frequency distribution.* Relative frequency is the individual class frequency divided by the total frequency. For example, from Table 2.3, the relative frequency for the class interval 5–under 7 is 4/40, or .10. Consideration of the relative frequency is preparatory to the study of probability in Chapter 4. Indeed, if values were selected randomly from the data in Table 2.1, the probability of drawing a number that is "5–under 7" would be .10, the relative frequency for that class interval. The fourth column of Table 2.3 lists the relative frequencies for the frequency distribution of Table 2.2.

## Cumulative Frequency

The **cumulative frequency** is *a running total of frequencies through the classes of a frequency distribution.* The cumulative frequency for each class interval is the frequency for that class interval added to the preceding cumulative total. In Table 2.3 the cumulative frequency for the first class is the same as the class frequency: 16. The cumulative frequency for the second class interval is the frequency of that interval (2) plus the frequency of the first interval (16), which yields a new cumulative frequency of 18. This process continues through the last interval, at which point the cumulative total equals the sum of the frequencies (40). The concept of cumulative frequency is used in many areas, including sales cumulated over a fiscal year, sports scores during a contest (cumulated points), years of service, points earned in a course, and costs of doing business over a period of time. Table 2.3 gives cumulative frequencies for the data in Table 2.2.

| TABLE 2.3 | | | | | |
|---|---|---|---|---|---|
| Class Midpoints, Relative Frequencies, and Cumulative Frequencies for Unemployment Data | Interval | Frequency | Class Midpoint | Relative Frequency | Cumulative Frequency |
| | 1–under 3 | 16 | 2 | .400 | 16 |
| | 3–under 5 | 2 | 4 | .050 | 18 |
| | 5–under 7 | 4 | 6 | .100 | 22 |
| | 7–under 9 | 3 | 8 | .075 | 25 |
| | 9–under 11 | 9 | 10 | .225 | 34 |
| | 11–under 13 | 6 | 12 | .150 | 40 |
| | Totals | 40 | | 1.000 | |

**DEMONSTRATION PROBLEM 2.1**

The following data are the average weekly mortgage interest rates for a 60-week period.

| | | | | |
|---|---|---|---|---|
| 7.29 | 7.03 | 7.14 | 6.77 | 6.35 |
| 6.69 | 7.02 | 7.40 | 7.16 | 6.96 |
| 6.98 | 7.56 | 6.75 | 6.87 | 7.11 |
| 7.39 | 7.28 | 6.97 | 6.90 | 6.57 |
| 7.11 | 6.95 | 7.23 | 7.31 | 7.00 |
| 7.30 | 7.17 | 6.96 | 6.78 | 7.30 |
| 7.16 | 6.78 | 6.79 | 7.07 | 7.03 |
| 6.87 | 6.80 | 7.10 | 7.13 | 6.95 |
| 7.08 | 7.24 | 7.34 | 7.47 | 7.31 |
| 6.96 | 6.70 | 6.57 | 6.88 | 6.84 |
| 7.02 | 7.40 | 7.12 | 7.16 | 7.16 |
| 6.99 | 6.94 | 7.29 | 7.05 | 6.84 |

Construct a frequency distribution for these data. Calculate and display the class midpoints, relative frequencies, and cumulative frequencies for this frequency distribution.

*Solution*

How many classes should this frequency distribution contain? The range of the data is 1.21 (7.56-6.35). If 13 classes are used, each class width is approximately:

$$\text{Class Width} = \frac{\text{Range}}{\text{Number of Classes}} = \frac{1.21}{13} = 0.093$$

If a class width of .10 is used, a frequency distribution can be constructed with endpoints that are more uniform looking and allow presentation of the information in categories more familiar to mortgage interest rate users.

The first class endpoint must be 6.35 or lower to include the smallest value; the last endpoint must be 7.56 or higher to include the largest value. In this case the frequency distribution begins at 6.30 and ends at 7.60. The resulting frequency distribution, class midpoints, relative frequencies, and cumulative frequencies are listed in the following table.

| Class Interval | Frequency | Class Midpoint | Relative Frequency | Cumulative Frequency |
|---|---|---|---|---|
| 6.30–under 6.40 | 1 | 6.35 | .0167 | 1 |
| 6.40–under 6.50 | 0 | 6.45 | .0000 | 1 |
| 6.50–under 6.60 | 2 | 6.55 | .0333 | 3 |
| 6.60–under 6.70 | 1 | 6.65 | .0167 | 4 |
| 6.70–under 6.80 | 6 | 6.75 | .1000 | 10 |
| 6.80–under 6.90 | 6 | 6.85 | .1000 | 16 |
| 6.90–under 7.00 | 10 | 6.95 | .1667 | 26 |
| 7.00–under 7.10 | 8 | 7.05 | .1333 | 34 |
| 7.10–under 7.20 | 11 | 7.15 | .1833 | 45 |
| 7.20–under 7.30 | 5 | 7.25 | .0833 | 50 |
| 7.30–under 7.40 | 6 | 7.35 | .1000 | 56 |
| 7.40–under 7.50 | 3 | 7.45 | .0500 | 59 |
| 7.50–under 7.60 | 1 | 7.55 | .0167 | 60 |
| Totals | 60 | | 1.0000 | |

The frequencies and relative frequencies of these data reveal the mortgage interest rate classes that are likely to occur during the period. Most of the mortgage interest rates (52 of the 60) are in the classes starting with (6.70–under 6.80) and going through (7.30–under 7.40). The rates with the greatest frequency, 11, are in the (7.10–under 7.20) class.

## 2.1 PROBLEMS

2.1 The following data represent the afternoon high temperatures for 50 construction days during a year in St. Louis.

| | | | | |
|---|---|---|---|---|
| 42 | 70 | 64 | 47 | 66 |
| 55 | 85 | 10 | 24 | 45 |
| 16 | 40 | 81 | 15 | 35 |
| 38 | 79 | 35 | 36 | 23 |
| 31 | 38 | 52 | 16 | 81 |
| 69 | 73 | 38 | 48 | 25 |
| 31 | 62 | 47 | 63 | 84 |
| 17 | 40 | 36 | 44 | 17 |
| 64 | 75 | 53 | 31 | 60 |
| 12 | 61 | 43 | 30 | 33 |

a. Construct a frequency distribution for the data using five class intervals.
b. Construct a frequency distribution for the data using 10 class intervals.
c. Examine the results of (a) and (b) and comment on the usefulness of the frequency distribution in terms of temperature summarization capability.

2.2 A packaging process is supposed to fill small boxes of raisins with approximately 50 raisins so that each box will weigh the same. However, the number of raisins in each box will vary. Suppose 100 boxes of raisins are randomly sampled, the raisins counted, and the following data are obtained.

| | | | | | | | | | |
|---|---|---|---|---|---|---|---|---|---|
| 57 | 51 | 53 | 52 | 50 | 60 | 51 | 51 | 52 | 52 |
| 44 | 53 | 45 | 57 | 39 | 53 | 58 | 47 | 51 | 48 |
| 49 | 49 | 44 | 54 | 46 | 52 | 55 | 54 | 47 | 53 |
| 49 | 52 | 49 | 54 | 57 | 52 | 52 | 53 | 49 | 47 |
| 51 | 48 | 55 | 53 | 55 | 47 | 53 | 43 | 48 | 46 |
| 54 | 46 | 51 | 48 | 53 | 56 | 48 | 47 | 49 | 57 |
| 55 | 53 | 50 | 47 | 57 | 49 | 43 | 58 | 52 | 44 |
| 46 | 59 | 57 | 47 | 61 | 60 | 49 | 53 | 41 | 48 |
| 59 | 53 | 45 | 45 | 56 | 40 | 46 | 49 | 50 | 57 |
| 47 | 52 | 48 | 50 | 45 | 56 | 47 | 47 | 48 | 46 |

Construct a frequency distribution for these data. What does the frequency distribution reveal about the box fills?

2.3 The owner of a fast-food restaurant ascertains the ages of a sample of customers. From these data, the owner constructs the frequency distribution shown. For each class interval of the frequency distribution, determine the class midpoint, the relative frequency, and the cumulative frequency.

| Class Interval | Frequency |
|---|---|
| 0–under 5 | 6 |
| 5–under 10 | 8 |
| 10–under 15 | 17 |
| 15–under 20 | 23 |
| 20–under 25 | 18 |
| 25–under 30 | 10 |
| 30–under 35 | 4 |

What does the relative frequency tell the fast-food restaurant owner about customer ages?

2.4 The human resources manager for a large company commissions a study in which the employment records of 500 company employees are examined for absenteeism during the past year. The business researcher conducting the study organizes the data into a frequency distribution to assist the human resources manager in analyzing the data. The frequency distribution is shown. For each class of the frequency distribution, determine the class midpoint, the relative frequency, and the cumulative frequency.

| Class Interval | Frequency |
|---|---|
| 0–under 2 | 218 |
| 2–under 4 | 207 |
| 4–under 6 | 56 |
| 6–under 8 | 11 |
| 8–under 10 | 8 |

2.5 List three specific uses of cumulative frequencies in business.

## 2.2 GRAPHICAL DEPICTION OF DATA

One of the most effective mechanisms for presenting data in a form meaningful to decision makers is graphical depiction. Through graphs and charts, the decision maker can often get an overall picture of the data and reach some useful conclusions merely by studying the chart or graph. Converting data to graphics can be creative and artful. Often the most difficult step in this process is to reduce important and sometimes expensive data to a graphic picture that is both clear and concise and yet consistent with the message of the original data. One of the most important uses of graphical depiction in statistics is to help the researcher determine the shape of a distribution. Six types of graphic depiction are presented here: (1) histogram, (2) frequency polygon, (3) ogive, (4) pie chart, (5) stem and leaf plot, and (6) Pareto chart.

### Histograms

A **histogram** is *a type of vertical bar chart that is used to depict a frequency distribution*. Construction involves labeling the $x$ axis (abscissa) with the class endpoints and the $y$ axis (ordinate) with the frequencies, drawing a horizontal line segment from class endpoint to class endpoint at each frequency value, and connecting each line segment vertically from the frequency value to the $x$ axis to form a series of rectangles. Figure 2.1 is a histogram of the frequency distribution in Table 2.2 produced by using the software package MINITAB.

A histogram is a useful tool for differentiating the frequencies of class intervals. A quick glance at a histogram reveals which class intervals produce the highest frequency totals. Figure 2.1 clearly shows that the class interval 1–under 3 yields by far the highest frequency count (16). Examination of the histogram reveals where large increases or decreases occur between classes, such as from the 1–under 3 class to the 3–under 5 class, a decrease of 14, and from the 7–under 9 class to the 9–under 11 class, an increase of 6.

Note that the scales used along the $x$ and $y$ axes for the histogram in Figure 2.1 are almost identical. However, because ranges of meaningful numbers for the two variables being graphed often differ considerably, the graph may have different scales on the two axes. Figure 2.2 shows what the histogram of unemployment rates would look like if the scale on the $y$ axis were more compressed than that on the $x$ axis. Notice that less difference in the length of the rectangles appears to represent the frequencies in Figure 2.2. It is important that the user of the graph clearly understands the scales used for the axes of a

**FIGURE 2.1**

MINITAB Histogram of French
Unemployment Data

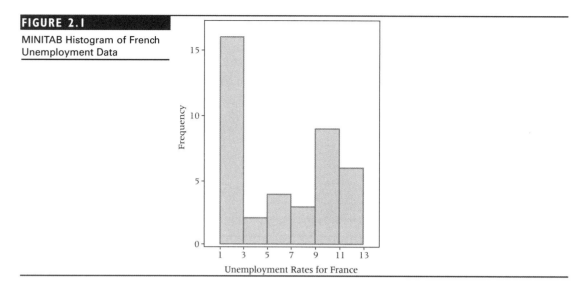

**FIGURE 2.2**

MINITAB Histogram of French
Unemployment Data (*y* axis
compressed)

histogram. Otherwise, a graph's creator can "lie with statistics" by stretching or compressing a graph to make a point.*

## Using Histograms to Get an Initial Overview of the Data

Because of the widespread availability of computers and statistical software packages to business researchers and decision makers, the histogram continues to become more important. Sometimes decision makers are presented with a large database of information and do not know where to begin in attempting to understand what the data mean. Histogram analysis of such data can yield initial information about the shape of the distribution of the data, the amount of variability of data, the central location of the data, and outlier data. Although most of these concepts are presented in Chapter 3, the notion of histogram as an initial tool to access these data characteristics is presented here.

For example, one of the variables in the Stock Market database (displayed on the CD-ROM) is Stock Volume. The database contains 324 stock volume observations. Suppose a

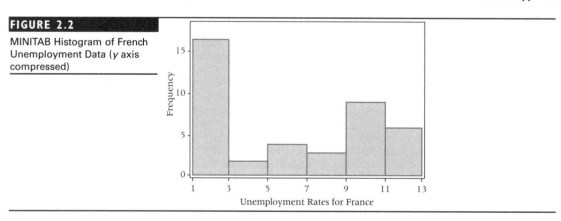

* It should be pointed out that the software package Excel uses the term *histogram* to refer to a frequency distribution. However, by checking Chart Output in the Excel histogram dialog box, a graphical histogram is also created.

financial decision maker wants to use these data to reach some conclusions about the stock market. Figure 2.3 shows a MINITAB-produced histogram of these data. What can we learn from this histogram? Virtually all stock market volumes fall between zero and 1 billion shares. The distribution takes on a shape that is high on the left end and tapered to the right. In Chapter 3 we will learn that the shape of this distribution is skewed toward the right end. In statistics, it is often useful to determine whether data are approximately normally distributed (bell-shaped curve) as shown in Figure 2.4. We can see by examining the histogram in Figure 2.3 that the stock market volume data are not normally distributed. Although the center of the histogram is located near 500 million shares, a large portion of stock volume observations falls in the lower end of the data somewhere between 100 million and 400 million shares. In addition, the histogram shows some outliers in the upper end of the distribution. Outliers are data points that appear outside of the main body of observations and may represent phenomena that differ from those represented by other data points. By observing the histogram, we notice a few data observations near 1 billion. One could conclude that on a few stock market days an unusually large volume of shares are traded. These and other insights can be gleaned by examining the histogram and show that histograms play an important role in the initial analysis of data.

## Frequency Polygons

A **frequency polygon** is *a graph in which line segments "connecting the dots" depict a frequency distribution*. Construction of a frequency polygon begins, as with a histogram, by scaling class endpoints along the $x$ axis and the frequency values along the $y$ axis. A dot is plotted for the frequency value at the midpoint of each class interval (class midpoint). Connecting these midpoint dots completes the graph. Figure 2.5 shows a frequency polygon of the distribution data from Table 2.2 produced by using the software package Excel. The information gleaned from frequency polygons and histograms is similar. As with the histogram, changing the scales of the axes can compress or stretch a frequency polygon, which affects the user's impression of what the graph represents.

## Ogives

An **ogive** (o-jive) is *a cumulative frequency polygon*. Again, construction begins by labeling the $x$ axis with the class endpoints and the $y$ axis with the frequencies. However, the use of cumulative frequency values requires that the scale along the $y$ axis be great enough to include the frequency total. A dot of zero frequency is plotted at the beginning of the first class and construction proceeds by marking a dot at the *end* of each class interval for the cumulative value. Connecting the dots then completes the ogive. Figure 2.6 presents an ogive produced by using Excel for the data in Table 2.2.

**FIGURE 2.3**

Histogram of Stock Volumes, 1990–1998

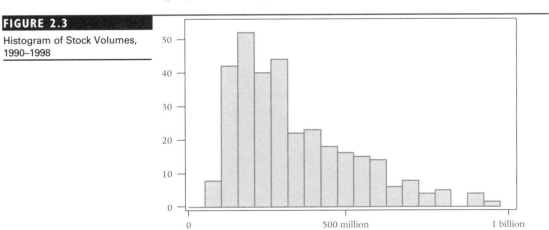

FIGURE 2.4

Normal Distribution

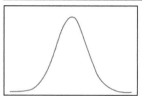

Ogives are most useful when the decision maker wants to see *running totals*. For example, if a comptroller is interested in controlling costs, an ogive could depict cumulative costs over a fiscal year.

Steep slopes in an ogive can be used to identify sharp increases in frequencies. In Figure 2.6 steep slopes occur in the 1–under 3 class and the 9–under 11 class, signifying large class frequency totals.

## Pie Charts

A **pie chart** is *a circular depiction of data where the area of the whole pie represents 100% of the data being studied and slices represent a percentage breakdown of the sublevels.* Pie charts show the relative magnitudes of parts to a whole. They are widely used in business, particularly to depict such things as budget categories, market share, and time and resource allocations. However, the use of pie charts is minimized in the sciences and technology because pie charts can lead to less accurate judgments than are possible with other

FIGURE 2.5

Excel-Produced Frequency Polygon of the Unemployment Data

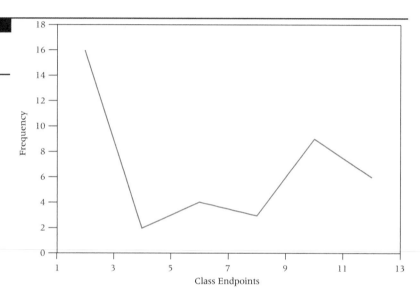

FIGURE 2.6

Excel Ogive of the Unemployment Data

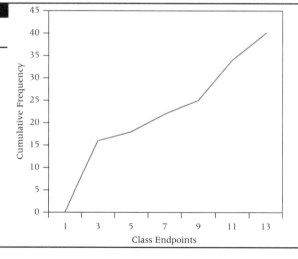

## Where Are Soft Drinks Sold?

The soft drink market is an extremely large and growing market in the United States and worldwide. In a recent year, 9.6 billion cases of soft drinks were sold in the United States alone. Where are soft drinks sold? The following data from Sanford C. Bernstein research indicate that the four leading places for soft drink sales are supermarkets, fountains, convenience/gas stores, and vending machines.

| Place of Sales | Percentage |
|---|---|
| Supermarket | 44 |
| Fountain | 24 |
| Convenience/gas stations | 16 |
| Vending | 11 |
| Mass merchandisers | 3 |
| Drugstores | 2 |

These data can be displayed graphically several ways. Displayed here is an Excel pie chart and a MINITAB bar chart of the data. Some statisticians prefer the histogram or the bar chart over the pie chart because they believe it is easier to compare categories that are similar in size with the histogram or the bar chart rather than the pie chart.

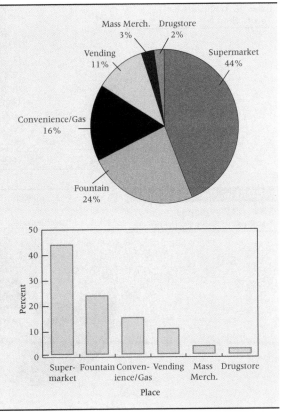

types of graphs.* Generally, it is more difficult for the viewer to interpret the relative size of angles in a pie chart than to judge the length of rectangles in a histogram or the relative distance of a frequency polygon dot from the $x$ axis. In the feature, Statistics in Business Today, "Where Are Soft Drinks Sold?" graphical depictions of the percentage of sales by place were displayed by both a pie chart and a vertical bar chart.

Construction of the pie chart begins by determining the proportion of the subunit to the whole. Table 2.4 contains sales figures generated by Information Resources, Inc., for the top 10 toothpaste brands for a recent year. First, the whole-number sales figures are converted to proportions by dividing each sales figure by the total sales figure. This proportion is analogous to the relative frequency computed for frequency distributions. Because a circle contains 360°, each proportion is multiplied by 360 to obtain the correct number of degrees to represent each item. For example, Aquafresh sales of $177,989,000 represent a .1319 proportion of the total sales (177,989,000/1,349,326,000 = .1319). Multiplying this value by 360° results in 47.48°. Aquafresh sales will account for 47.48° of the pie. The pie chart is then completed by using a compass to lay out the slices. The pie chart in Figure 2.7, constructed by using MINITAB, depicts the data from Table 2.4.

*William S. Cleveland, *The Elements of Graphing Data* (Monterey, CA: Wadsworth Advanced Books and Software, 1985).

| TABLE 2.4 | Brand | Sales | Proportion | Degrees |
|---|---|---|---|---|
| Sales of Toothpaste for Top 10 Brands | Crest | $370,437,000 | .2745 | 98.82 |
| | Colgate | 321,084,000 | .2380 | 85.68 |
| | Aquafresh | 177,989,000 | .1319 | 47.48 |
| | Mentadent | 170,630,000 | .1265 | 45.55 |
| | Arm & Hammer | 109,512,000 | .0812 | 29.23 |
| | Rembrandt | 52,067,000 | .0386 | 13.90 |
| | Sensodyn | 50,133,000 | .0372 | 13.39 |
| | Listerine | 40,107,000 | .0297 | 10.69 |
| | Closeup | 32,009,000 | .0237 | 8.53 |
| | Ultrabrite | 25,358,000 | .0187 | 6.73 |
| | Totals | $1,349,326,000 | 1.0000 | 360.00 |

## FIGURE 2.7

MINITAB Pie Chart of Toothpaste Sales by Brand

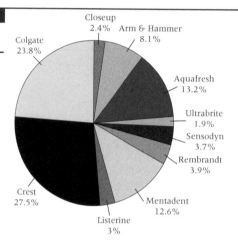

## DEMONSTRATION PROBLEM 2.2

According to the National Retail Federation and Center for Retailing Education at the University of Florida, the four main sources of inventory shrinkage are employee theft, shoplifting, administrative error, and vendor fraud. The estimated annual dollar amount in shrinkage ($ millions) associated with each of these sources follows:

| | |
|---|---|
| Employee theft | $17,918.6 |
| Shoplifting | 15,191.9 |
| Administrative error | 7,617.6 |
| Vendor fraud | 2,553.6 |
| Total | $43,281.7 |

Construct a pie chart to depict these data.

### Solution

Convert each raw dollar amount to a proportion by dividing each individual amount by the total.

| | |
|---|---|
| Employee theft | 17,918.6/43,281.7 = .414 |
| Shoplifting | 15,191.9/43,281.7 = .351 |
| Administrative error | 7,617.6/43,281.7 = .176 |
| Vendor fraud | 2,553.6/43,281.7 = .059 |
| Total | 1.000 |

Convert each proportion to degrees by multiplying each proportion by 360°.

| | | | |
|---|---|---|---|
| Employee theft | .414 · 360° | = | 149.0° |
| Shoplifting | .351 · 360° | = | 126.4° |
| Administrative error | .176 · 360° | = | 63.4° |
| Vendor fraud | .059 · 360° | = | 21.2° |
| Total | | | 360.0° |

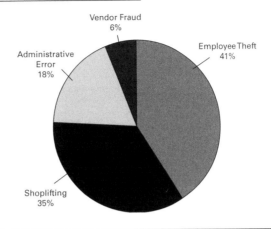

## Stem and Leaf Plots

Another way to organize raw data into groups is by a **stem and leaf plot.** This technique is simple and provides a unique view of the data. A stem and leaf plot is *constructed by sepa-rating the digits for each number of the data into two groups, a stem and a leaf.* The leftmost digits are the stem and consist of the higher valued digits. The rightmost digits are the leaves and contain the lower values. If a set of data has only two digits, the stem is the value on the left and the leaf is the value on the right. For example, if 34 is one of the numbers, the stem is 3 and the leaf is 4. For numbers with more than two digits, division of stem and leaf is a matter of researcher preference.

Table 2.5 contains scores from an examination on plant safety policy and rules given to a group of 35 job trainees. A stem and leaf plot of these data is displayed in Table 2.6. One advantage of such a distribution is that the instructor can readily see whether the scores are in the upper or lower end of each bracket and also determine the spread of the scores. A second advantage of stem and leaf plots is that the values of the original raw data

**TABLE 2.5**

Safety Examination Scores for Plant Trainees

| | | | | |
|---|---|---|---|---|
| 86 | 77 | 91 | 60 | 55 |
| 76 | 92 | 47 | 88 | 67 |
| 23 | 59 | 72 | 75 | 83 |
| 77 | 68 | 82 | 97 | 89 |
| 81 | 75 | 74 | 39 | 67 |
| 79 | 83 | 70 | 78 | 91 |
| 68 | 49 | 56 | 94 | 81 |

**TABLE 2.6**

Stem and Leaf Plot for Plant Safety Examination Data

| Stem | Leaf | | | | | | | | |
|---|---|---|---|---|---|---|---|---|---|
| 2 | 3 | | | | | | | | |
| 3 | 9 | | | | | | | | |
| 4 | 7 | 9 | | | | | | | |
| 5 | 5 | 6 | 9 | | | | | | |
| 6 | 0 | 7 | 7 | 8 | 8 | | | | |
| 7 | 0 | 2 | 4 | 5 | 5 | 6 | 7 | 7 | 8 | 9 |
| 8 | 1 | 1 | 2 | 3 | 3 | 6 | 8 | 9 | |
| 9 | 1 | 1 | 2 | 4 | 7 | | | | |

are retained (whereas most frequency distributions and graphic depictions use the class midpoint to represent the values in a class).

| DEMONSTRATION PROBLEM 2.3 |
|---|

The following data represent the costs (in dollars) of a sample of 30 postal mailings by a company.

| | | | | | |
|---|---|---|---|---|---|
| 3.67 | 2.75 | 5.47 | 4.65 | 3.32 | 2.09 |
| 1.83 | 10.94 | 1.93 | 3.89 | 7.20 | 2.78 |
| 3.34 | 7.80 | 3.20 | 3.21 | 3.55 | 3.53 |
| 3.64 | 4.95 | 5.42 | 8.64 | 4.84 | 4.10 |
| 9.15 | 3.45 | 5.11 | 1.97 | 2.84 | 4.15 |

Using dollars as a stem and cents as a leaf, construct a stem and leaf plot of the data.

Solution

| Stem | Leaf | | | | | | | | |
|---|---|---|---|---|---|---|---|---|---|
| 1 | 83 | 93 | 97 | | | | | | |
| 2 | 09 | 75 | 78 | 84 | | | | | |
| 3 | 20 | 21 | 32 | 34 | 45 | 53 | 55 | 64 | 67 | 89 |
| 4 | 10 | 15 | 65 | 84 | 95 | | | | |
| 5 | 11 | 42 | 47 | | | | | | |
| 6 | | | | | | | | | |
| 7 | 20 | 80 | | | | | | | |
| 8 | 64 | | | | | | | | |
| 9 | 15 | | | | | | | | |
| 10 | 94 | | | | | | | | |

## Pareto Charts

An important concept and movement in business is Total Quality Management (see Chapter 18). One of the important aspects of total quality management is the constant search for causes of problems in products and processes. A graphical technique for displaying problem causes is Pareto analysis. Pareto analysis is a quantitative tallying of the number and types of defects that occur with a product or service. Analysts use this tally to produce *a vertical bar chart that displays the most common types of defects, ranked in order of occurrence from left to right*. The bar chart is called a **Pareto chart.**

Pareto charts were named after an Italian economist, Vilfredo Pareto, who observed more than 100 years ago that most of Italy's wealth was controlled by a few families who were the major drivers behind the Italian economy. Quality expert J. M. Juran applied this notion to the quality field by observing that poor quality can often be addressed by attacking a few major causes that result in most of the problems. A Pareto chart enables quality control decision makers to separate the most important defects from trivial defects, which helps them to set priorities for needed quality improvement work.

Suppose the number of electric motors being rejected by inspectors for a company has been increasing. Company officials examine the records of several hundred of the motors in which at least one defect was found to determine which defects occurred more frequently. They find that 40% of the defects involved poor wiring, 30% involved a short in the coil, 25% involved a defective plug, and 5% involved cessation of bearings. Figure 2.8 is a Pareto chart constructed from this information. It shows that the main three problems with defective motors—poor wiring, a short in the coil, and a defective plug—account for 95% of the problems. From the Pareto chart, decision makers can formulate a logical plan for reducing the number of defects.

Company officials and workers would probably begin to improve quality by examining the segments of the production process that involve the wiring. Next, they would study the construction of the coil, then examine the plugs used and the plug-supplier process.

**FIGURE 2.8**

Pareto Chart for Electric
Motor Problems

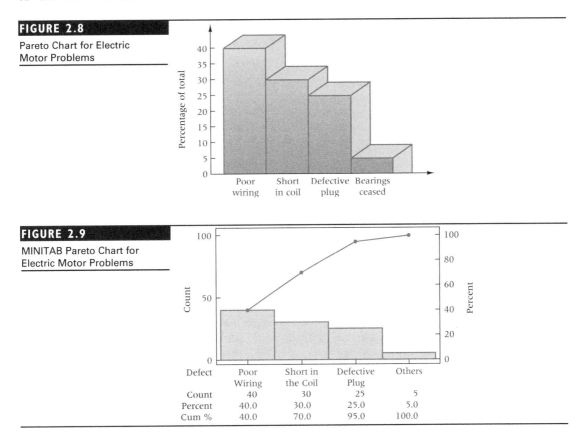

**FIGURE 2.9**

MINITAB Pareto Chart for
Electric Motor Problems

| Defect | Poor Wiring | Short in the Coil | Defective Plug | Others |
|---|---|---|---|---|
| Count | 40 | 30 | 25 | 5 |
| Percent | 40.0 | 30.0 | 25.0 | 5.0 |
| Cum % | 40.0 | 70.0 | 95.0 | 100.0 |

Figure 2.9 is a MINITAB rendering of this Pareto chart. In addition to the bar chart analysis, the MINITAB Pareto analysis contains a cumulative percentage line graph. Observe the slopes on the line graph. The steepest slopes represent the more frequently occurring problems. As the slopes level off, the problems occur less frequently. The line graph gives the decision maker another tool for determining which problems to solve first.

## 2.2 PROBLEMS

2.6    Construct a histogram and a frequency polygon for the following data.

| Class Interval | Frequency |
|---|---|
| 30–under 32 | 5 |
| 32–under 34 | 7 |
| 34–under 36 | 15 |
| 36–under 38 | 21 |
| 38–under 40 | 34 |
| 40–under 42 | 24 |
| 42–under 44 | 17 |
| 44–under 46 | 8 |

2.7    Construct a histogram and a frequency polygon for the following data.

| Class Interval | Frequency |
|---|---|
| 10–under 20 | 9 |
| 20–under 30 | 7 |
| 30–under 40 | 10 |
| 40–under 50 | 6 |
| 50–under 60 | 13 |
| 60–under 70 | 18 |
| 70–under 80 | 15 |

2.8    Construct an ogive for the following data.

| Class Interval | Frequency |
|---|---|
| 3–under 6 | 2 |
| 6–under 9 | 5 |
| 9–under 12 | 10 |
| 12–under 15 | 11 |
| 15–under 18 | 17 |
| 18–under 21 | 5 |

2.9    Construct a stem and leaf plot using two digits for the stem.

| | | | | | | | |
|---|---|---|---|---|---|---|---|
| 212 | 239 | 240 | 218 | 222 | 249 | 265 | 224 |
| 257 | 271 | 266 | 234 | 239 | 219 | 255 | 260 |
| 243 | 261 | 249 | 230 | 246 | 263 | 235 | 229 |
| 218 | 238 | 254 | 249 | 250 | 263 | 229 | 221 |
| 253 | 227 | 270 | 257 | 261 | 238 | 240 | 239 |
| 273 | 220 | 226 | 239 | 258 | 259 | 230 | 262 |
| 255 | 226 | | | | | | |

2.10   A list of the largest accounting firms in the United States along with their net revenue figures for 1997 ($ millions) according to the Public Accounting Report follows.

| Firm | Revenue |
|---|---|
| Andersen Worldwide | $5,445 |
| Ernst & Young | 4,416 |
| Deloitte & Touche | 3,600 |
| KPMG Peat Marwick | 2,698 |
| Coopers & Lybrand | 2,504 |
| PriceWaterhouse | 2,344 |
| Grant Thornton | 289 |
| McGladrey & Pullen | 270 |
| BDO Seidman | 240 |

Construct a pie chart to represent these data. Label the slices with the appropriate percentages. Comment on the effectiveness of using a pie chart to display the revenue of these top accounting firms.

2.11   According to the Air Transport Association of America, Delta Airlines led all U.S. carriers in the number of passengers flown in a recent year. The top five airlines were Delta, United, American, US Airways, and Southwest. The number of passengers flown (in thousands) by each of these airlines follows:

**TABLE 2.7**

Value of New Construction
Over a 35-Year Period

| Residential | Nonresidential |
|---|---|
| 169635 | 96497 |
| 155113 | 115372 |
| 149410 | 96407 |
| 175822 | 129275 |
| 162706 | 140569 |
| 134605 | 145054 |
| 195028 | 131289 |
| 231396 | 155261 |
| 234955 | 178925 |
| 266481 | 163740 |
| 267063 | 160363 |
| 263385 | 164191 |
| 252745 | 169173 |
| 228943 | 167896 |
| 197526 | 135389 |
| 232134 | 120921 |
| 249757 | 122222 |
| 274956 | 127593 |
| 251937 | 139711 |
| 281229 | 153866 |
| 280748 | 166754 |
| 297886 | 177639 |
| 315757 | 175048 |

*Source:* U.S. Census Bureau, *Current Construction Reports* (in millions of constant dollars).

| Airline | Passengers |
|---|---|
| Delta | 103,133 |
| United | 84,203 |
| American | 81,083 |
| US Airways | 58,659 |
| Southwest | 55,946 |

Construct a pie chart to depict this information.

2.12 Information Resources, Inc., reports that in a recent year, Huggies was the top-selling diaper brand in the United States with 41.3% of the market share. Other leading brands included Pampers with 25.6%, Luvs with 12.1%, Drypers with 3.3%, Fitti with 0.9%, and private labels with 15.8%. Use this information to construct a pie chart of the diaper market shares.

2.13 The following data represent the number of passengers per flight in a sample of 50 flights from Wichita, Kansas, to Kansas City, Missouri.

| | | | | | | | | | |
|---|---|---|---|---|---|---|---|---|---|
| 23 | 46 | 66 | 67 | 13 | 58 | 19 | 17 | 65 | 17 |
| 25 | 20 | 47 | 28 | 16 | 38 | 44 | 29 | 48 | 29 |
| 69 | 34 | 35 | 60 | 37 | 52 | 80 | 59 | 51 | 33 |
| 48 | 46 | 23 | 38 | 52 | 50 | 17 | 57 | 41 | 77 |
| 45 | 47 | 49 | 19 | 32 | 64 | 27 | 61 | 70 | 19 |

Construct a stem and leaf plot for these data. What does the stem and leaf plot tell you about the number of passengers per flight?

2.14 An airline company uses a central telephone bank and a semiautomated telephone process to take reservations. It has been receiving an unusually high number of customer complaints about its reservation system. The company conducted a survey of customers, asking them whether they had encountered any of the following problems in making reservations: busy signal, disconnection, poor connection, too long a wait to talk to someone, could not get through to an agent, connected with the wrong person. Suppose a survey of 744 complaining customers resulted in the following frequency tally.

| Number of Complaints | Complaint |
|---|---|
| 184 | Too long a wait |
| 10 | Transferred to the wrong person |
| 85 | Could not get through to an agent |
| 37 | Got disconnected |
| 420 | Busy signal |
| 8 | Poor connection |

Construct a Pareto diagram from this information to display the various problems encountered in making reservations.

## 2.3 GRAPHICAL DEPICTION OF TWO-VARIABLE NUMERICAL DATA: SCATTER PLOTS

Many times in business research it is important to explore the relationship between two numerical variables. More detailed statistical approaches are given in Chapters 3 and 13, but here we present a graphical mechanism for examining the relationship between two numerical variables, the scatter plot (or scatter diagram). A **scatter plot** is *a two-dimensional graph plot of pairs of points from two numerical variables.*

As an example of two numerical variables, consider the data in Table 2.7. Displayed are the values of new residential and new nonresidential buildings in the United States for

## FIGURE 2.10

MINITAB Scatter Plot of New
Residential and New
Nonresidential Construction

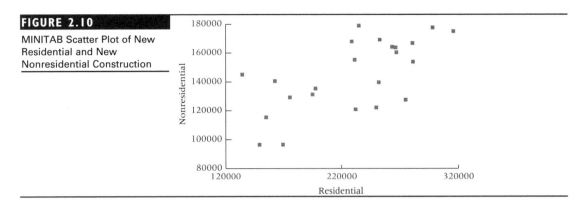

various years over a 35-year period. Do these two numerical variables exhibit any relationship? It might seem logical when new construction booms that it would boom in both residential building and in nonresidential building at the same time. However, the MINITAB scatter plot of these data displayed in Figure 2.10 shows somewhat mixed results. The apparent tendency is that more new residential building construction occurs when more new nonresidential building construction is also taking place and less new residential building construction when new nonresidential building construction is also at lower levels. The scatter plot also shows that in some years more new residential building and less new nonresidential building happened at the same time, and vice versa.

## 2.3 PROBLEMS

2.15    The U.S. National Oceanic and Atmospheric Administration, National Marine Fisheries Service, publishes data on the quantity and value of domestic fishing in the United States. The quantity (in millions of pounds) of fish caught and used for human food and for industrial products (oil, bait, animal food, etc.) over a decade follows. Is a relationship evident between the quantity used for human food and the quantity used for industrial products for a given year? Construct a scatter plot of the data. Examine the plot and discuss the strength of the relationship of the two variables.

| Human Food | Industrial Product |
|------------|--------------------|
| 3654 | 2828 |
| 3547 | 2430 |
| 3285 | 3082 |
| 3238 | 3201 |
| 3320 | 3118 |
| 3294 | 2964 |
| 3393 | 2638 |
| 3946 | 2950 |
| 4588 | 2604 |
| 6204 | 2259 |

2.16    Are the advertising dollars spent by a company related to total sales revenue? The following data represent the advertising dollars and the sales revenues for various companies in a given industry during a recent year. Construct a scatter plot of the data from the two variables and discuss the relationship between the two variables.

| Advertising (in $millions) | Sales (in $millions) |
|---|---|
| 4.2 | 155.7 |
| 1.6 | 87.3 |
| 6.3 | 135.6 |
| 2.7 | 99.0 |
| 10.4 | 168.2 |
| 7.1 | 136.9 |
| 5.5 | 101.4 |
| 8.3 | 158.2 |

# State of Auto Manufacturing

Because the raw data in the Decision Dilemma are in the millions, it is advantageous to represent the data graphically for the reader/listener. As examples of what can be done graphically, the 1999 market share data are shown in a MINITAB pie chart in Figure 2.11; the 2000 data are shown in an Excel histogram in Figure 2.12.

The dealership data can be summarized using either a frequency distribution or a stem and leaf plot. The following frequency distribution of the data shows the range of the data to be $69 - 30 = 39$. If the class widths are 5 and the frequency distribution begins at 30, 8 classes are needed.

| | |
|---|---|
| 30–under 35 | 6 |
| 35–under 40 | 0 |
| 40–under 45 | 7 |
| 45–under 50 | 6 |
| 50–under 55 | 2 |
| 55–under 60 | 6 |
| 60–under 65 | 6 |
| 65–under 70 | 7 |

## ETHICAL CONSIDERATIONS

Ethical considerations for techniques learned in Chapter 2 begin with the data chosen for representation. With the abundance of available data in business, the person constructing the data summary must be selective in choosing the reported variables. The potential is great for the analyst to select variables or even data within variables that are favorable to his or her own situation or that are perceived to be well received by the listener.

Section 2.1 noted that the number of classes and the size of the intervals in frequency distributions are usually selected by the researcher. The researcher should be careful to select values and sizes that will give an honest, accurate reflection of the situation and not a biased over- or understated case.

Sections 2.2 and 2.3 discussed the construction of charts and graphs. It pointed out that in many instances, it makes sense to use unequal scales on the axes. However, doing so opens the possibility of "cheating with statistics" by stretching or compressing of the axes to underscore the researcher's or analyst's point. It is imperative that frequency distributions and charts and graphs be constructed in a manner that most reflects actual data and not merely the researcher's own agenda.

A stem and leaf plot of these data would appear as follows.

| Stem | Leaf |
|------|------|
| 3 | 0 1 3 4 4 4 |
| 4 | 0 3 4 4 4 4 4 5 5 7 7 9 9 |
| 5 | 1 2 7 7 7 8 8 9 |
| 6 | 0 1 1 2 3 4 5 5 6 7 7 8 9 |

A scatter plot can be used to examine the relationship between the 1999 and the 2000 data. An Excel plot of these two numerical variables is shown in Figure 2.13.

**FIGURE 2.11**

Pie Chart of Company

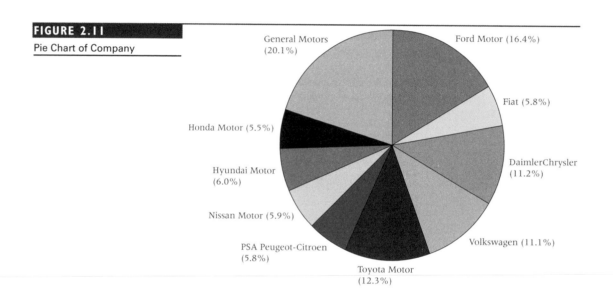

**FIGURE 2.12**

Histogram of Company
Sales Data

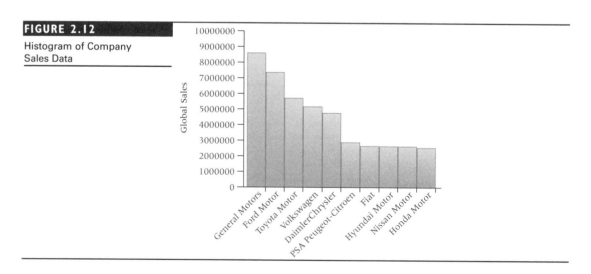

**FIGURE 2.13**

A Scatter Plot of Company Sales Data for 1999 and 2000

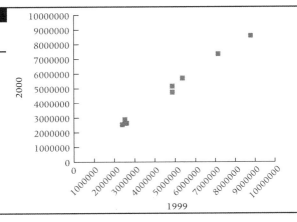

# SUMMARY

The two types of data are grouped and ungrouped. Most statistical analysis is performed on ungrouped, or raw, data. Grouped data are data organized into a frequency distribution. Differentiating between grouped and ungrouped data is important, because statistical operations on the two types are computed differently.

Constructing a frequency distribution involves several steps. The first step is to determine the range of the data, which is the difference between the largest value and the smallest value. Next, the number of classes is determined, which is an arbitrary choice of the researcher. However, too few classes overaggregate the data into meaningless categories, and too many classes do not summarize the data enough to be useful. The third step in constructing the frequency distribution is to determine the width of the class interval. Dividing the range of values by the number of classes yields the approximate width of the class interval.

The class midpoint is the midpoint of a class interval. It is the average of the class endpoints and represents the halfway point of the class interval. Relative frequency is a value computed by dividing an individual frequency by the sum of the frequencies. Relative frequency represents the proportion of total values that is in a given class interval. It is analogous to the probability of randomly drawing a value from a given class interval out of all values. The cumulative frequency is a running total frequency tally that starts with the first frequency value and adds each ensuing frequency to the total.

The types of graphic depictions presented in this chapter are histograms, frequency polygons, ogives, pie charts, stem and leaf plots, Pareto charts, and scatter plots. Graphical depiction of data is especially useful in helping statisticians to determine the shape of distributions. A histogram is a vertical bar chart in which a line segment connects class endpoints at the value of the frequency. Two vertical lines connect this line segment down to the $x$ axis, forming a rectangle. Histograms are taking on a growing importance as an initial analysis tool. The statistician can learn much about the shape of the distribution and other important characteristics of the data by examining a histogram of the data. A frequency polygon is constructed by plotting a dot at the midpoint of each class interval for the value of each frequency and then connecting the dots. Ogives are cumulative frequency polygons. Points on an ogive are plotted at the class endpoints. The ogive graph starts at the beginning of the first class interval with a value of zero and continues through the values of the cumulative frequencies to the class endpoints.

A pie chart is a circular depiction of data. The amount of each category is represented as a slice of the pie proportionate to the total. The slices are determined by multiplying the proportion of each category by 360° to compute the number of degrees of the circle allotted to each category. The researcher is cautioned in using pie charts because it is sometimes difficult to differentiate the relative sizes of the slices. Stem and leaf plots are another way to organize data. The numbers are divided into two parts, a stem and a leaf. The stems are the leftmost digits of the numbers and the leaves are the rightmost digits. The business researcher determines how to divide the digits into stems and leaves. The stems are listed individually, with all leaf values corresponding to each stem displayed beside that stem.

A Pareto chart is a vertical bar chart that is used in Total Quality Management to graphically display the causes of problems. The Pareto chart presents problem causes in descending order to assist the decision maker in prioritizing problem causes. The scatter plot is a two-dimensional plot of pairs of points from two numerical variables. It is used to graphically determine whether any apparent relationship exists between the two variables.

## KEY TERMS

| | | | |
|---|---|---|---|
| class mark | frequency polygon | Pareto chart | scatter plot |
| class midpoint | grouped data | pie chart | stem and leaf plot |
| cumulative frequency | histogram | range | ungrouped data |
| frequency distribution | ogive | relative frequency | |

## SUPPLEMENTARY PROBLEMS

### CALCULATING THE STATISTICS

2.17 For the following data, construct a frequency distribution with six classes.

| | | | | |
|---|---|---|---|---|
| 57 | 23 | 35 | 18 | 21 |
| 26 | 51 | 47 | 29 | 21 |
| 46 | 43 | 29 | 23 | 39 |
| 50 | 41 | 19 | 36 | 28 |
| 31 | 42 | 52 | 29 | 18 |
| 28 | 46 | 33 | 28 | 20 |

2.18 For each class interval of the frequency distribution given, determine the class midpoint, the relative frequency, and the cumulative frequency.

| Class Interval | Frequency |
|---|---|
| 20–under 25 | 17 |
| 25–under 30 | 20 |
| 30–under 35 | 16 |
| 35–under 40 | 15 |
| 40–under 45 | 8 |
| 45–under 50 | 6 |

2.19 Construct a histogram, a frequency polygon, and an ogive for the following frequency distribution.

| Class Interval | Frequency |
|---|---|
| 50–under 60 | 13 |
| 60–under 70 | 27 |
| 70–under 80 | 43 |
| 80–under 90 | 31 |
| 90–under 100 | 9 |

2.20 Construct a pie chart from the following data.

| Label | Value |
|---|---|
| A | 55 |
| B | 121 |
| C | 83 |
| D | 46 |

2.21 Construct a stem and leaf plot for the following data. Let the leaf contain one digit.

| | | | | |
|---|---|---|---|---|
| 312 | 324 | 289 | 335 | 298 |
| 314 | 309 | 294 | 326 | 317 |
| 290 | 311 | 317 | 301 | 316 |
| 306 | 286 | 308 | 284 | 324 |

2.22 An examination of rejects shows at least 10 problems. A frequency tally of the problems follows. Construct a Pareto chart for these data.

| Problem | Frequency |
|---|---|
| 1 | 673 |
| 2 | 29 |
| 3 | 108 |
| 4 | 379 |
| 5 | 73 |
| 6 | 564 |
| 7 | 12 |
| 8 | 402 |
| 9 | 54 |
| 10 | 202 |

2.23 Construct a scatter plot for the following two numerical variables.

| $x$ | $y$ |
|---|---|
| 12 | 5 |
| 17 | 3 |
| 9 | 10 |
| 6 | 15 |
| 10 | 8 |
| 14 | 9 |
| 8 | 8 |

### TESTING YOUR UNDERSTANDING

2.24 The Whitcomb Company manufactures a metal ring for industrial engines that usually weighs about 50 ounces. A random sample of 50 of these metal rings produced the following weights (in ounces).

| | | | | | |
|---|---|---|---|---|---|
| 51 | 53 | 56 | 50 | 44 | 47 |
| 53 | 53 | 42 | 57 | 46 | 55 |
| 41 | 44 | 52 | 56 | 50 | 57 |
| 44 | 46 | 41 | 52 | 69 | 53 |
| 57 | 51 | 54 | 63 | 42 | 47 |
| 47 | 52 | 53 | 46 | 36 | 58 |
| 51 | 38 | 49 | 50 | 62 | 39 |
| 44 | 55 | 43 | 52 | 43 | 42 |
| 57 | 49 | | | | |

Construct a frequency distribution for these data using eight classes. What can you observe about the data from the frequency distribution?

**2.25** A northwestern distribution company surveyed 53 of its midlevel managers. The survey obtained the ages of these managers, which later were organized into the frequency distribution shown. Determine the class midpoint, relative frequency, and cumulative frequency for these data.

| Class Interval | Frequency |
|---|---|
| 20–under 25 | 8 |
| 25–under 30 | 6 |
| 30–under 35 | 5 |
| 35–under 40 | 12 |
| 40–under 45 | 15 |
| 45–under 50 | 7 |

**2.26** The following data are shaped roughly like a normal distribution (discussed in Chapter 6).

| | | | | | |
|---|---|---|---|---|---|
| 61.4 | 27.3 | 26.4 | 37.4 | 30.4 | 47.5 |
| 63.9 | 46.8 | 67.9 | 19.1 | 81.6 | 47.9 |
| 73.4 | 54.6 | 65.1 | 53.3 | 71.6 | 58.6 |
| 57.3 | 87.8 | 71.1 | 74.1 | 48.9 | 60.2 |
| 54.8 | 60.5 | 32.5 | 61.7 | 55.1 | 48.2 |
| 56.8 | 60.1 | 52.9 | 60.5 | 55.6 | 38.1 |
| 76.4 | 46.8 | 19.9 | 27.3 | 77.4 | 58.1 |
| 32.1 | 54.9 | 32.7 | 40.1 | 52.7 | 32.5 |
| 35.3 | 39.1 | | | | |

Construct a frequency distribution starting with 10 as the lowest class beginning point and use a class width of 10. Construct a histogram and a frequency polygon for this frequency distribution and observe the shape of a normal distribution. On the basis of your results from these graphs, what does a normal distribution look like?

**2.27** Use the data from Problem 2.25.

**a.** Construct a histogram and a frequency polygon.

**b.** Construct an ogive.

**2.28** In a medium-sized southern city, 86 houses are for sale, each having about 2000 square feet of floor space. The asking prices vary. The frequency distribution shown contains the price categories for the 86 houses. Construct a histogram, a frequency polygon, and an ogive from these data.

| Asking Price | Frequency |
|---|---|
| $ 60,000–under $ 70,000 | 21 |
| 70,000–under 80,000 | 27 |
| 80,000–under 90,000 | 18 |
| 90,000–under 100,000 | 11 |
| 100,000–under 110,000 | 6 |
| 110,000–under 120,000 | 3 |

**2.29** Good, relatively inexpensive prenatal care often can prevent a lifetime of expense owing to complications resulting from a baby's low birth weight. A survey of a random sample of 57 new mothers asked them to estimate how much they spent on prenatal care. The researcher tallied the results and presented them in the frequency distribution shown. Use these data to construct a histogram, a frequency polygon, and an ogive.

| Amount Spent on Prenatal Care | Frequency of New Mothers |
|---|---|
| $ 0–under $100 | 3 |
| 100–under 200 | 6 |
| 200–under 300 | 12 |
| 300–under 400 | 19 |
| 400–under 500 | 11 |
| 500–under 600 | 6 |

**2.30** A consumer group surveyed food prices at 87 stores on the East Coast. Among the food prices being measured was that of sugar. From the data collected, the group constructed the frequency distribution of the prices of 5 pounds of Domino's sugar in the stores surveyed. Compute a histogram, a frequency polygon, and an ogive for the following data.

| Price | Frequency |
|---|---|
| $1.75–under $1.90 | 9 |
| 1.90–under 2.05 | 14 |
| 2.05–under 2.20 | 17 |
| 2.20–under 2.35 | 16 |
| 2.35–under 2.50 | 18 |
| 2.50–under 2.65 | 8 |
| 2.65–under 2.80 | 5 |

**2.31** The top music genres according to SoundScan for a recent year are R&B, Alternative (Rock) Music, Rap, and Country. These and other music genres along with the number of albums sold in each (in millions) are shown.

| Genre | Albums Sold |
|---|---|
| R&B | 146.4 |
| Alternative | 102.6 |
| Rap | 73.7 |
| Country | 64.5 |
| Soundtrack | 56.4 |
| Metal | 26.6 |
| Classical | 14.8 |
| Latin | 14.5 |

Construct a pie chart for these data displaying the percentage of the whole that each of these genres represents.

**2.32** The following figures for U.S. imports of agricultural products and manufactured goods were taken from selected years between 1970 and 2000 (in $ billions). The source of the data is the U.S. International Trade Administration. Construct a scatter plot for these data and determine whether any relationship is apparent between the U.S. imports of agricultural products and the U.S. imports of manufactured goods during this time period.

| Agricultural Products | Manufactured Goods |
|---|---|
| 5.8 | 27.3 |
| 9.5 | 54.0 |
| 17.4 | 133.0 |
| 19.5 | 257.5 |
| 22.3 | 388.8 |
| 29.3 | 629.7 |

**2.33** We show a list of the industries with the largest total release of toxic chemicals in 1998 according to the U.S. Environmental Protection Agency. Construct a pie chart to depict this information.

| Industry | Total Release (pounds) |
|---|---|
| Chemicals | 737,100,000 |
| Primary metals | 566,400,000 |
| Paper | 229,900,000 |
| Plastics and rubber | 109,700,000 |
| Transportation equipment | 102,500,000 |
| Food | 89,300,000 |
| Fabricated metals | 85,900,000 |
| Petroleum | 63,300,000 |
| Electrical equipment | 29,100,000 |

**2.34** A manufacturing company produces plastic bottles for the dairy industry. Some of the bottles are rejected because of poor quality. Causes of poor-quality bottles include faulty plastic, incorrect labeling, discoloration, incorrect thickness, broken handle, and others. The following data for 500 plastic bottles that were rejected include the problems and the frequency of the problems. Use these data to construct a Pareto chart. Discuss the implications of the chart.

| Problem | Number |
|---|---|
| Discoloration | 32 |
| Thickness | 117 |
| Broken handle | 86 |
| Fault in plastic | 221 |
| Labeling | 44 |

**2.35** A research organization selected 50 U.S. towns with Census 2000 populations between 4,000 and 6,000 as a sample to represent small towns for survey purposes. The populations of these towns follow.

| | | | | |
|---|---|---|---|---|
| 4420 | 5221 | 4299 | 5831 | 5750 |
| 5049 | 5556 | 4361 | 5737 | 4654 |
| 4653 | 5338 | 4512 | 4388 | 5923 |
| 4730 | 4963 | 5090 | 4822 | 4304 |
| 4758 | 5366 | 5431 | 5291 | 5254 |
| 4866 | 5858 | 4346 | 4734 | 5919 |
| 4216 | 4328 | 4459 | 5832 | 5873 |
| 5257 | 5048 | 4232 | 4878 | 5166 |
| 5366 | 4212 | 5669 | 4224 | 4440 |
| 4299 | 5263 | 4339 | 4834 | 5478 |

Construct a stem and leaf plot for the data, letting each leaf contain two digits.

**2.36** Listed here are 30 different weekly Dow Jones industrial stock averages.

| | | | | |
|---|---|---|---|---|
| 2656 | 2301 | 2975 | 3002 | 2468 |
| 2742 | 2830 | 2405 | 2677 | 2990 |
| 2200 | 2764 | 2337 | 2961 | 3010 |
| 2976 | 2375 | 2602 | 2670 | 2922 |
| 2344 | 2760 | 2555 | 2524 | 2814 |
| 2996 | 2437 | 2268 | 2448 | 2460 |

Construct a stem and leaf plot for these 30 values. Let the stem contain two digits.

**INTERPRETING THE OUTPUT**

**2.37** Suppose 150 shoppers at an upscale mall are interviewed and one of the questions asked is the household income. Study the MINITAB histogram of the following data and discuss what can be learned about the shoppers.

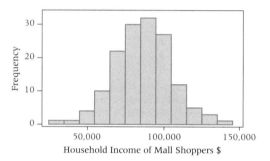

**2.38** Shown here is an Excel-produced pie chart representing physician specialties. What does the chart tell you about the various specialties?

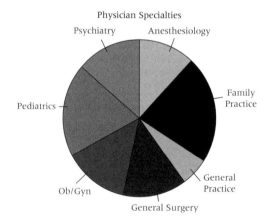

**2.39** Suppose 100 CPA firms are surveyed to determine how many audits they perform over a certain time. The data are summarized using the MINITAB stem and leaf plot shown. What can you learn about the number of audits being performed by these firms from this plot?

### Character Stem and Leaf Display

Stem and leaf of Number of Audits    N = 100
Leaf Unit = 1.0

| | | |
|---|---|---|
| 9 | 1 | 222333333 |
| 16 | 1 | 4445555 |
| 26 | 1 | 6666667777 |
| 35 | 1 | 888899999 |
| 39 | 2 | 0001 |
| 44 | 2 | 22333 |
| 49 | 2 | 55555 |
| (9) | 2 | 677777777 |
| 42 | 2 | 8888899 |
| 35 | 3 | 000111 |
| 29 | 3 | 223333 |
| 23 | 3 | 44455555 |
| 15 | 3 | 67777 |
| 10 | 3 | 889 |
| 7 | 4 | 0011 |
| 3 | 4 | 222 |

2.40 The following Excel ogive shows toy sales by a company over a 12-month period. What conclusions can you reach about toy sales at this company?

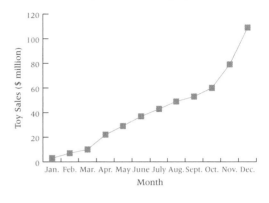

## ANALYZING THE DATABASES

*see* www.wiley.com/college/black

1. Using the manufacturing database, construct a frequency distribution for the variable, Number of Production Workers Across All Industries. In Excel the frequency distribution is referred to a histogram. In MINITAB, produce a frequency distribution by constructing a histogram checking *Frequency* under *Options* and by checking *Show Data Labels* under *Annotation*, thereby revealing the class frequency counts. What does the frequency distribution reveal about the number of production workers?

2. Using the stock market database, construct a histogram for the variable, Reported Trades. How is the histogram shaped? Is it high in the middle or near one or both of the endpoints? Is it relatively

constant in size across the classes (uniform) or does it appear to have no shape? Does it appear to be "normally" distributed?

3. Construct an ogive for the variable, Type, in the financial database. The 100 companies in this database are each categorized into one of seven types of companies. These types are listed at the end of Chapter 1. Construct a pie chart of these types and discuss the output. For example, which type is most prevalent in the database and which is the least?

4. Using the international unemployment database, construct a stem and leaf plot for Italy. What does the plot show about unemployment for Italy over the past 40 years? What does the plot fail to show?

## CASE: SOAP COMPANIES DO BATTLE

Procter & Gamble has been the leading soap manufacturer in the United States since 1879, when it introduced Ivory soap. However, late in 1991 its major rival, Lever Bros. (Unilever), overtook it by grabbing 31.5% of the $1.6 billion personal soap market, of which Procter & Gamble had a 30.5% share. Lever Bros. had trailed Procter & Gamble since it entered the soap market with Lifebuoy in 1895. In 1990 Lever Bros. introduced a new soap, Lever 2000, into its product mix as a soap for the entire family. A niche for such a soap had been created because of the segmentation of the soap market into specialty soaps for children, women, and men. Lever Bros. felt that it could sell a soap for everyone in the family. Consumer

response was strong; Lever 2000 rolled up $113 million in sales in 1991, putting Lever Bros. ahead of Procter & Gamble for the first time in the personal-soap revenue contest. Procter & Gamble still sells more soap, but Lever's brands cost more, thereby resulting in greater overall sales.

Needless to say, Procter & Gamble was quick to search for a response to the success of Lever 2000. Procter & Gamble looked at several possible strategies, including repositioning Safeguard, which has been seen as a male soap. Ultimately, Procter & Gamble responded to the challenge by introducing its Oil of Olay Moisturizing Bath Bar. In its first year of national distribution, this product was backed by a $24 million media effort. The new bath bar was quite successful and helped Procter & Gamble regain market share.

The following represent the latest figures on the leading personal soaps in the United States with their respective sales figures. Each of these soaps is produced by one of four soap manufacturers: Unilever, Procter & Gamble, Dial, and Colgate-Palmolive.

| Soap | Manufacturer | Sales ($ millions) |
|------|--------------|---------------------|
| Dove | Unilever | 271 |
| Dial | Dial | 193 |
| Lever 2000 | Unilever | 138 |
| Irish Spring | Colgate-Palmolive | 121 |
| Zest | Procter & Gamble | 115 |
| Ivory | Procter & Gamble | 94 |
| Caress | Unilever | 93 |
| Olay | Procter & Gamble | 69 |
| Safeguard | Procter & Gamble | 48 |
| Coast | Dial | 44 |

In 1983 the market shares for soap were Procter & Gamble with 37.1%, Lever Bros. (Unilever) with 24%, Dial with 15%, Colgate-Palmolive with 6.5%, and all others with 17.4%. By 1991 the market shares for soap were Lever Bros. (Unilever) with 31.5%, Procter & Gamble with 30.5%, Dial with 19%, Colgate-Palmolive with 8%, and all others with 11%.

### DISCUSSION

1. Suppose you are making a report for Procter & Gamble displaying their share of the market along with the share of other companies for the years 1983, 1991, and the latest figures. Using either Excel or MINITAB, produce graphs for the market shares of personal soap for each of these years. For the latest figures data, assume that the "all others" total is about $119 million. What do you observe about the market shares of the various companies by studying the graphs? In particular, how is Procter & Gamble doing relative to previous years?

2. Suppose Procter & Gamble sells about 20 million bars of soap per week, but the demand is not constant and production management would like to get a better handle on how sales are distributed over the year. Let the following sales figures given in units of million bars represent the sales of bars per week over one year.

Construct a histogram to represent these data. What do you see in the graph that might be helpful to the production (and sales) people?

| | | | | | | | |
|---|---|---|---|---|---|---|---|
| 17.1 | 19.6 | 15.4 | 17.4 | 15.0 | 18.5 | 20.6 | 18.4 |
| 20.0 | 20.9 | 19.3 | 18.2 | 14.7 | 17.1 | 12.2 | 19.9 |
| 18.7 | 20.4 | 20.3 | 15.5 | 16.8 | 19.1 | 20.4 | 15.4 |
| 20.3 | 17.5 | 17.0 | 18.3 | 13.6 | 39.8 | 20.7 | 21.3 |
| 22.5 | 21.4 | 23.4 | 23.1 | 22.8 | 21.4 | 24.0 | 25.2 |
| 26.3 | 23.9 | 30.6 | 25.2 | 26.2 | 26.9 | 32.8 | 26.3 |
| 26.6 | 24.3 | 26.2 | 23.8 | | | | |

Construct a stem and leaf plot using the whole numbers as the stems. What advantages does the stem and leaf plot of these sales figures offer over the histogram? What are some disadvantages? Which would you use in discussions with production people and why?

3. A random sample of finished soap bars in their packaging is tested for quality. All defective bars are examined for problem causes. Among the problems found were improper packaging, poor labeling, bad seal, shape of bar wrong, bar surface marred, wrong color in bar, wrong bar fragrance, wrong soap consistency, and others. Some of the leading problem causes and the number of each are given here. Use a Pareto chart to analyze these problem causes. Based on your findings, what would you recommend to the company?

| Problem Cause | Frequency |
|---------------|-----------|
| Bar surface | 89 |
| Color | 17 |
| Fragrance | 2 |
| Label | 32 |
| Shape | 8 |
| Seal | 47 |
| Labeling | 5 |
| Soap consistency | 3 |

*Source:* Adapted from Valerie Reitman, "Buoyant Sales of Lever 2000 Soap Bring Sinking Sensation to Procter & Gamble," *Wall Street Journal*, 19 March 1992, p. B1. Reprinted by permission of The Wall Street Journal © 1992, Dow Jones & Company, Inc. All rights reserved worldwide; Pam Weisz, "$40 M Extends Lever 2000 Family," *Brandweek*, vol. 36, no. 32 (21 August 1995), p. 6; Laurie Freeman, "P&G Pushes Back against Unilever in Soap," *Advertising Age*, vol. 65, no. 41 (28 September 1994), p. 21; Jeanne Whalen and Pat Sloan, "Intros Help Boost Soap Coupons," *Advertising Age*, vol. 65, no. 19 (2 May 1994), p. 30; and "P&G Places Coast Soap Up for Sale," *The Post*, World Wide Web Edition of *The Cincinnati Post*, 2 February 1999, http://www.cincypost.com.business /pg022599.html.

## USING THE COMPUTER

### EXCEL

With **Chart Wizard,** Excel offers the capability of producing many of the charts and graphs presented in this chapter. In addition, Excel can generate frequency distributions and histograms using **Data Analysis.**

Many of the techniques in this course can be done on Excel using a tool called **Data Analysis.** To access the **Data** Analysis feature, select **Tools** on the menu bar. **Data Analysis** is located at the bottom of the **Tools** pull-down menu. If **Data Analysis** does not appear on this menu, it must be added in. This add-in need only be done once. To add in **Data Analysis,** select **Add-ins** on the **Tools** menu. On the **Add-ins** dialog box that appears, check **Analysis ToolPak** (not **Analysis ToolPak—VBA**). Click OK and **Analysis ToolPak** will be added to the **Tools** capability.

Excel refers to frequency distributions as histograms. In Excel the classes are called bins. If you do not specify bins, Excel will automatically determine the number of bins. If you want to specify the bins, load the class endpoints into a column. To compute the frequency distribution, select **Tools** on the Excel menu bar. Select **Data Analysis** from the **Tools** pull-down menu and select **Histogram** from the **Data Analysis** dialog box. Place the location of the raw values of data into **Input Range.** If you want to specify class endpoints, place the location of the endpoints into **Bin Range.** If you want Excel to automatically determine the bins, leave this blank. If you have labels, then check **Labels.** If you want a histogram graph, check **Chart Output** at the bottom of the dialog box. If you want an ogive, select **Cumulative Percentage** along with **Chart Output,** and Excel will yield a histogram graph with an ogive overlaid on it. Select one of the output options. After clicking OK you will get a frequency distribution as output with bins and frequencies along with a histogram graph.

After constructing a frequency distribution, you can construct histograms, frequency polygons, and ogives with the **Chart Wizard** feature. To access the **Chart Wizard** select **Insert** on the menu bar. From the pull-down menu select **Chart.** A variety of charts and graphs are available here. The first is called **Column.** With it a histogram-type chart can be constructed. These Column charts are actually vertical bar charts with spaces between the classes. Select **Column,** and then move through the four dialog boxes that follow, filling in the appropriate information. In the data range box place the location of the bins and the frequencies from the frequency distribution. In the **Chart Wizard** it is possible to modify the titles, axes, legend, and location of the output as desired. To convert a vertical bar graph into a histogram by eliminating the gap between bars, right click on one of the bars of the graph. From the menu that appears, select **Format Data Series.** From the dialog box that appears, select **Options.** In the space beside **Gap width,** place a zero or reduce the number to zero. Click OK. The gap will disappear.

A frequency polygon can be constructed by selecting **Line** on the **Chart Wizard.** The steps are virtually the same for the Line chart as for the Column chart.

To construct an ogive, the data must be cumulated first when the frequency distribution is being constructed by checking **Cumulative Percentage** in the Histogram dialog box. The **Chart Wizard** can then be used to construct the ogive by selecting **Line** chart. The four-step dialog boxes are virtually the same as those used to construct vertical bar charts and frequency polygons except that at step 2 you must select the **Series** tab. Under **Series,** highlight **Frequency** and select **Remove,** which leaves you with just the cumulative percentages or an ogive.

To construct a pie chart in Excel, load the labels (company, person, etc.) into one column and the values (frequency, dollar value, percentage, etc.) into another column. Select **Insert** from the menu bar, then select **Chart** from the pull-down menu. Select **Pie** from this menu and follow the directions through the four steps. You have the option of including

a legend, determining what data labels to use if any, and determining the final location of the pie chart.

To construct a scatter plot in Excel, load the data for each variable in a separate column. Select **Insert** from the menu bar, then select **Chart** from the pull-down menu. Select **XY (Scatter)** from this menu and follow the directions through the four steps. You have the option of including a legend, determining what data labels to use if any, and determining the final location of the scatter plot.

## MINITAB

MINITAB has the capability of constructing histograms, frequency polygons, ogives, pie charts, stem and leaf charts, Pareto charts, and scatter plots along with the essentials needed to construct a frequency distribution. With the exception of Pareto charts, which are accessed through **Stat,** all of these charts and graphs are accessed by selecting **Graph** on the menu bar.

Histograms, frequency polygons, and ogives are constructed in MINITAB using the **Histogram** option on the **Graph** pull-down menu. To begin, insert the column location of the raw data into the first line under **Graph variables** in the **Histogram** dialog box. Multiple graphs can be made by inserting locations in several lines under **Graph variables.** Under **Data display,** select the type of graph desired. Use **Bar** for a histogram and **Connect** for a frequency polygon or an ogive. Several options are available in this dialog box for setting the number of classes, giving the graph a title, modifying the axes, and so on. The **Options** dialog box is especially important in modifying the number of classes, determining the type of intervals used, and constructing an ogive. To construct an ogive, select **Cumulative Frequency** in the **Options** dialog box. To construct a frequency polygon, a histogram, or to determine frequencies for a frequency distribution, select **Frequency.** Most of the essentials of a frequency distribution can be obtained by constructing a histogram, selecting **Annotation** from the Histogram dialog box, and then selecting **Data Labels.** In the **Data Labels** dialog box, check **Show data labels.** This option will add frequencies to the graph. From these frequencies and the class endpoints displayed on the graph, a frequency distribution can be constructed.

Pie charts are constructed by selecting **Pie Chart** on the **Graph** pull-down menu. In the **Pie Chart** dialog box, the two main options are **Chart data in** and **Chart table.** Use the **Chart data in** option if the values to be used in constructing the pie chart are in a single column. Use the **Chart table** option if the categories are in one column and the frequencies (values) are in another column. Other options are available, such as how to order the pie slices, exploding slices, colors, or labels.

Stem and leaf plots are constructed by selecting **Stem-and-leaf...** from the **Graph** pull-down menu. In the **Stem-and-leaf...** dialog box, enter the location of the data and click OK. The output contains stems and leaves but in addition gives a cumulative frequency count above and below the median value (displayed on the left of the output).

To construct a Pareto chart, begin by selecting <u>S</u>tat from the menu bar. From the pull-down menu that appears, select **Quality Tools.** From the **Quality Tools** pull-down menu select **<u>P</u>areto Chart.** From the **<u>P</u>areto Chart** dialog box select **C<u>h</u>art defects table** if you have a summary of the defects with the reasons (**<u>L</u>abels**) in one column and the frequency of occurrence (**<u>F</u>requencies**) in another column. Enter the location of the reasons in **<u>L</u>abels** and the location of the frequencies in **<u>F</u>requencies.** If you have unsummarized data, you can select **<u>C</u>hart defects data in.** In the space provided, give the location of the column with all the defects that occurred. It is possible to have the defects either by name or with some code. If you want to have the labels in one column and the defects in another, then select **<u>B</u>Y variable in** and place the location of the labels there.

To construct a scatter plot, select **<u>G</u>raph,** then select **<u>P</u>lot.** In the **<u>P</u>lot** dialog box under **<u>G</u>raph variables,** place the location of the $y$ variable in the first space under **Y** and the location of the $x$ variable in the second space under **X.** Multiple scatter plots can be created by filling in the spaces beside **Graph 2, Graph 3,** and so on. To get a scatter plot (instead of a line plot, etc.), select **Symbol** under **Display** in the **Data display** portion of the dialog box.

# Descriptive Statistics

**LEARNING OBJECTIVES**

The focus of Chapter 3 is the use of statistical techniques to describe data, thereby enabling you to:

1. Distinguish between measures of central tendency, measures of variability, measures of shape, and measures of association.
2. Understand the meanings of mean, median, mode, quartile, percentile, and range.
3. Compute mean, median, mode, percentile, quartile, range, variance, standard deviation, and mean absolute deviation on ungrouped data.
4. Differentiate between sample and population variance and standard deviation.
5. Understand the meaning of standard deviation as it is applied by using the empirical rule and Chebyshev's theorem.
6. Compute the mean, mode, standard deviation, and variance on grouped data.
7. Understand skewness, kurtosis, and box and whisker plots.
8. Compute a coefficient of correlation and interpret it.

*Business Statistics For Contemporary Decision Making 4th Edition Update,*
Ken Black . ISBN-10 0-471-70563-2 ©2006 John Wiley & Sons, Inc.

## Laundry Statistics

According to Procter & Gamble, 35 billion loads of laundry are run in the United States each year. Every second, 1,100 loads are started. Statistics show that one person in the United States generates a quarter of a ton of dirty clothing each year. Americans appear to be spending more time doing laundry than they did 40 years ago. Today, the average American woman spends seven to nine hours a week on laundry. However, industry research shows that the result is dirtier laundry than in other developed countries. Various companies market new and improved versions of washers and detergents. Yet, Americans seem to be resistant to manufacturers' innovations in this area. In the United States, the average washing machine uses about 16 gallons of water. In Europe, the figure is about 4 gallons. The average wash cycle of an American wash is about 35 minutes compared to 90 minutes in Europe. Americans prefer top loading machines because they do not have to bend over, and the top loading machines are larger. Europeans use the smaller front-loading machines because of smaller living spaces.

### Managerial and Statistical Questions

Virtually all of the statistics cited here are gleaned from studies or surveys.

1. Suppose a study of laundry usage is done in 50 U.S. households that contain washers and dryers. Water measurements are taken for the number of gallons of water used by each washing machine in completing a cycle. The following data are the number of gallons used by each washing machine during the washing cycle. Summarize the data so that study findings can be reported.

   | | | | | | | | | | |
   |---|---|---|---|---|---|---|---|---|---|
   | 15 | 17 | 16 | 15 | 16 | 17 | 18 | 15 | 14 | 15 |
   | 16 | 16 | 17 | 16 | 15 | 15 | 17 | 14 | 15 | 16 |
   | 16 | 17 | 14 | 15 | 12 | 15 | 16 | 14 | 14 | 16 |
   | 15 | 13 | 16 | 17 | 17 | 15 | 16 | 16 | 16 | 14 |
   | 17 | 16 | 17 | 14 | 16 | 13 | 16 | 15 | 16 | 15 |

2. The average wash cycle for an American wash is 35 minutes. Suppose the standard deviation of a wash cycle for an American wash is 5 minutes. Within what range of time do most American wash cycles fall?

3. Is the amount of laundry done by a household each year related in some way to the household income? Suppose eight households of two adults and two children are randomly chosen for a study. Over a year period, a record is kept of the weight of clothing washed by each household, and their annual household income is ascertained. From the following study data, determine whether a relationship exists between a household's income and the amount of laundry done (in weight).

   | Amount of Laundry (weight in lbs.) | Household Income ($1,000s) |
   |---|---|
   | 1,210 | 42 |
   | 875 | 31 |
   | 1,890 | 60 |
   | 1,450 | 68 |
   | 2,040 | 110 |
   | 1,330 | 45 |
   | 660 | 56 |
   | 1,490 | 72 |
   | 1,950 | 93 |

*Source:* Adapted from Emily Nelson, "In Doing Laundry, Americans Cling to Outmoded Ways," *Wall Street Journal*, 16 May 2002, pp. A1 & A10.

Chapter 2 described graphical techniques for organizing and presenting data. For example, we attempted to summarize 40 years of unemployment rates for France with a frequency distribution, a histogram, a frequency polygon, and an ogive. Even though these graphs allow the researcher to make some general observations about the shape and spread of the data, a more complete understanding of the data can be attained by summarizing the data using statistics. This chapter presents such statistical measures, including measures of central tendency, measures of variability, and measures of shape. The computation of these measures is different for ungrouped and grouped data. Hence we present some measures for both ungrouped and grouped data. In addition, one of the statistics presented can be used to compute the correlation or relatedness of two numerical variables.

## 3.1 MEASURES OF CENTRAL TENDENCY: UNGROUPED DATA

One type of measure that is used to describe a set of data is the **measure of central tendency.** Measures of central tendency *yield information about the center, or middle part, of a group of numbers.* Table 3.1 displays offer price for the 20 largest U.S. initial public offerings in a recent year according to Securities Data. For these data, measures of central tendency can yield such information as the average offer price, the middle offer price, and the most frequently occurring offer price. Measures of central tendency do not focus on the span of the data set or how far values are from the middle numbers. The measures of central tendency presented here for ungrouped data are the mode, the median, the mean, percentiles, and quartiles.

### Mode

The **mode** is *the most frequently occurring value in a set of data.* For the data in Table 3.1 the mode is $19.00 because the offer price that recurred the most times (4) was $19.00. Organizing the data into an ordered array (an ordering of the numbers from smallest to largest) helps to locate the mode. The following is an ordered array of the values from Table 3.1.

| 7.00 | 11.00 | 14.25 | 15.00 | 15.00 | 15.50 | 19.00 | 19.00 | 19.00 | 19.00 |
|---|---|---|---|---|---|---|---|---|---|
| 21.00 | 22.00 | 23.00 | 24.00 | 25.00 | 27.00 | 27.00 | 28.00 | 34.22 | 43.25 |

This grouping makes it easier to see that 19.00 is the most frequently occurring number.

In the case of a tie for the most frequently occurring value, two modes are listed. Then the data are said to be **bimodal.** If a set of data is not exactly bimodal but contains two values that are more dominant than others, some researchers take the liberty of referring to the data set as bimodal even without an exact tie for the mode. Data sets with more than two modes are referred to as **multimodal.**

In the world of business, the concept of mode is often used in determining sizes. For example, shoe manufacturers might produce inexpensive shoes in three widths only: small, medium, and large. Each width size represents a modal width of feet. By reducing the number of sizes to a few modal sizes, companies can reduce total product costs by limiting machine setup costs. Similarly, the garment industry produces shirts, dresses, suits, and many other clothing products in modal sizes. For example, all size M shirts in a given lot are produced in the same size. This size is some modal size for medium-sized men.

The mode is an appropriate measure of central tendency for nominal-level data. The mode can be used to determine which category occurs most frequently.

**TABLE 3.1**

Offer Prices for the 20 Largest U.S. Initial Public Offerings in a Recent Year

| $14.25 | $19.00 | $11.00 | $28.00 |
|---|---|---|---|
| 24.00 | 23.00 | 43.25 | 19.00 |
| 27.00 | 25.00 | 15.00 | 7.00 |
| 34.22 | 15.50 | 15.00 | 22.00 |
| 19.00 | 19.00 | 27.00 | 21.00 |

### Median

The **median** is *the middle value in an ordered array of numbers.* For an array with an odd number of terms, the median is the middle number. For an array with an even number of terms, the median is the average of the two middle numbers. The following steps are used to determine the median.

STEP 1. Arrange the observations in an ordered data array.

STEP 2. For an odd number of terms, find the middle term of the ordered array. It is the median.

STEP 3. For an even number of terms, find the average of the middle two terms. This average is the median.

Suppose a business researcher wants to determine the median for the following numbers.

15   11   14   3   21   17   22   16   19   16   5   7   19   8   9   20   4

The researcher arranges the numbers in an ordered array.

3   4   5   7   8   9   11   14   15   16   16   17   19   19   20   21   22

Because the array contains 17 terms (an odd number of terms), the median is the middle number, or 15.

If the number 22 is eliminated from the list, the array would contain only 16 terms.

3   4   5   7   8   9   11   14   15   16   16   17   19   19   20   21

Now, for an even number of terms, the statistician determines the median by averaging the two middle values, 14 and 15. The resulting median value is 14.5.

Another way to locate the median is by finding the $(n + 1)/2$ term in an ordered array. For example, if a data set contains 77 terms, the median is the 39th term. That is,

$$\frac{n+1}{2} = \frac{77+1}{2} = \frac{78}{2} = 39\text{th term}$$

This formula is helpful when a large number of terms must be manipulated.

Consider the offer price data in Table 3.1. Because this data set contains 20 values, or $n = 20$, the median for these data is located at the $(20+ 1)/2$ term, or the 10.5th term. This equation indicates that the median is located halfway between the 10th and 11th terms or the average of 19.00 and 21.00. Thus, the median offer price for the largest 20 U.S. initial public offerings is $20.00.

The median is unaffected by the magnitude of extreme values. This characteristic is an advantage, because large and small values do not inordinately influence the median. For this reason, the median is often the best measure of location to use in the analysis of variables such as house costs, income, and age. Suppose, for example, that a real estate broker wants to determine the median selling price of 10 houses listed at the following prices.

| $67,000 | $105,000 | $148,000 | $5,250,000 |
|---------|----------|----------|------------|
| 91,000  | 116,000  | 167,000  |            |
| 95,000  | 122,000  | 189,000  |            |

The median is the average of the two middle terms, $116,000 and $122,000, or $119,000. This price is a reasonable representation of the prices of the 10 houses. Note that the house priced at $5,250,000 did not enter into the analysis other than to count as one of the 10 houses. If the price of the tenth house were $200,000, the results would be the same. However, if all the house prices were averaged, the resulting average price of the original 10 houses would be $635,000, higher than nine of the 10 individual prices.

A disadvantage of the median is that not all the information from the numbers is used. For example, information about the specific asking price of the most expensive house does not really enter into the computation of the median. The level of data measurement must be at least ordinal for a median to be meaningful.

## Mean

The **arithmetic mean** is *the average of a group of numbers* and is computed by summing all numbers and dividing by the number of numbers. Because the arithmetic mean is so widely used, most statisticians refer to it simply as the *mean*.

The population mean is represented by the Greek letter mu ($\mu$). The sample mean is represented by $\bar{x}$. The formulas for computing the population mean and the sample mean are given in the boxes that follow.

| POPULATION MEAN | $\mu = \dfrac{\Sigma x}{N} = \dfrac{x_1 + x_2 + x_3 + \cdots + x_N}{N}$ |
|---|---|
| SAMPLE MEAN | $\bar{x} = \dfrac{\Sigma x}{n} = \dfrac{x_1 + x_2 + x_3 \cdots + x_n}{n}$ |

The capital Greek letter sigma ($\Sigma$) is commonly used in mathematics to represent a summation of all the numbers in a grouping.* Also, $N$ is the number of terms in the population, and $n$ is the number of terms in the sample. The algorithm for computing a mean is to sum all the numbers in the population or sample and divide by the number of terms.

A more formal definition of the mean is

$$\mu = \frac{\sum_{i=1}^{N} x_i}{N}$$

However, for the purposes of this text,

$$\Sigma x \text{ denotes } \sum_{i=1}^{N} x_i$$

It is inappropriate to use the mean to analyze data that are not at least interval level in measurement.

Suppose a company has five departments with 24, 13, 19, 26, and 11 workers each. The *population mean* number of workers in each department is 18.6 workers. The computations follow.

$$
\begin{array}{r}
24 \\
13 \\
19 \\
26 \\
\underline{11} \\
\Sigma x = \quad 93
\end{array}
$$

and

$$\mu = \frac{\Sigma x}{n} = \frac{93}{5} = 18.6$$

The calculation of a sample mean uses the same algorithm as for a population mean and will produce the same answer if computed on the same data. However, it is inappropriate to compute a sample mean for a population or a population mean for a sample. Because both populations and samples are important in statistics, a separate symbol is necessary for the population mean and for the sample mean.

---

| DEMONSTRATION PROBLEM 3.1 | The number of U.S. cars in service by top car rental companies in a recent year according to *Auto Rental News* follows. |
|---|---|

| Company | Number of Cars in Service |
|---|---|
| Enterprise | 460,000 |
| Hertz | 350,000 |
| ANC Rental Group | 322,000 |
| Avis | 220,000 |
| Budget | 146,000 |
| Dollar | 78,000 |
| Thrifty | 51,000 |
| U-Save | 15,000 |
| Toyota | 12,000 |
| Rent-a-Wreck | 12,000 |
| Advantage | 12,000 |
| Payless | 8,000 |
| ACE | 8,000 |

---

* The mathematics of summations is not discussed here. A more detailed explanation is given on the CD-ROM.

Compute the mode, the median, and the mean.

Solution

Mode: 12,000

Median: With 13 different companies in this group, $n = 13$. The median is located at the $(13 + 1)/2 = $ 7th position. Because the data are already ordered, the 7th term is 51,000, which is the median.

Mean: The total number of cars in service is $1,694,000 = \Sigma x$

$$\mu = \frac{\Sigma x}{n} = \frac{1,694,000}{13} = 130,307.7$$

The mean is affected by each and every value, which is an advantage. The mean uses all the data and each data item influences the mean. It is also a disadvantage, because extremely large or small values can cause the mean to be pulled toward the extreme value. Recall the preceding discussion of the 10 house prices. If the mean is computed for the 10 houses, the mean price is higher than the prices of nine of the houses because the $5,250,000 house is included in the calculation. The total price of the 10 houses is $6,350,000, and the mean price is $635,000.

The mean is the most commonly used measure of central tendency because it uses each data item in its computation, it is a familiar measure, and it has mathematical properties that make it attractive to use in inferential statistics analysis.

## Percentiles

**Percentiles** are *measures of central tendency that divide a group of data into 100 parts.* There are 99 percentiles, because it takes 99 dividers to separate a group of data into 100 parts. The $n$th percentile is the value such that at least $n$ percent of the data are below that value and at most $(100 - n)$ percent are above that value. Specifically, the 87th percentile is a value such that at least 87% of the data are below the value and no more than 13% are above the value. Percentiles are "stair-step" values, as shown in Figure 3.1, because the 87th percentile and the 88th percentile have no percentile between. If a plant operator takes a safety examination and 87.6% of the safety exam scores are below that person's score, he or she still scores at only the 87th percentile, even though more than 87% of the scores are lower.

Percentiles are widely used in reporting test results. Almost all college or university students have taken the SAT, ACT, GRE, or GMAT examination. In most cases, the results for these examinations are reported in percentile form and also as raw scores. Shown next is a summary of the steps used in determining the location of a percentile.

### Steps in Determining the Location of a Percentile

1. Organize the numbers into an ascending-order array.
2. Calculate the percentile location ($i$) by:

$$i = \frac{P}{100}(n)$$

where

$P = $ the percentile of interest

$i = $ percentile location

$n = $ number in the data set

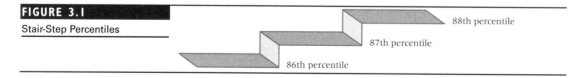

**FIGURE 3.1**

Stair-Step Percentiles

88th percentile

87th percentile

86th percentile

3.  Determine the location by either (a) or (b).

   a.  If $i$ is a whole number, the $P$th percentile is the average of the value at the $i$th location and the value at the $(i + 1)^{st}$ location.

   b.  If $i$ is not a whole number, the $P$th percentile value is located at the whole number part of $i + 1$.

For example, suppose you want to determine the 80th percentile of 1240 numbers. $P$ is 80 and $n$ is 1240. First, order the numbers from lowest to highest. Next, calculate the location of the 80th percentile.

$$i = \frac{80}{100}(1240) = 992$$

Because $i = 992$ is a whole number, follow the directions in step 3(a). The 80th percentile is the average of the 992nd number and the 993rd number.

$$P_{80} = \frac{(992\text{nd number} + 993\text{rd number})}{2}$$

| **DEMONSTRATION PROBLEM 3.2** | Determine the 30th percentile of the following eight numbers: 14, 12, 19, 23, 5, 13, 28, 17. |

**Solution**

For these eight numbers, we want to find the value of the 30th percentile, so $n = 8$ and $P = 30$.

First, organize the data into an ascending-order array.

   5        12        13        14        17        19        23        28

Next, compute the value of $i$.

$$i = \frac{30}{100}(8) = 2.4$$

Because $i$ is not a whole number, step 3(b) is used. The value of $i + 1$ is 2.4 + 1, or 3.4. The whole-number part of 3.4 is 3. The 30th percentile is located at the third value. The third value is 13, so 13 is the 30th percentile. Note that a percentile may or may not be one of the data values.

## Quartiles

**Quartiles** are *measures of central tendency that divide a group of data into four subgroups or parts.* The three quartiles are denoted as $Q_1$, $Q_2$, and $Q_3$. The first quartile, $Q_1$, separates the first, or lowest, one-fourth of the data from the upper three-fourths and is equal to the 25th percentile. The second quartile, $Q_2$, separates the second quarter of the data from the third quarter. $Q_2$ is located at the 50th percentile and equals the median of the data. The third quartile, $Q_3$, divides the first three-quarters of the data from the last quarter and is equal to the value of the 75th percentile. These three quartiles are shown in Figure 3.2.

Suppose we want to determine the values of $Q_1$, $Q_2$, and $Q_3$ for the following numbers.

   106        109        114        116        121        122        125        129

| **FIGURE 3.2** Quartiles | |
|---|---|

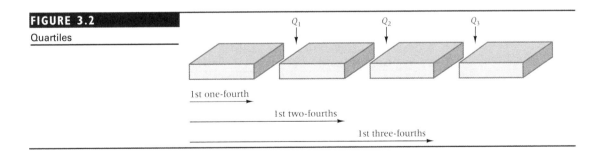

The value of $Q_1$ is found at the 25th percentile, $P_{25}$, by:

$$\text{For } n = 8, \ i = \frac{25}{100}(8) = 2$$

Because $i$ is a whole number, $P_{25}$ is found as the average of the second and third numbers.

$$P_{25} = \frac{(109 + 114)}{2} = 111.5$$

The value of $Q_1$ is $P_{25}$ = 111.5. Notice that one-fourth, or two, of the values (106 and 109) are less than 111.5.

The value of $Q_2$ is equal to the median. Because the array contains an even number of terms, the median is the average of the two middle terms.

$$Q_2 = \text{median} = \frac{(116 + 121)}{2} = 118.5$$

Notice that exactly half of the terms are less than $Q_2$ and half are greater than $Q_2$.

The value of $Q_3$ is determined by $P_{75}$ as follows.

$$i = \frac{75}{100}(8) = 6$$

Because $i$ is a whole number, $P_{75}$ is the average of the sixth and the seventh numbers.

$$P_{75} = \frac{(122 + 125)}{2} = 123.5$$

The value of $Q_3$ is $P_{75}$ = 123.5. Notice that three-fourths, or six, of the values are less than 123.5 and two of the values are greater than 123.5.

---

| **DEMONSTRATION PROBLEM 3.3** | The following shows revenues for the world's top advertising organizations according to *Advertising Age*. Determine the first, the second, and the third quartiles for these data. |
|---|---|

| Ad Organization | Headquarters | Worldwide Gross Income ($ millions) |
|---|---|---|
| WPP Group | London | 8165 |
| Interpublic Group of Cos. | New York | 7981 |
| Omnicom Group | New York | 7404 |
| Publicis Communication | Paris | 4770 |
| Dentsu | Tokyo | 2796 |
| Havas Advertising | Paris | 2733 |
| Grey Advertising | New York | 1864 |
| Cordiant Communications Group | London | 1175 |
| Hakuhodo | Tokyo | 874 |
| Asatsu | Tokyo | 396 |
| TMP Worldwide | New York | 359 |
| Carlson Marketing Group | Minneapolis | 356 |
| Incepta Group | London | 248 |
| DigitasA | Boston | 236 |
| Tokyu Agency | Tokyo | 204 |
| Daiko Advertising | Tokyo | 203 |

**Solution**

For 16 advertising organizations, $n$ = 16. $Q_1 = P_{25}$ is found by

$$i = \frac{25}{100}(16) = 4$$

Because $i$ is a whole number, $Q_1$ is found to be the average of the fourth and fifth values from the bottom.

$$Q_1 = \frac{248 + 356}{2} = 302$$

$Q_2 = P_{50}$ = median; with 16 terms, the median is the average of the eighth and ninth terms.

$$Q_2 = \frac{874 + 1175}{2} = 1024.5$$

$Q_3 = P_{75}$ is solved by

$$i = \frac{75}{100}(16) = 12$$

$Q_3$ is found by averaging the twelfth and thirteenth terms.

$$Q_3 = \frac{2796 + 4770}{2} = 3783$$

## 3.1 PROBLEMS

**3.1**   Determine the mode for the following numbers.

  2   4   8   4   6   2   7   8   4   3   8   9   4   3   5

**3.2**   Determine the median for the numbers in Problem 3.1.

**3.3**   Determine the median for the following numbers.

  213   345   609   073   167   243   444   524   199   682

**3.4**   Compute the mean for the following numbers.

  17.3   44.5   31.6   40.0   52.8   38.8   30.1   78.5

**3.5**   Compute the mean for the following numbers.

  7   −2   5   9   0   −3   −6   −7   −4   −5   2   −8

**3.6**   Compute the 35th percentile, the 55th percentile, $Q_1$, $Q_2$, and $Q_3$ for the following data.

  16   28   29   13   17   20   11   34   32   27   25   30   19   18   33

**3.7**   Compute $P_{20}$, $P_{47}$, $P_{83}$, $Q_1$, $Q_2$, and $Q_3$ for the following data.

| 120 | 138 | 97  | 118 | 172 | 144 |
|-----|-----|-----|-----|-----|-----|
| 138 | 107 | 94  | 119 | 139 | 145 |
| 162 | 127 | 112 | 150 | 143 | 80  |
| 105 | 116 | 142 | 128 | 116 | 171 |

**3.8**   The following data show the number of cars and light trucks for a recent year for the largest automakers in the world, as reported by *AutoFacts*, a unit of Coopers & Lybrand Consulting. Compute the mean and median. Which of these two measures do you think is most appropriate for summarizing these data and why? What is the value of $Q_2$? Determine the 63rd percentile for the data. Determine the 29th percentile for the data.

| Automaker | Production (1,000s) |
|---|---|
| General Motors | 7880 |
| Ford Motors | 6359 |
| Toyota | 4580 |
| Volkswagen | 4161 |
| Chrysler | 2968 |
| Nissan | 2646 |
| Honda | 2436 |
| Fiat | 2264 |
| Peugeot | 1767 |
| Renault | 1567 |
| Mitsubishi | 1535 |
| Hyundai | 1434 |
| BMW | 1341 |
| Daimler-Benz | 1227 |
| Daewoo | 898 |

**3.9** The following lists the biggest banks in the world ranked by assets according to *American Banker*. Compute the median, $Q_3$, $P_{20}$, $P_{60}$, $P_{80}$, and $P_{93}$.

| Bank | Assets ($ billions) |
|---|---|
| Citigroup (New York) | 902 |
| Deutsche Bank (Frankfurt) | 873 |
| Bank of Tokyo-Mitsubishi | 721 |
| J.P.Morgan Chase (New York) | 715 |
| UBS (Zurich) | 674 |
| HSBC Holdings (London) | 673 |
| BHV AG (Munich) | 654 |
| BNP-SG-Paribas (Paris) | 652 |
| BankAmerica (Charlotte) | 642 |
| ING NV (Amsterdam) | 613 |

**3.10** The following lists the number of fatal accidents by scheduled commercial airline over a 17-year period according to the Air Transport Association of America. Using these data, compute the mean, median, and mode. What is the value of the third quartile? Determine $P_{11}$, $P_{35}$, $P_{58}$, and $P_{67}$.

4  4  4  1  4  2  4  3  8  6  4  4  1  4  2  3  3

## 3.2 MEASURES OF VARIABILITY: UNGROUPED DATA

Measures of central tendency yield information about particular points of a data set. However, business researchers can use another group of analytic tools to describe a set of data. These tools are **measures of variability,** which *describe the spread or the dispersion of a set of data.* Using measures of variability in conjunction with measures of central tendency makes possible a more complete numerical description of the data.

For example, a company has 25 salespeople in the field, and the median annual sales figure for these people is $1.2 million. Are the salespeople being successful as a group or not? The median provides information about the sales of the person in the middle, but what about the other salespeople? Are all of them selling $1.2 million annually, or do the sales figures vary widely, with one person selling $5 million annually and another selling only $150,000 annually? Measures of variability provide the additional information necessary to answer that question.

Figure 3.3 shows three distributions in which the mean of each distribution is the same ($\mu = 50$) but the variabilities differ. Observation of these distributions shows that a measure of variability is necessary to complement the mean value in describing the data. Methods of computing measures of variability differ for ungrouped data and grouped data. This section focuses on seven measures of variability for ungrouped data: range, interquartile range, mean absolute deviation, variance, standard deviation, $Z$ scores, and coefficient of variation.

## Range

The **range** is *the difference between the largest value of a data set and the smallest value.* Although it is usually a single numeric value, some business researchers define the range as the ordered pair of smallest and largest numbers (smallest, largest). It is a crude measure of variability, describing the distance to the outer bounds of the data set. It reflects those extreme values because it is constructed from them. An advantage of the range is its ease of computation. One important use of the range is in quality assurance, where the range is used to construct control charts. A disadvantage of the range is that, because it is computed with the values that are on the extremes of the data, it is affected by extreme values. Therefore its application as a measure of variability is limited.

The data in Table 3.1 represent the offer prices for the 20 largest U.S. initial public offerings in a recent year. The lowest offer price was $7.00 and the highest price was $43.25. The range of the offer prices can be computed as the difference of the highest and lowest values:

$$\text{Range} = \text{Highest} - \text{Lowest} = \$43.25 - \$7.00 = \$36.25$$

## Interquartile Range

Another measure of variability is the **interquartile range**. The interquartile range is *the range of values between the first and third quartile.* Essentially, it is the range of the middle 50% of the data and is determined by computing the value of $Q_3 - Q_1$. The interquartile range is especially useful in situations where data users are more interested in values toward the middle and less interested in extremes. In describing a real estate housing market, realtors might use the interquartile range as a measure of housing prices when describing the middle half of the market for buyers who are interested in houses in the midrange. In addition, the interquartile range is used in the construction of box and whisker plots.

| INTERQUARTILE RANGE | $Q_3 - Q_1$ |
|---|---|

The following data indicate the top 15 trading partners of the United States by U.S. exports to the country in a recent year according to the U.S. Census Bureau.

| Country | Exports ($ billions) |
|---|---|
| Canada | $151.8 |
| Mexico | 71.4 |
| Japan | 65.5 |
| United Kingdom | 36.4 |
| South Korea | 25.0 |
| Germany | 24.5 |
| Taiwan | 20.4 |
| Netherlands | 19.8 |
| Singapore | 17.7 |
| France | 16.0 |
| Brazil | 15.9 |
| Hong Kong | 15.1 |
| Belgium | 13.4 |
| China | 12.9 |
| Australia | 12.1 |

FIGURE 3.3

Three Distributions with the
Same Mean but Different
Dispersions

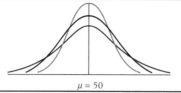

$\mu = 50$

What is the interquartile range for these data? The process begins by computing the first
and third quartiles as follows.

Solving for $Q_1 = P_{25}$ when $n = 15$:

$$i = \frac{25}{100}(15) = 3.75$$

Because $i$ is not a whole number, $P_{25}$ is found as the fourth term from the bottom.

$$Q_1 = P_{25} = 15.1$$

Solving for $Q_3 = P_{75}$:

$$i = \frac{75}{100}(15) = 11.25$$

Because $i$ is not a whole number, $P_{75}$ is found as the 12th term from the bottom.

$$Q_3 = P_{75} = 36.4$$

The interquartile range is:

$$Q_3 - Q_1 = 36.4 - 15.1 = 21.3$$

The middle 50% of the exports for the top 15 U.S. trading partners spans a range of
21.3 ($ billions).

### Telecommuting Statistics

A study by Telework America sponsored by AT&T in 2001
revealed that 28 million Americans are teleworking. Of these,
24.1% work on the road, 21.7% work out of their home,
7.5% work in telework centers, and 4.2% work at satellite
offices. More than 40% of these people work in more than
one location. An estimated 30 million regular teleworkers
will be working in the United States by the end of 2004.

The typical telecommuter lives in the West or the
Northeast, is male, has a college education, is between 35
and 44 years of age, is married, and earns at least $ 40,000
per year. The mean income for teleworkers is $ 44,000.
Most of telecommuters work in IT, real estate, or enterprise
management. Teleworkers typically drive 18 miles to work
and save nearly 53 minutes of commuting time each work-
day they telecommute. On average, teleworkers work one
to two days per week away from home.

Teleworkers are relatively satisfied with their work.
Seventy-five percent of home workers reported a quantifiable

increase in productivity and work quality when they
switched from traditional at-work jobs to telecommuting.
Two-thirds of teleworkers expressed increased job satisfaction. Teleworkers say that they work longer hours than non-
teleworkers but that their job interferes less with their
personal lives.

Teleworking can result in cost savings for companies
due to lack of absenteeism, reduced real estate costs, and
job retention. It is estimated that employees who telework can save their employers an average of $10,000 each
in reduced absenteeism and job retention. Real estate
costs can be reduced from 25% to 90%. AT&T saves
$3,000 per teleworker annually and has saved $25 million
a year in real estate costs through employees who are full-
time teleworkers.

*Source:*  Adapted  from  YouCanWorkFromAnywhere.com  at
http://www.ycwfa.com/infocenter/facts.htm; Toni Kistner, "Annual Survey
Helps Debunk Telework Myths," *Net.Worker*, 29 October 2001, at
http://www.nwfusion.com/net.worker/columnists/2001/1029kistner.html.

## Mean Absolute Deviation, Variance, and Standard Deviation

Three other measures of variability are the variance, the standard deviation, and the mean absolute deviation. They are obtained through similar processes and are, therefore, presented together. These measures are not meaningful unless the data are at least interval-level data. The variance and standard deviation are widely used in statistics. Although the standard deviation has some stand-alone potential, the importance of variance and standard deviation lies mainly in their role as tools used in conjunction with other statistical devices.

Suppose a small company started a production line to build computers. During the first five weeks of production, the output is 5, 9, 16, 17, and 18 computers, respectively. Which descriptive statistics could the owner use to measure the early progress of production? In an attempt to summarize these figures, the owner could compute a mean.

$$x$$
$$5$$
$$9$$
$$16$$
$$17$$
$$18$$

$$\Sigma x = 65 \qquad \mu = \frac{\Sigma x}{N} = \frac{65}{5} = 13$$

What is the variability in these five weeks of data? One way for the owner to begin to look at the spread of the data is to subtract the mean from each data value. *Subtracting the mean from each value of data* yields the **deviation from the mean** $(x - \mu)$. Table 3.2 shows these deviations for the computer company production. Note that some deviations from the mean are positive and some are negative. Figure 3.4 shows that geometrically the negative deviations represent values that are below (to the left of) the mean and positive deviations represent values that are above (to the right of) the mean.

An examination of deviations from the mean can reveal information about the variability of data. However, the deviations are used mostly as a tool to compute other measures of variability. Note that in both Table 3.2 and Figure 3.4 these deviations total zero. This phenomenon applies to all cases. For a given set of data, the sum of all deviations from the arithmetic mean is always zero.

| TABLE 3.2 | |
|---|---|
| Deviations from the Mean for Computer Production | |

| Number ($x$) | Deviations from the Mean ($x - \mu$) |
|:---:|:---:|
| 5 | $5 - 13 = -8$ |
| 9 | $9 - 13 = -4$ |
| 16 | $16 - 13 = +3$ |
| 17 | $17 - 13 = +4$ |
| 18 | $18 - 13 = \underline{+5}$ |
| $\Sigma x = 65$ | $\Sigma(x - \mu) = 0$ |

| FIGURE 3.4 | |
|---|---|
| Geometric Distances from the Mean (from Table 3.2) | |

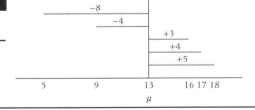

| SUM OF DEVIATIONS FROM THE ARITHMETIC MEAN IS ALWAYS ZERO | $\Sigma(x - \mu) = 0$ |
| --- | --- |

This property requires considering alternative ways to obtain measures of variability.

One obvious way to force the sum of deviations to have a nonzero total is to take the absolute value of each deviation around the mean. Utilizing the absolute value of the deviations about the mean makes solving for the mean absolute deviation possible.

## Mean Absolute Deviation

The **mean absolute deviation** (**MAD**) is *the average of the absolute values of the deviations around the mean for a set of numbers.*

| MEAN ABSOLUTE DEVIATION | $\mathrm{MAD} = \dfrac{\Sigma |x - \mu|}{N}$ |
| --- | --- |

Using the data from Table 3.2, the computer company owner can compute a mean absolute deviation by taking the absolute values of the deviations and averaging them, as shown in Table 3.3. The mean absolute deviation for the computer production data is 4.8.

Because it is computed by using absolute values, the mean absolute deviation is less useful in statistics than other measures of dispersion. However, in the field of forecasting, it is used occasionally as a measure of error.

## Variance

Because absolute values are not conducive to easy manipulation, mathematicians developed an alternative mechanism for overcoming the zero-sum property of deviations from the mean. This approach utilizes the square of the deviations from the mean. The result is the variance, an important measure of variability.

The **variance** is *the average of the squared deviations about the arithmetic mean for a set of numbers.* The population variance is denoted by $\sigma^2$.

| POPULATION VARIANCE | $\sigma^2 = \dfrac{\Sigma(x - \mu)^2}{N}$ |
| --- | --- |

Table 3.4 shows the original production numbers for the computer company, the deviations from the mean, and the squared deviations from the mean.

*The sum of the squared deviations about the mean of a set of values*—called the **sum of squares of x** and sometimes abbreviated as $SS_x$—is used throughout statistics. For the computer company, this value is 130. Dividing it by the number of data values (5 weeks) yields the variance for computer production.

$$\sigma^2 = \frac{130}{5} = 26.0$$

| **TABLE 3.3** | | | |
| --- | --- | --- | --- |
| MAD for Computer Production Data | $x$ | $x - \mu$ | $|x - \mu|$ |
| | 5 | −8 | +8 |
| | 9 | −4 | +4 |
| | 16 | +3 | +3 |
| | 17 | +4 | +4 |
| | 18 | +5 | +5 |
| | $\Sigma x = 65$ | $\Sigma(x - \mu) = 0$ | $\Sigma|x - \mu| = 24$ |

$$\mathrm{MAD} = \frac{\Sigma|x - \mu|}{n} = \frac{24}{5} = 4.8$$

Because the variance is computed from squared deviations, the final result is expressed in terms of squared units of measurement. Statistics measured in squared units are problematic to interpret. Consider, for example, Mattel Toys attempting to interpret production costs in terms of squared dollars or Troy-Bilt measuring production output variation in terms of squared lawn mowers. Therefore, when used as a descriptive measure, variance can be considered as an intermediate calculation in the process of obtaining the sample standard deviation.

## Standard Deviation

The standard deviation is a popular measure of variability. It is used both as a separate entity and as a part of other analyses, such as computing confidence intervals and in hypothesis testing (see Chapters 8, 9, and 10).

| POPULATION STANDARD DEVIATION | $\sigma = \sqrt{\dfrac{\Sigma(x-\mu)^2}{N}}$ |
|---|---|

The **standard deviation** is *the square root of the variance*. The population standard deviation is denoted by $\sigma$.

Like the variance, the standard deviation utilizes the sum of the squared deviations about the mean ($SS_x$). It is computed by averaging these squared deviations ($SS_x/N$) and taking the square root of that average. One feature of the standard deviation that distinguishes it from a variance is that the standard deviation is expressed in the same units as the raw data, whereas the variance is expressed in those units squared. Table 3.4 shows the standard deviation for the computer production company: $\sqrt{26}$, or 5.1.

What does a standard deviation of 5.1 mean? The meaning of standard deviation is more readily understood from its use, which is explored in the next section. Although the standard deviation and the variance are closely related and can be computed from each other, differentiating between them is important, because both are widely used in statistics.

## Meaning of Standard Deviation

What is a standard deviation? What does it do, and what does it mean? The most precise way to define standard deviation is by reciting the formula used to compute it. However, insight into the concept of standard deviation can be gleaned by viewing the manner in which it is applied. Two ways of applying the standard deviation are the empirical rule and Chebyshev's theorem.

---

**TABLE 3.4**

Computing a Variance and a Standard Deviation from the Computer Production Data

| $x$ | $x-\mu$ | $(x-\mu)^2$ |
|---|---|---|
| 5 | −8 | 64 |
| 9 | −4 | 16 |
| 16 | +3 | 9 |
| 17 | +4 | 16 |
| 18 | +5 | 25 |
| $\Sigma x = 65$ | $\Sigma(x-\mu)=0$ | $\Sigma(x-\mu)^2 = 130$ |

$$SS_x = \Sigma(x-\mu)^2 = 130$$

$$\text{Variance} = \sigma^2 = \frac{SS_x}{N} = \frac{\Sigma(x-\mu)^2}{N} = \frac{130}{5} = 26.0$$

$$\text{Standard Deviation} = \sigma = \sqrt{\frac{\Sigma(x-\mu)^2}{N}} = \sqrt{\frac{130}{5}} = 5.1$$

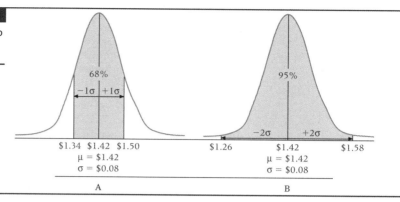

**FIGURE 3.5**

Empirical Rule for One and Two Standard Deviations of Gasoline Prices

## Empirical Rule

The **empirical rule** is an important rule of thumb that *is used to state the approximate percentage of values that lie within a given number of standard deviations from the mean of a set of data if the data are normally distributed.*

The empirical rule is used only for three numbers of standard deviations: $1\sigma$, $2\sigma$, and $3\sigma$. More detailed analysis of other numbers of $\sigma$ values is presented in Chapter 6. Also discussed in further detail in Chapter 6 is the normal distribution, a unimodal, symmetrical distribution that is bell (or mound) shaped. The requirement that the data be normally distributed contains some tolerance, and the empirical rule generally applies as long as the data are approximately mound shaped.

| EMPIRICAL RULE* | Distance from the Mean | Values within Distance |
|---|---|---|
| | $\mu \pm 1\sigma$ | 68% |
| | $\mu \pm 2\sigma$ | 95% |
| | $\mu \pm 3\sigma$ | 99.7% |

*Based on the assumption that the data are approximately normally distributed.

If a set of data is normally distributed, or bell shaped, approximately 68% of the data values are within one standard deviation of the mean, 95% are within two standard deviations, and almost 100% are within three standard deviations.

Suppose a recent report states that for California, the average statewide price of a gallon of regular gasoline was $1.42. Suppose regular gasoline prices varied across the state with a standard deviation of $0.08 and were normally distributed. According to the empirical rule, approximately 68% of the prices should fall within $\mu \pm 1\sigma$, or $1.42 \pm 1$ ($0.08). Approximately 68% of the prices would be between $1.34 and $1.50, as shown in Figure 3.5A. Approximately 95% should fall within $\mu \pm 2\sigma$ or $1.42 \pm 2($0.08) = $1.42 \pm $0.16, or between $1.26 and $1.58, as shown in Figure 3.5B. Nearly all regular gasoline prices (99.7%) should fall between $1.16 and $1.66 ($\mu \pm 3\sigma$).

Note that with 68% of the gasoline prices falling within one standard deviation of the mean, approximately 32% are outside this range. Because the normal distribution is symmetrical, the 32% can be split in half such that 16% lie in each tail of the distribution. Thus, approximately 16% of the gasoline prices should be less than $1.34 and approximately 16% of the prices should be greater than $1.50.

Many phenomena are distributed approximately in a bell shape, including most human characteristics such as height and weight; therefore the empirical rule applies in many situations and is widely used.

| DEMONSTRATION PROBLEM 3.4 | A company produces a lightweight valve that is specified to weigh 1365 grams. Unfortunately, because of imperfections in the manufacturing process not all of the valves produced weigh exactly 1365 grams. In fact, the weights of the valves produced are normally distributed with a mean weight of 1365 grams and a standard deviation of 294 grams. Within what range of weights would approximately 95% of the valve weights fall? Approximately 16% of the weights would be more than what value? Approximately 0.15% of the weights would be less than what value? |
|---|---|

### Solution

Because the valve weights are normally distributed, the empirical rule applies. According to the empirical rule, approximately 95% of the weights should fall within $\mu \pm 2\sigma = 1365 \pm 2(294) = 1365 \pm 588$. Thus, approximately 95% should fall between 777 and 1953. Approximately 68% of the weights should fall within $\mu \pm 1\sigma$ and 32% should fall outside this interval. Because the normal distribution is symmetrical, approximately 16% should lie above $\mu + 1\sigma = 1365 + 294 = 1659$. Approximately 99.7% of the weights should fall within $\mu \pm 3\sigma$ and .3% should fall outside this interval. Half of these or .15% should lie below $\mu - 3\sigma = 1365 - 3(294) = 1365 - 882 = 483$.

## Chebyshev's Theorem

The empirical rule applies only when data are known to be approximately normally distributed. What do researchers use when data are not normally distributed or when the shape of the distribution is unknown? Chebyshev's theorem applies to all distributions regardless of their shape and thus can be used whenever the data distribution shape is unknown or is nonnormal. Even though Chebyshev's theorem can in theory be applied to data that are normally distributed, the empirical rule is more widely known and is preferred whenever appropriate. Chebyshev's theorem is not a rule of thumb, as is the empirical rule, but rather it is presented in formula format and therefore can be more widely applied. **Chebyshev's theorem** states that *at least $1 - 1/k^2$ values will fall within $\pm k$ standard deviations of the mean regardless of the shape of the distribution.*

| CHEBYSHEV'S THEOREM | Within $k$ standard deviations of the mean, $\mu \pm k\sigma$, lie at least $$1 - \frac{1}{k^2}$$ proportion of the values. Assumption: $k > 1$ |
|---|---|

Specifically, Chebyshev's theorem says that at least 75% of all values are within $\pm 2\sigma$ of the mean regardless of the shape of a distribution because if $k = 2$, then $1 - 1/k^2 = 1 - 1/2^2 = 3/4 = .75$. Figure 3.6 provides a graphic illustration. In contrast, the empirical rule states that if the data are normally distributed 95% of all values are within $\mu \pm 2\sigma$. According to Chebyshev's theorem, the percentage of values within three standard deviations of the mean is at least 89%, in contrast to 99.7% for the empirical rule. Because a formula is used to compute proportions with Chebyshev's theorem, any value of $k$ greater than 1 $(k > 1)$ can be used. For example, if $k = 2.5$, at least .84 of all values are within $\mu \pm 2.5\sigma$, because $1 - 1/k^2 = 1 - 1/(2.5)^2 = .84$.

| FIGURE 3.6 | |
|---|---|
| Application of Chebyshev's Theorem for Two Standard Deviations | 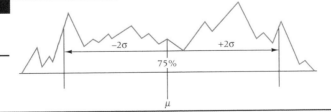 |

**DEMONSTRATION PROBLEM 3.5**

In the computing industry the average age of professional employees tends to be younger than in many other business professions. Suppose the average age of a professional employed by a particular computer firm is 28 with a standard deviation of 5 years. A histogram of professional employee ages with this firm reveals that the data are not normally distributed but rather are amassed in the twenties and that few workers are over 40. Apply Chebyshev's theorem to determine within what range of ages would at least 85% of the workers' ages fall.

### Solution

Because the ages are not normally distributed, it is not appropriate to apply the empirical rule; and therefore, Chebyshev's theorem must be applied to answer the question.

Chebyshev's theorem states that at least $1 - 1/k^2$ proportion of the values are within $\mu \pm k\sigma$. Because 85% of the values are within this range, let

$$1 - \frac{1}{k^2} = .85$$

Solving for $k$ yields

$$.15 = \frac{1}{k^2}$$
$$k^2 = 6.667$$
$$k = 2.58$$

Chebyshev's theorem says that at least .85 of the values are within $\pm 2.58\sigma$ of the mean. For $\mu = 28$ and $\sigma = 5$, at least .85, or 85%, of the values are within $28 \pm 2.58(5)$ $= 28 \pm 12.9$ years of age or between 15.1 and 40.9 years old.

## Population versus Sample Variance and Standard Deviation

The sample variance is denoted by $s^2$ and the sample standard deviation by $s$. The main use for sample variances and standard deviations is as estimators of population variances and standard deviations. Because of this, computation of the sample variance and standard deviation differs slightly from computation of the population variance and standard deviation. Both the sample variance and sample standard deviation use $n - 1$ in the denominator instead of $n$ because using $n$ in the denominator of a sample variance results in a statistic that tends to underestimate the population variance. While discussion of the properties of *good estimators* is beyond the scope of this text, one of the properties of a good estimator is being *unbiased*. Whereas, using $n$ in the denominator of the sample variance makes it a *biased* estimator, using $n - 1$ allows it to be an *unbiased* estimator, which is a desirable property in inferential statistics.

| SAMPLE VARIANCE | $s^2 = \dfrac{\Sigma(x - \bar{x})^2}{n - 1}$ |
|---|---|

| SAMPLE STANDARD DEVIATION | $s = \sqrt{\dfrac{\Sigma(x - \bar{x})^2}{n - 1}}$ |
|---|---|

Shown here is a sample of six of the largest accounting firms in the United States and the number of partners associated with each firm as reported by the *Public Accounting Report*.

| Firm | Number of Partners |
|---|---|
| PriceWaterhouse | 1062 |
| McGladrey & Pullen | 381 |
| Deloitte & Touche | 1719 |
| Andersen Worldwide | 1673 |
| Coopers & Lybrand | 1277 |
| BDO Seidman | 217 |

The sample variance and sample standard deviation can be computed by:

| $x$ | $(x-\bar{x})^2$ |
|---|---|
| 1062 | 51.41 |
| 381 | 454,046.87 |
| 1719 | 441,121.79 |
| 1673 | 382,134.15 |
| 1277 | 49,359.51 |
| 217 | 701,959.11 |
| $\Sigma x = 6329$ | $\Sigma(x-\bar{x})^2 = 2,028,672.84$ |

$$\bar{x} = \frac{6329}{6} = 1054.83$$

$$s^2 = \frac{\Sigma(x-\bar{x})^2}{n-1} = \frac{2,028,672.84}{5} = 405,734.57$$

$$s = \sqrt{s^2} = \sqrt{405,734.57} = 636.97$$

The sample variance is 405,734.57 and the sample standard deviation is 636.97.

## Computational Formulas for Variance and Standard Deviation

An alternative method of computing variance and standard deviation, sometimes referred to as the computational method or shortcut method, is available. Algebraically,

$$\Sigma(x-\mu)^2 = \Sigma x^2 - \frac{(\Sigma x)^2}{N}$$

and

$$\Sigma(x-\bar{x})^2 = \Sigma x^2 - \frac{(\Sigma x)^2}{n}$$

Substituting these equivalent expressions into the original formulas for variance and standard deviation yields the following computational formulas.

| COMPUTATIONAL FORMULA FOR POPULATION VARIANCE AND STANDARD DEVIATION | $\sigma^2 = \dfrac{\Sigma x^2 - \dfrac{(\Sigma x)^2}{N}}{N}$ <br> $\sigma = \sqrt{\sigma^2}$ |
|---|---|

| COMPUTATIONAL FORMULA FOR SAMPLE VARIANCE AND STANDARD DEVIATION | $s^2 = \dfrac{\Sigma x^2 - \dfrac{(\Sigma x)^2}{n}}{n-1}$ <br> $s = \sqrt{s^2}$ |
|---|---|

These computational formulas utilize the sum of the $x$ values and the sum of the $x^2$ values instead of the difference between the mean and each value and computed deviations. In the precalculator/computer era, this method usually was faster and easier than using the original formulas.

For situations in which the mean is already computed or is given, alternative forms of these formulas are

$$\sigma^2 = \frac{\Sigma x^2 - N\mu^2}{N}$$

$$s^2 = \frac{\Sigma x^2 - n(\bar{x})^2}{n-1}$$

**TABLE 3.5**

Computational Formula
Calculations of Variance and
Standard Deviation for
Computer Production Data

| $x$ | $x^2$ |
|---|---|
| 5 | 25 |
| 9 | 81 |
| 16 | 256 |
| 17 | 289 |
| 18 | 324 |
| $\Sigma x = 65$ | $\Sigma x^2 = 975$ |

$$\sigma^2 = \frac{975 - \frac{(65)^2}{5}}{5} = \frac{975 - 845}{5} = \frac{130}{5} = 26$$

$$\sigma = \sqrt{26} = 5.1$$

Using the computational method, the owner of the start-up computer production company can compute a population variance and standard deviation for the production data, as shown in Table 3.5. (Compare these results with those in Table 3.4.)

**DEMONSTRATION PROBLEM 3.6**

The effectiveness of district attorneys can be measured by several variables, including the number of convictions per month, the number of cases handled per month, and the total number of years of conviction per month. A researcher uses a sample of five district attorneys in a city and determines the total number of years of conviction that each attorney won against defendants during the past month, as reported in the first column in the following tabulations. Compute the mean absolute deviation, the variance, and the standard deviation for these figures.

Solution

The researcher computes the mean absolute deviation, the variance, and the standard deviation for these data in the following manner.

| $x$ | $|x-\bar{x}|$ | $(x-\bar{x})^2$ |
|---|---|---|
| 55 | 41 | 1,681 |
| 100 | 4 | 16 |
| 125 | 29 | 841 |
| 140 | 44 | 1,936 |
| 60 | 36 | 1,296 |
| $\Sigma x = 480$ | $\Sigma|x-\bar{x}| = 154$ | $\Sigma(x-\bar{x})^2 = 5,770$ |

$$\bar{x} = \frac{\Sigma x}{n} = \frac{480}{5} = 96$$

$$MAD = \frac{154}{5} = 30.8$$

$$s^2 = \frac{5,770}{4} = 1,442.5 \text{ and } s = \sqrt{s^2} = 37.98$$

She then uses computational formulas to solve for $s^2$ and $s$ and compares the results.

| $x$ | $x^2$ |
|---|---|
| 55 | 3,025 |
| 100 | 10,000 |
| 125 | 15,625 |
| 140 | 19,600 |
| 60 | 3,600 |
| $\Sigma x = 480$ | $\Sigma x^2 = 51,850$ |

$$s^2 = \frac{51,850 - \frac{(480)^2}{5}}{4} = \frac{51,850 - 46,080}{4} = \frac{5,770}{4} = 1,442.5$$

$$s = \sqrt{1,442.5} = 37.98$$

The results are the same. The sample standard deviation obtained by both methods is 37.98, or 38, years.

## *z* Scores

A **z score** represents the number of standard deviations a value (*x*) is above or below the mean of a set of numbers when the data are normally distributed. Using *z* scores allows translation of a value's raw distance from the mean into units of standard deviations.

| *z* SCORE | $$z = \frac{x - \mu}{\sigma}$$ |
|---|---|

For samples,

$$z = \frac{x - \overline{x}}{s}$$

If a *z* score is negative, the raw value (*x*) is below the mean. If the *z* score is positive, the raw value (*x*) is above the mean.

For example, for a data set that is normally distributed with a mean of 50 and a standard deviation of 10, suppose a statistician wants to determine the *z* score for a value of 70. This value (*x* = 70) is 20 units above the mean, so the *z* value is

$$z = \frac{70 - 50}{10} = +2.00$$

This *z* score signifies that the raw score of 70 is two standard deviations above the mean. How is this *z* score interpreted? The empirical rule states that 95% of all values are within two standard deviations of the mean if the data are approximately normally distributed. Figure 3.7 shows that because the value of 70 is two standard deviations above the mean (*z* = +2.00) 95% of the values are between 70 and the value (*x* = 30), that is two standard deviations below the mean, or *z* = (30 − 50)/10= −2.00. Because 5% of the values are outside the range of two standard deviations from the mean and the normal distribution is symmetrical, 2½% (½ of the 5%) are below the value of 30. Thus 97½% of the values are below the value of 70. Because a *z* score is the number of standard deviations an individual data value is from the mean, the empirical rule can be restated in terms of *z* scores.

Between *z* = −1.00 and *z* = +1.00 are approximately 68% of the values.
Between *z* = −2.00 and *z* = +2.00 are approximately 95% of the values.
Between *z* = −3.00 and *z* = +3.00 are approximately 99.7% of the values.

The topic of *z* scores is discussed more extensively in Chapter 6.

## Coefficient of Variation

The **coefficient of variation** is a statistic that is *the ratio of the standard deviation to the mean expressed in percentage* and is denoted CV.

| **COEFFICIENT OF VARIATION** | $$CV = \frac{\sigma}{\mu}(100)$$ |
|---|---|

The coefficient of variation essentially is a relative comparison of a standard deviation to its mean. The coefficient of variation can be useful in comparing standard deviations that have been computed from data with different means.

Suppose five weeks of average prices for stock A are 57, 68, 64, 71, and 62. To compute a coefficient of variation for these prices, first determine the mean and standard deviation: $\mu = 64.40$ and $\sigma = 4.84$. The coefficient of variation is:

$$CV_A = \frac{\sigma_A}{\mu_A}(100) = \frac{4.84}{64.40}(100) = .075 = 7.5\%$$

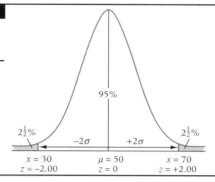

**FIGURE 3.7**

Percentage Breakdown of
Scores Two Standard
Deviations from the Mean

95%

$2\frac{1}{2}\%$

$-2\sigma$        $+2\sigma$

$2\frac{1}{2}\%$

$x = 30$         $\mu = 50$        $x = 70$
$z = -2.00$      $z = 0$          $z = +2.00$

The standard deviation is 7.5% of the mean.

Sometimes financial investors use the coefficient of variation or the standard deviation or both as measures of risk. Imagine a stock with a price that never changes. An investor bears no risk of losing money from the price going down because no variability occurs in the price. Suppose, in contrast, that the price of the stock fluctuates wildly. An investor who buys at a low price and sells for a high price can make a nice profit. However, if the price drops below what the investor buys it for, the stock owner is subject to a potential loss. The greater the variability is, the more the potential for loss. Hence, investors use measures of variability such as standard deviation or coefficient of variation to determine the risk of a stock. What does the coefficient of variation tell us about the risk of a stock that the standard deviation does not?

Suppose the average prices for a second stock, B, over these same five weeks are 12, 17, 8, 15, and 13. The mean for stock B is 13.00 with a standard deviation of 3.03. The coefficient of variation can be computed for stock B as:

$$CV_B = \frac{\sigma_B}{\mu_B}(100) = \frac{3.03}{13}(100) = .233 = 23.3\%$$

The standard deviation for stock B is 23.3% of the mean.

With the standard deviation as the measure of risk, stock A is more risky over this period of time because it has a larger standard deviation. However, the average price of stock A is almost five times as much as that of stock B. Relative to the amount invested in stock A, the standard deviation of $4.84 may not represent as much risk as the standard deviation of $3.03 for stock B, which has an average price of only $13.00. The coefficient of variation reveals the risk of a stock in terms of the size of standard deviation relative to the size of the mean (in percentage). Stock B has a coefficient of variation that is nearly three times as much as the coefficient of variation for stock A. Using coefficient of variation as a measure of risk indicates that stock B is riskier.

The choice of whether to use a coefficient of variation or raw standard deviations to compare multiple standard deviations is a matter of preference. The coefficient of variation also provides an optional method of interpreting the value of a standard deviation.

## 3.2 PROBLEMS

3.11  A data set contains the following seven values.

   6    2    4    9    1    3    5

   **a.**  Find the range.
   **b.**  Find the mean absolute deviation.
   **c.**  Find the population variance.
   **d.**  Find the population standard deviation.

   e.   Find the interquartile range.

   f.   Find the $z$ score for each value.

**3.12** A data set contains the following eight values.

| 4 | 3 | 0 | 5 | 2 | 9 | 4 | 5 |
|---|---|---|---|---|---|---|---|

   a.   Find the range.

   b.   Find the mean absolute deviation.

   c.   Find the sample variance.

   d.   Find the sample standard deviation.

   e.   Find the interquartile range.

**3.13** A data set contains the following six values.

| 12 | 23 | 19 | 26 | 24 | 23 |
|----|----|----|----|----|----|

   a.   Find the population standard deviation using the formula containing the mean (the original formula).

   b.   Find the population standard deviation using the computational formula.

   c.   Compare the results. Which formula was faster to use? Which formula do you prefer? Why do you think the computational formula is sometimes referred to as the "shortcut" formula?

**3.14** Use your calculator or computer to find the sample variance and sample standard deviation for the following data.

| 57 | 88 | 68 | 43 | 93 |
|----|----|----|----|----|
| 63 | 51 | 37 | 77 | 83 |
| 66 | 60 | 38 | 52 | 28 |
| 34 | 52 | 60 | 57 | 29 |
| 92 | 37 | 38 | 17 | 67 |

**3.15** Use your calculator or computer to find the population variance and population standard deviation for the following data.

| 123 | 090 | 546 | 378 |
|-----|-----|-----|-----|
| 392 | 280 | 179 | 601 |
| 572 | 953 | 749 | 075 |
| 303 | 468 | 531 | 646 |

**3.16** Determine the interquartile range on the following data.

| 44 | 18 | 39 | 40 | 59 |
|----|----|----|----|----|
| 46 | 59 | 37 | 15 | 73 |
| 23 | 19 | 90 | 58 | 35 |
| 82 | 14 | 38 | 27 | 24 |
| 71 | 25 | 39 | 84 | 70 |

**3.17** According to Chebyshev's theorem, at least what proportion of the data will be within $\mu \pm k\sigma$ for each value of $k$?

   a.   $k = 2$

   b.   $k = 2.5$

   c.   $k = 1.6$

   d.   $k = 3.2$

**3.18** Compare the variability of the following two sets of data by using both the standard deviation and the coefficient of variation.

| Data Set 1 | Data Set 2 |
|:----------:|:----------:|
| 49 | 159 |
| 82 | 121 |
| 77 | 138 |
| 54 | 152 |

**3.19** A sample of 12 small accounting firms reveals the following numbers of professionals per office.

| | | | | | |
|---|---|---|---|---|---|
| 7 | 10 | 9 | 14 | 11 | 8 |
| 5 | 12 | 8 | 3 | 13 | 6 |

**a.** Determine the mean absolute deviation.

**b.** Determine the variance.

**c.** Determine the standard deviation.

**d.** Determine the interquartile range.

**e.** What is the $z$ score for the firm that has six professionals?

**f.** What is the coefficient of variation for this sample?

**3.20** The following, supplied by Marketing Intelligence Service, is a list of the companies with the most new products in a recent year.

| Company | Number of New Products |
|---|---|
| Avon Products | 768 |
| L'Oreal | 429 |
| Unilever U.S. | 323 |
| Revlon | 306 |
| Garden Botanika | 286 |
| Philip Morris | 262 |
| Procter & Gamble | 215 |
| Nestlé | 172 |
| Paradiso | 162 |
| Tsumura International | 148 |
| Grand Metropolitan | 145 |

**a.** Find the range.

**b.** Find the mean absolute deviation.

**c.** Find the population variance.

**d.** Find the population standard deviation.

**e.** Find the interquartile range.

**f.** Find the $z$ score for Nestlé.

**g.** Find the coefficient of variation.

**3.21** A distribution of numbers is approximately bell shaped. If the mean of the numbers is 125 and the standard deviation is 12, between what two numbers would approximately 68% of the values fall? Between what two numbers would 95% of the values fall? Between what two values would 99.7% of the values fall?

**3.22** Some numbers are not normally distributed. If the mean of the numbers is 38 and the standard deviation is 6, what proportion of values would fall between 26 and 50? What proportion of values would fall between 14 and 62? Between what two values would 89% of the values fall?

**3.23** According to Chebyshev's theorem, how many standard deviations from the mean would include at least 80% of the values?

**3.24** The time needed to assemble a particular piece of furniture with experience is normally distributed with a mean time of 43 minutes. If 68% of the assembly times are between 40 and 46 minutes, what is the value of the standard deviation? Suppose 99.7% of the assembly times are between 35 and 51 minutes and the mean is still 43 minutes. What would the value of the standard deviation be now? Suppose the time needed to assemble another piece of furniture is not normally distributed and that the mean assembly time is 28 minutes. What is the value of the standard deviation if at least 77% of the assembly times are between 24 and 32 minutes?

3.25 Environmentalists are concerned about emissions of sulfur dioxide into the air. The average number of days per year in which sulfur dioxide levels exceed 150 milligrams per cubic meter in Milan, Italy, is 29. The number of days per year in which emission limits are exceeded is normally distributed with a standard deviation of 4.0 days. What percentage of the years would average between 21 and 37 days of excess emissions of sulfur dioxide? What percentage of the years would exceed 37 days? What percentage of the years would exceed 41 days? In what percentage of the years would there be fewer than 25 days with excess sulfur dioxide emissions?

3.26 The *Runzheimer Guide* publishes a list of the most inexpensive cities in the world for the business traveler. Listed are the 10 most inexpensive cities with their respective per diem costs. Use this list to calculate the *z* scores for Bordeaux, Montreal, Edmonton, and Hamilton. Treat this list as a sample.

| City | Per Diem ($) |
|---|---|
| Hamilton, Ontario | 97 |
| London, Ontario | 109 |
| Edmonton, Alberta | 111 |
| Jakarta, Indonesia | 118 |
| Ottawa | 120 |
| Montreal | 130 |
| Halifax, Nova Scotia | 132 |
| Winnipeg, Manitoba | 133 |
| Bordeaux, France | 137 |
| Bangkok, Thailand | 137 |

## 3.3 MEASURES OF CENTRAL TENDENCY AND VARIABILITY: GROUPED DATA

Grouped data do not provide information about individual values. Hence, measures of central tendency and variability for grouped data must be computed differently from those for ungrouped or raw data.

### Measures of Central Tendency

Two measures of central tendency are presented here for grouped data: the mean and the mode.

### Mean

For ungrouped data, the mean is computed by summing the data values and dividing by the number of values. With grouped data, the specific values are unknown. What can be used to represent the data values? The midpoint of each class interval is used to represent all the values in a class interval. This midpoint is weighted by the frequency of values in that class interval. The mean for grouped data is then computed by summing the products of the class midpoint and the class frequency for each class and dividing that sum by the total number of frequencies. The formula for the mean of grouped data follows.

---

**MEAN OF GROUPED DATA**

$$\mu_{\text{grouped}} = \frac{\sum fM}{N} = \frac{\sum fM}{\sum f} = \frac{f_1 M_1 + f_2 M_2 + \cdots + f_i M_i}{f_1 + f_2 + \cdots + f_i}$$

where

$i$ = the number of classes
$f$ = class frequency
$N$ = total frequencies

---

**TABLE 3.6**

Frequency Distribution of the
Unemployment Rates of France

| Class Interval | Frequency |
|----------------|-----------|
| 1–under 3 | 16 |
| 3–under 5 | 2 |
| 5–under 7 | 4 |
| 7–under 9 | 3 |
| 9–under 11 | 9 |
| 11–under 13 | 6 |

Table 3.6 gives the frequency distribution of the unemployment rates of France from Table 2.2. To find the mean of these data, we need $\Sigma f$ and $\Sigma fM$. The value of $\Sigma f$ can be determined by summing the values in the frequency column. To calculate $\Sigma fM$, we must first determine the values of $M$, or the class midpoints. Next we multiply each of these class midpoints by the frequency in that class interval, $f$, resulting in $fM$. Summing these values of $fM$ yields the value of $\Sigma fM$.

Table 3.7 contains the calculations needed to determine the group mean. The group mean for the unemployment data is 6.25. Remember that because each class interval was represented by its class midpoint rather than by actual values, the group mean is only approximate.

## Mode

The *mode* for grouped data is *the class midpoint of the modal class. The modal class is the class interval with the greatest frequency.* Using the data from Table 3.7, the 1–under 3 class interval contains the greatest frequency, 16. Thus, the modal class is 1–under 3. The class midpoint of this modal class is 2. Therefore, the mode for the frequency distribution shown in Table 3.7 is 2. The modal unemployment rate is 2%.

## Measures of Variability

Two measures of variability for grouped data are presented here: the variance and the standard deviation. Again, the standard deviation is the square root of the variance. Both measures have original and computational formulas.

| FORMULAS FOR POPULATION VARIANCE AND STANDARD DEVIATION OF GROUPED DATA | Original Formula | Computational Version |
|---|---|---|
| | $$\sigma^2 = \frac{\Sigma f(M-\mu)^2}{N}$$ $$\sigma = \sqrt{\sigma^2}$$ | $$\sigma^2 = \frac{\Sigma fM^2 - \frac{(\Sigma fM)^2}{N}}{N}$$ |

where:
  $f$ = frequency
  $M$ = class midpoint
  $N$ = $\Sigma f$, or total frequencies of the population
  $\mu$ = grouped mean for the population

**TABLE 3.7**

Calculation of Grouped Mean

| Class Interval | Frequency ($f$) | Class Midpoint ($M$) | $fM$ |
|----------------|-----------------|----------------------|------|
| 1–under 3 | 16 | 2 | 32 |
| 3–under 5 | 2 | 4 | 8 |
| 5–under 7 | 4 | 6 | 24 |
| 7–under 9 | 3 | 8 | 24 |
| 9–under 11 | 9 | 10 | 90 |
| 11–under 13 | 6 | 12 | 72 |
| | $\Sigma f = N = 40$ | | $\Sigma fM = 250$ |

$$\mu = \frac{\Sigma fM}{\Sigma f} = \frac{250}{40} = 6.25$$

**TABLE 3.8**

Calculating Grouped Variance and Standard Deviation with the Original Formula

| Class Interval | $f$ | $M$ | $fM$ | $M-\mu$ | $(M-\mu)^2$ | $f(M-\mu)^2$ |
|---|---|---|---|---|---|---|
| 1–under 3 | 16 | 2 | 32 | −4.25 | 18.063 | 289.008 |
| 3–under 5 | 2 | 4 | 8 | −2.25 | 5.063 | 10.126 |
| 5–under 7 | 4 | 6 | 24 | −0.25 | 0.063 | 0.252 |
| 7–under 9 | 3 | 8 | 24 | 1.75 | 3.063 | 9.189 |
| 9–under 11 | 9 | 10 | 90 | 3.75 | 14.063 | 126.567 |
| 11–under 13 | 6 | 12 | 72 | 5.75 | 33.063 | 198.378 |
| | $\Sigma f = N = 40$ | | $\Sigma fM = 250$ | | | $\Sigma f(M-\mu)^2 = 633.520$ |

$$\mu = \frac{\Sigma fM}{\Sigma f} = \frac{250}{40} = 6.25$$

$$\sigma^2 = \frac{\Sigma f(M-\mu)^2}{N} = \frac{633.520}{40} = 15.838$$

$$\sigma = \sqrt{15.838} = 3.980$$

**TABLE 3.9**

Calculating Grouped Variance and Standard Deviation with the Computational Formula

| Class Interval | $f$ | $M$ | $fM$ | $fM^2$ |
|---|---|---|---|---|
| 1–under 3 | 16 | 2 | 32 | 64 |
| 3–under 5 | 2 | 4 | 8 | 32 |
| 5–under 7 | 4 | 6 | 24 | 144 |
| 7–under 9 | 3 | 8 | 24 | 192 |
| 9–under 11 | 9 | 10 | 90 | 900 |
| 11–under 13 | 6 | 12 | 72 | 864 |
| | $f = N = 40$ | | $fM = 250$ | $fM^2 = 2196$ |

$$\sigma^2 = \frac{\Sigma fM^2 - \frac{(\Sigma fM)^2}{n}}{n} = \frac{2196 - \frac{(250)^2}{40}}{40} = \frac{2196 - 1562.5}{40} = \frac{633.5}{40} = 15.838$$

$$\sigma = \sqrt{15.838} = 3.980$$

**FORMULAS FOR SAMPLE VARIANCE AND STANDARD DEVIATION OF GROUPED DATA**

Original Formula

$$s^2 = \frac{\Sigma f(M - \bar{x})^2}{n-1}$$

$$s = \sqrt{s^2}$$

Computational Version

$$s^2 = \frac{\Sigma fM^2 - \frac{(\Sigma fM)^2}{n}}{n-1}$$

where:

$f$ = frequency

$M$ = class midpoint

$N$ = $\Sigma f$, or total of the frequencies of the population

$\mu$ = grouped mean for the sample

For example, let us calculate the variance and standard deviation of the French unemployment data grouped as a frequency distribution in Table 3.6. If the data are treated as a population, the computations are as follows.

For the original formula, the computations are given in Table 3.8. The method of determining $\sigma^2$ and $\sigma$ by using the computational formula is shown in Table 3.9. In either case, the variance of the unemployment data is 15.838 (squared percent) and the standard deviation is 3.98%. As with the computation of the grouped mean, the class midpoint is used to represent all values in a class interval. This approach may or may not be appropriate, depending on whether the average value in a class is at the midpoint. If this situation does not occur, then the variance and the standard deviation are only approximations. Because grouped statistics are usually computed without knowledge of the actual data, the statistics computed potentially may be only approximations.

| DEMONSTRATION PROBLEM 3.7 | |
|---|---|

Compute the mean, mode, variance, and standard deviation on the following sample data.

| Class Interval | Frequency |
|---|---|
| 10–under 15 | 6 |
| 15–under 20 | 22 |
| 20–under 25 | 35 |
| 25–under 30 | 29 |
| 30–under 35 | 16 |
| 35–under 40 | 8 |
| 40–under 45 | 4 |
| 45–under 50 | 2 |

### Solution

The mean is computed as follows.

| Class | f | M | fM |
|---|---|---|---|
| 10–under 15 | 6 | 12.5 | 75.0 |
| 15–under 20 | 22 | 17.5 | 385.0 |
| 20–under 25 | 35 | 22.5 | 787.5 |
| 25–under 30 | 29 | 27.5 | 797.5 |
| 30–under 35 | 16 | 32.5 | 520.0 |
| 35–under 40 | 8 | 37.5 | 300.0 |
| 40–under 45 | 4 | 42.5 | 170.0 |
| 45–under 50 | 2 | 47.5 | 95.0 |
| | $\Sigma f = n = 122$ | | $\Sigma fM = 3130.0$ |

$$\bar{x} = \frac{\Sigma fM}{\Sigma f} = \frac{3130}{122} = 25.66$$

The grouped mean is 25.66.

The grouped mode can be determined by finding the class midpoint of the class interval with the greatest frequency. The class with the greatest frequency is 20–under 25 with a frequency of 35. The midpoint of this class is 22.5, which is the grouped mode.

The variance and standard deviation can be found as shown next. First, use the original formula.

| Class | f | M | $M - \bar{x}$ | $(M - \bar{x})^2$ | $f(M - \bar{x})^2$ |
|---|---|---|---|---|---|
| 10–under 15 | 6 | 12.5 | –13.16 | 173.19 | 1039.14 |
| 15–under 20 | 22 | 17.5 | –8.16 | 66.59 | 1464.98 |
| 20–under 25 | 35 | 22.5 | –3.16 | 9.99 | 349.65 |
| 25–under 30 | 29 | 27.5 | 1.84 | 3.39 | 98.31 |
| 30–under 35 | 16 | 32.5 | 6.84 | 46.79 | 748.64 |
| 35–under 40 | 8 | 37.5 | 11.84 | 140.19 | 1121.52 |
| 40–under 45 | 4 | 42.5 | 16.84 | 283.59 | 1134.36 |
| 45–under 50 | 2 | 47.5 | 21.84 | 476.99 | 953.98 |
| | $\Sigma f = n = 122$ | | | | $\Sigma f(M - \bar{x})^2 = 6910.58$ |

$$s^2 = \frac{\Sigma f(M - \bar{x})^2}{n-1} = \frac{6910.58}{121} = 57.11$$

$$s = \sqrt{57.11} = 7.56$$

Next, use the computational formula.

| Class | f | M | fM | fM² |
|---|---|---|---|---|
| 10–under 15 | 6 | 12.5 | 75.0 | 937.50 |
| 15–under 20 | 22 | 17.5 | 385.0 | 6,737.50 |
| 20–under 25 | 35 | 22.5 | 787.5 | 17,718.75 |
| 25–under 30 | 29 | 27.5 | 797.5 | 21,931.25 |
| 30–under 35 | 16 | 32.5 | 520.0 | 16,900.00 |
| 35–under 40 | 8 | 37.5 | 300.0 | 11,250.00 |
| 40–under 45 | 4 | 42.5 | 170.0 | 7,225.00 |
| 45–under 50 | 2 | 47.5 | 95.0 | 4,512.50 |
| | $\Sigma f = n = 122$ | | $\Sigma fM = 3{,}130.0$ | $\Sigma fM^2 = 87{,}212.50$ |

$$s^2 = \frac{\Sigma fM^2 - \frac{(\Sigma fM)^2}{n}}{n-1} = \frac{87{,}212.5 - \frac{(3{,}130)^2}{122}}{121} = \frac{6{,}910.04}{121} = 57.11$$

$$s = \sqrt{57.11} = 7.56$$

The sample variance is 57.11 and the standard deviation is 7.56.

# 3.3 PROBLEMS

**3.27** Compute the mean and the mode for the following data.

| Class | $f$ |
|---|---|
| 0–under 2 | 39 |
| 2–under 4 | 27 |
| 4–under 6 | 16 |
| 6–under 8 | 15 |
| 8–under 10 | 10 |
| 10–under 12 | 8 |
| 12–under 14 | 6 |

**3.28** Compute the mean and the mode for the following data.

| Class | $f$ |
|---|---|
| 1.2–under 1.6 | 220 |
| 1.6–under 2.0 | 150 |
| 2.0–under 2.4 | 90 |
| 2.4–under 2.8 | 110 |
| 2.8–under 3.2 | 280 |

**3.29** Determine the population variance and standard deviation for the following data by using the original formula.

| Class | $f$ |
|---|---|
| 20–under 30 | 7 |
| 30–under 40 | 11 |
| 40–under 50 | 18 |
| 50–under 60 | 13 |
| 60–under 70 | 6 |
| 70–under 80 | 4 |

**3.30** Determine the sample variance and standard deviation for the following data by using the computational formula.

| Class | $f$ |
|---|---|
| 5–under 9 | 20 |
| 9–under 13 | 18 |
| 13–under 17 | 8 |
| 17–under 21 | 6 |
| 21–under 25 | 2 |

**3.31** A random sample of voters in Nashville, Tennessee, is classified by age group, as shown by the following data.

| Age Group | Frequency |
|---|---|
| 18–under 24 | 17 |
| 24–under 30 | 22 |
| 30–under 36 | 26 |
| 36–under 42 | 35 |
| 42–under 48 | 33 |
| 48–under 54 | 30 |
| 54–under 60 | 32 |
| 60–under 66 | 21 |
| 66–under 72 | 15 |

a. Calculate the mean of the data.

b. Calculate the mode.

c. Calculate the variance.

d. Calculate the standard deviation.

**3.32** The following data represent the number of appointments made per 15-minute interval by telephone solicitation for a lawn-care company.

| Number of Appointments | Frequency of Occurrence |
|---|---|
| 0–under 1 | 31 |
| 1–under 2 | 57 |
| 2–under 3 | 26 |
| 3–under 4 | 14 |
| 4–under 5 | 6 |
| 5–under 6 | 3 |

a. Calculate the mean of the data.

b. Calculate the mode.

c. Calculate the variance.

d. Calculate the standard deviation.

3.33 The Air Transport Association of America publishes figures on the busiest airports in the United States. The following frequency distribution has been constructed from these figures for a recent year.

| Number of Passengers Arriving and Departing (millions) | Number of Airports |
|---|---|
| 20–under 30 | 8 |
| 30–under 40 | 7 |
| 40–under 50 | 1 |
| 50–under 60 | 0 |
| 60–under 70 | 3 |
| 70–under 80 | 1 |

a. Calculate the mean of these data.

b. Calculate the mode.

c. Calculate the variance.

d. Calculate the standard deviation.

3.34 The frequency distribution shown represents the number of farms per state for 49 of the 50 states, based on information from the U.S. Department of Agriculture. Determine the average number of farms per state from these data. The mean computed from the original ungrouped data was 37,816 and the standard deviation was 29,341. How do your answers for these grouped data compare? Why might they differ?

| Number of Farms per State | $f$ |
|---|---|
| 0–under 20,000 | 16 |
| 20,000–under 40,000 | 11 |
| 40,000–under 60,000 | 10 |
| 60,000–under 80,000 | 6 |
| 80,000–under 100,000 | 5 |
| 100,000–under 120,000 | 1 |

## 3.4 MEASURES OF SHAPE

**Measures of shape** are *tools that can be used to describe the shape of a distribution of data.* In this section, we examine two measures of shape, skewness and kurtosis. We also look at box and whisker plots.

### Skewness

A distribution of data in which the right half is a mirror image of the left half is said to be *symmetrical.* One example of a symmetrical distribution is the normal distribution, or bell curve, which is presented in more detail in Chapter 6.

**Skewness** is when *a distribution is asymmetrical or lacks symmetry.* The distribution in Figure 3.8 has no skewness because it is symmetric. Figure 3.9 shows a distribution that is skewed left, or negatively skewed, and Figure 3.10 shows a distribution that is skewed right, or positively skewed.

The skewed portion is the long, thin part of the curve. Many researchers use skewed distribution to denote that the data are sparse at one end of the distribution and piled up at the other end. Instructors sometimes refer to a grade distribution as skewed, meaning that few students scored at one end of the grading scale, and many students scored at the other end.

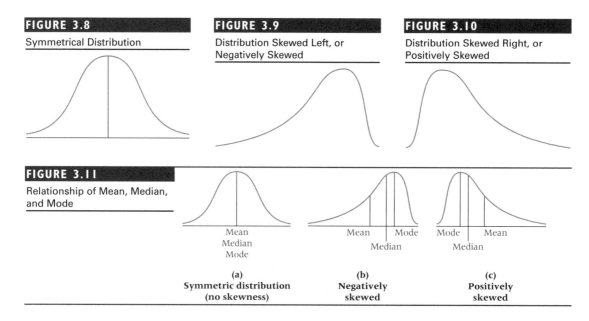

**FIGURE 3.8**
Symmetrical Distribution

**FIGURE 3.9**
Distribution Skewed Left, or
Negatively Skewed

**FIGURE 3.10**
Distribution Skewed Right, or
Positively Skewed

**FIGURE 3.11**
Relationship of Mean, Median,
and Mode

(a)
**Symmetric distribution
(no skewness)**

(b)
**Negatively
skewed**

(c)
**Positively
skewed**

### Skewness and the Relationship of the Mean, Median, and Mode

The concept of skewness helps to understand the relationship of the mean, median, and mode. In a unimodal distribution (distribution with a single peak or mode) that is skewed, the mode is the apex (high point) of the curve and the median is the middle value. The mean tends to be located toward the tail of the distribution, because the mean is affected by all values, including the extreme ones. A bell-shaped or normal distribution with the mean, median, and mode all at the center of the distribution has no skewness. Figure 3.11 displays the relationship of the mean, median, and mode for different types of skewness.

### Coefficient of Skewness

Statistician Karl Pearson is credited with developing at least two coefficients of skewness that can be used to determine the degree of skewness in a distribution. We present one of these coefficients here, referred to as a Pearsonian **coefficient of skewness.** This coefficient *compares the mean and median in light of the magnitude of the standard deviation.* Note that if the distribution is symmetrical, the mean and median are the same value and hence the coefficient of skewness is equal to zero.

**COEFFICIENT OF SKEWNESS**

$$S_k = \frac{3(\mu - M_d)}{\sigma}$$

where
$S_k$ = coefficient of skewness
$M_d$ = median

Suppose, for example, that a distribution has a mean of 29, a median of 26, and a standard deviation of 12.3. The coefficient of skewness is computed as

$$S_k = \frac{3(29 - 26)}{12.3} = +0.73$$

Because the value of $S_k$ is positive, the distribution is positively skewed. If the value of $S_k$ is negative, the distribution is negatively skewed. The greater the magnitude of $S_k$, the more skewed is the distribution.

**FIGURE 3.12**

Types of Kurtosis

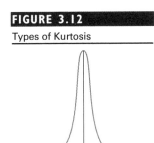

Leptokurtic distribution

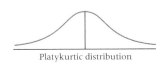

Platykurtic distribution

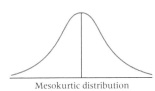

Mesokurtic distribution

## Kurtosis

**Kurtosis** *describes the amount of peakedness of a distribution.* Distributions that are high and thin are referred to as **leptokurtic** distributions. Distributions that are flat and spread out are referred to as **platykurtic** distributions. Between these two types are distributions that are more "normal" in shape, referred to as **mesokurtic** distributions. These three types of kurtosis are illustrated in Figure 3.12.

## Box and Whisker Plots

Another way to describe a distribution of data is by using a box and whisker plot. A **box and whisker plot**, sometimes called a *box plot*, is *a diagram that utilizes the upper and lower quartiles along with the median and the two most extreme values to depict a distribution graphically.* The plot is constructed by using a box to enclose the median. This *box* is extended outward from the median along a continuum to the lower and upper quartiles, enclosing not only the median but also the middle 50% of the data. From the lower and upper quartiles, lines referred to as *whiskers* are extended out from the box toward the outermost data values. The box and whisker plot is determined from five specific numbers.

1. The median ($Q_2$).
2. The lower quartile ($Q_1$).
3. The upper quartile ($Q_3$).
4. The smallest value in the distribution.
5. The largest value in the distribution.

The box of the plot is determined by locating the median and the lower and upper quartiles on a continuum. A box is drawn around the median with the lower and upper quartiles ($Q_1$ and $Q_3$) as the box endpoints. These box endpoints ($Q_1$ and $Q_3$) are referred to as the *hinges* of the box.

Next the value of the interquartile range (IQR) is computed by $Q_3 - Q_1$. The interquartile range includes the middle 50% of the data and should equal the length of the box. However, here the interquartile range is used outside of the box also. At a distance of $1.5 \cdot \text{IQR}$ outward from the lower and upper quartiles are what are referred to as *inner fences*. A *whisker*, a line segment, is drawn from the lower hinge of the box outward to the smallest data value. A second whisker is drawn from the upper hinge of the box outward to the largest data value. The inner fences are established as follows.

$$Q_1 - 1.5 \cdot \text{IQR}$$
$$Q_3 + 1.5 \cdot \text{IQR}$$

If data fall beyond the inner fences, then *outer* fences can be constructed:

$$Q_1 - 3.0 \cdot \text{IQR}$$
$$Q_3 + 3.0 \cdot \text{IQR}$$

Figure 3.13 shows the features of a box and whisker plot.

Data values outside the mainstream of values in a distribution are viewed as *outliers*. Outliers can be merely the more extreme values of a data set. However, sometimes outliers occur due to measurement or recording errors. Other times they are values so unlike the other values that they should not be considered in the same analysis as the rest of the distribution. Values in the data distribution that are outside the inner fences but within the outer fences are referred to as *mild outliers*. Values that are outside the outer fences are called

**FIGURE 3.13**

Box and Whisker Plot

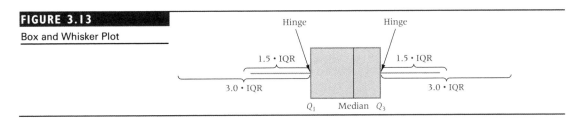

*extreme outliers.* Thus, one of the main uses of a box and whisker plot is to identify outliers. In some computer-produced box and whisker plots, the whiskers are drawn to the largest and smallest data values within the inner fences. An asterisk is then printed for each data value located between the inner and outer fences to indicate a mild outlier. Values outside the outer fences are indicated by a zero on the graph. These values are extreme outliers.

Another use of box and whisker plots is to determine whether a distribution is skewed. The location of the median in the box can relate information about the skewness of the middle 50% of the data. If the median is located on the right side of the box, then the middle 50% are skewed to the left. If the median is located on the left side of the box, then the middle 50% are skewed to the right. By examining the length of the whiskers on each side of the box, a business researcher can make a judgment about the skewness of the outer values. If the longest whisker is to the right of the box, then the outer data are skewed to the right and vice versa. We shall use the data given in Table 3.10 to construct a box and whisker plot.

After organizing the data into an ordered array, as shown in Table 3.11, it is relatively easy to determine the values of the lower quartile ($Q_1$), the median, and the upper quartile ($Q_3$). From these, the value of the interquartile range can be computed.

The hinges of the box are located at the lower and upper quartiles, 69 and 80.5. The median is located within the box at distances of 4 from the lower quartile and 6.5 from the upper quartile. The distribution of the middle 50% of the data is skewed right, because the median is nearer to the lower or left hinge. The inner fence is constructed by

$$Q_1 - 1.5 \cdot IQR = 69 - 1.5(11.5) = 69 - 17.25 = 51.75$$

and

$$Q_3 + 1.5 \cdot IQR = 80.5 + 1.5(11.5) = 80.5 + 17.25 = 97.75$$

The whiskers are constructed by drawing a line segment from the lower hinge outward to the smallest data value and a line segment from the upper hinge outward to the largest data value. An examination of the data reveals that no data values in this set of numbers are outside the inner fence. The whiskers are constructed outward to the lowest value, which is 62, and to the highest value, which is 87.

To construct an outer fence, we calculate $Q_1 - 3 \cdot IQR$ and $Q_3 + 3 \cdot IQR$, as follows.

$$Q_1 - 3 \cdot IQR = 69 - 3(11.5) = 69 - 34.5 = 34.5$$
$$Q_3 + 3 \cdot IQR = 80.5 + 3(11.5) = 80.5 + 34.5 = 115.0$$

Figure 3.14 is the MINITAB computer printout for this box and whisker plot.

## TABLE 3.10

Data for Box and Whisker Plot

| | | | | | | | |
|---|---|---|---|---|---|---|---|
| 71 | 87 | 82 | 64 | 72 | 75 | 81 | 69 |
| 76 | 79 | 65 | 68 | 80 | 73 | 85 | 71 |
| 70 | 79 | 63 | 62 | 81 | 84 | 77 | 73 |
| 82 | 74 | 74 | 73 | 84 | 72 | 81 | 65 |
| 74 | 62 | 64 | 68 | 73 | 82 | 69 | 71 |

## TABLE 3.11

Data in Ordered Array with Quartiles and Median

| | | | | | | | | | |
|---|---|---|---|---|---|---|---|---|---|
| 87 | 85 | 84 | 84 | 82 | 82 | 82 | 81 | 81 | 81 |
| 80 | 79 | 79 | 77 | 76 | 75 | 74 | 74 | 74 | 73 |
| 73 | 73 | 73 | 72 | 72 | 71 | 71 | 71 | 70 | 69 |
| 69 | 68 | 68 | 65 | 65 | 64 | 64 | 63 | 62 | 62 |

$Q_1 = 69$

$Q_2 = \text{median} = 73$

$Q_3 = 80.5$

$IQR = Q_3 - Q_1 = 80.5 - 69 = 11.5$

## FIGURE 3.14

MINITAB Box and Whisker Plot

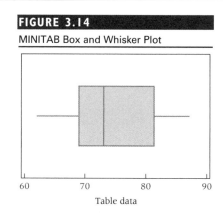

Table data

## 3.4 PROBLEMS

**3.35** On a certain day the average closing price of a group of stocks on the New York Stock Exchange is $35 (to the nearest dollar). If the median value is $33 and the mode is $21, is the distribution of these stock prices skewed? If so, how?

**3.36** A local hotel offers ballroom dancing on Friday nights. A researcher observes the customers and estimates their ages. Discuss the skewness of the distribution of ages if the mean age is 51, the median age is 54, and the modal age is 59.

**3.37** The sales volumes for the top real estate brokerage firms in the United States for a recent year were analyzed using descriptive statistics. The mean annual dollar volume for these firms was $5.51 billion, the median was $3.19 billion, and the standard deviation was $9.59 billion. Compute the value of the Pearsonian coefficient of skewness and discuss the meaning of it. Is the distribution skewed? If so, to what extent?

**3.38** Suppose the following data are the ages of Internet users obtained from a sample. Use these data to compute a Pearsonian coefficient of skewness. What is the meaning of the coefficient?

| | | | | |
|---|---|---|---|---|
| 41 | 15 | 31 | 25 | 24 |
| 23 | 21 | 22 | 22 | 18 |
| 30 | 20 | 19 | 19 | 16 |
| 23 | 27 | 38 | 34 | 24 |
| 19 | 20 | 29 | 17 | 23 |

**3.39** Construct a box and whisker plot on the following data. Do the data contain any outliers? Is the distribution of data skewed?

| | | | | | |
|---|---|---|---|---|---|
| 540 | 690 | 503 | 558 | 490 | 609 |
| 379 | 601 | 559 | 495 | 562 | 580 |
| 510 | 623 | 477 | 574 | 588 | 497 |
| 527 | 570 | 495 | 590 | 602 | 541 |

**3.40** Suppose a consumer group asked 18 consumers to keep a yearly log of their shopping practices and that the following data represent the number of coupons used by each consumer over the yearly period. Use the data to construct a box and whisker plot. List the median, $Q_1$, $Q_3$, the endpoints for the inner fences, and the endpoints for the outer fences. Discuss the skewness of the distribution of these data and point out any outliers.

| | | | | | | | | |
|---|---|---|---|---|---|---|---|---|
| 81 | 68 | 70 | 100 | 94 | 47 | 66 | 70 | 82 |
| 110 | 105 | 60 | 21 | 70 | 66 | 90 | 78 | 85 |

## 3.5 MEASURES OF ASSOCIATION

Measures of association are statistics that yield information about the relatedness of numerical variables. In this chapter, we discuss only one measure of association, correlation, and do so only for two numerical variables.

### Correlation

**Correlation** is *a measure of the degree of relatedness of variables*. It can help a business researcher determine, for example, whether the stocks of two airlines rise and fall in any related manner. Logically, the prices of two stocks in the same industry should be related. For a sample of pairs of data, correlation analysis can yield a numerical value that represents the degree of relatedness of the two stock prices over time. In the transportation industry, is a correlation evident between the price of transportation and the weight of the

## TABLE 3.12

Data for the
Economics Example

| Day | Interest Rate | Futures Index |
|-----|---------------|---------------|
| 1   | 7.43          | 221           |
| 2   | 7.48          | 222           |
| 3   | 8.00          | 226           |
| 4   | 7.75          | 225           |
| 5   | 7.60          | 224           |
| 6   | 7.63          | 223           |
| 7   | 7.68          | 223           |
| 8   | 7.67          | 226           |
| 9   | 7.59          | 226           |
| 10  | 8.07          | 235           |
| 11  | 8.03          | 233           |
| 12  | 8.00          | 241           |

object being shipped? Do price and distance show any correlation? How strong are the correlations? Pricing decisions can be based in part on shipment costs that are correlated with other variables. In economics and finance, how strong is the correlation between the producer price index and the unemployment rate? In retail sales, what variables are related to a particular store's sales? Are sales related to population density, number of competitors, size of the store, amount of advertising, or other variables?

Several measures of correlation are available, the selection of which depends mostly on the level of data being analyzed. Ideally, researchers would like to solve for $\rho$, the population coefficient of correlation. However, because researchers virtually always deal with sample data, this section introduces a widely used sample **coefficient of correlation,** $r$. This measure is applicable only if both variables being analyzed have at least an interval level of data. Chapter 17 presents a correlation measure that can be used when the data are ordinal.

The statistic $r$ is the **Pearson product-moment correlation coefficient,** named after Karl Pearson (1857–1936), an English statistician who developed several coefficients of correlation along with other significant statistical concepts. The term $r$ is a *measure of the linear correlation of two variables.* It is a number that ranges from −1 to 0 to +1, representing the strength of the relationship between the variables. An $r$ value of +1 denotes a perfect positive relationship between two sets of numbers. An $r$ value of −1 denotes a perfect negative correlation, which indicates an inverse relationship between two variables: as one variable gets larger, the other gets smaller. An $r$ value of 0 means no linear relationship is present between the two variables.

**PEARSON PRODUCT-MOMENT CORRELATION COEFFICIENT**

$$r = \frac{\Sigma(x-\bar{x})(y-\bar{y})}{\sqrt{\Sigma(x-\bar{x})^2\Sigma(y-\bar{y})^2}} = \frac{\Sigma xy - \frac{(\Sigma x \Sigma y)}{n}}{\sqrt{\left[\Sigma x^2 - \frac{(\Sigma x)^2}{n}\right]\left[\Sigma y^2 - \frac{(\Sigma y)^2}{n}\right]}}$$

Figure 3.15 depicts five different degrees of correlation: (a) represents strong negative correlation, (b) represents moderate negative correlation, (c) represents moderate positive correlation, (d) represents strong positive correlation, and (e) contains no correlation.

## TABLE 3.13

Computation of $r$ for the
Economics Example

| Day | Interest $x$ | Futures Index $y$ | $x^2$ | $y^2$ | $xy$ |
|-----|------|------|-------|-------|------|
| 1  | 7.43 | 221 | 55.205 | 48,841 | 1,642.03 |
| 2  | 7.48 | 222 | 55.950 | 49,284 | 1,660.56 |
| 3  | 8.00 | 226 | 64.000 | 51,076 | 1,808.00 |
| 4  | 7.75 | 225 | 60.063 | 50,625 | 1,743.75 |
| 5  | 7.60 | 224 | 57.760 | 50,176 | 1,702.40 |
| 6  | 7.63 | 223 | 58.217 | 49,729 | 1,701.49 |
| 7  | 7.68 | 223 | 58.982 | 49,729 | 1,712.64 |
| 8  | 7.67 | 226 | 58.829 | 51,076 | 1,733.42 |
| 9  | 7.59 | 226 | 57.608 | 51,076 | 1,715.34 |
| 10 | 8.07 | 235 | 65.125 | 55,225 | 1,896.45 |
| 11 | 8.03 | 233 | 64.481 | 54,289 | 1,870.99 |
| 12 | 8.00 | 241 | 64.000 | 58,081 | 1,928.00 |
| | $\Sigma x = 92.93$ | $\Sigma y = 2{,}725$ | $\Sigma x^2 = 720.220$ | $\Sigma y^2 = 619{,}207$ | $\Sigma xy = 21{,}115.07$ |

$$r = \frac{(21{,}115.07) - \frac{(92.93)(2725)}{12}}{\sqrt{\left[(720.22) - \frac{(92.93)^2}{12}\right]\left[(619{,}207) - \frac{(2725)^2}{12}\right]}} = .815$$

| FIGURE 3.15 | Five Correlations |
|---|---|

(a) Strong Negative Correlation ($r = -.933$)

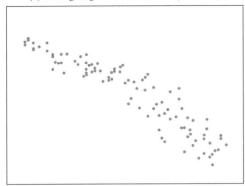

(b) Moderate Negative Correlation ($r = -.674$)

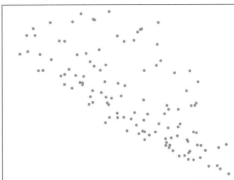

(c) Moderate Positive Correlation ($r = .518$)

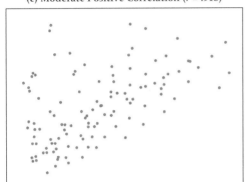

(d) Strong Positive Correlation ($r = .909$)

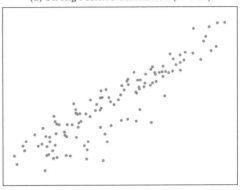

(e) Virtually No Correlation ($r = -.004$)

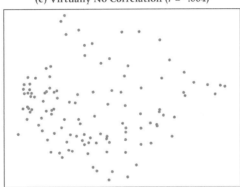

| FIGURE 3.16 | Excel Output |
|---|---|
| Excel and MINITAB Output for the Economics Example | |

**Excel Output**

|  | A | B | C |
|---|---|---|---|
| 1 | | Interest Rate | Futures Index |
| 2 | Interest Rate | 1 | |
| 3 | Futures Index | 0.815 | 1 |

**MINITAB Output**

Correlations: INTEREST RATE, FUTURES INDEX

Pearson correlation of INTEREST RATE and FUTURES INDEX = 0.815

What is the measure of correlation between the interest rate of federal funds and the commodities futures index? With data such as those shown in Table 3.12, which represent the values for interest rates of federal funds and commodities futures indexes for a sample of 12 days, a correlation coefficient, $r$, can be computed.

Examination of the formula for computing a Pearson product-moment correlation coefficient reveals that the following values must be obtained to compute $r$: $\Sigma x$, $\Sigma x^2$, $\Sigma y$, $\Sigma y^2$, $\Sigma xy$, and $n$. In correlation analysis, it does not matter which variable is designated $x$ and which is designated $y$. For this example, the correlation coefficient is computed as shown in Table 3.13. The $r$ value obtained ($r = .815$) represents a relatively strong positive relationship between interest rates and commodities futures index over this 12-day period.

Figure 3.16 shows both Excel and MINITAB output for this problem.

## 3.5 PROBLEMS

**3.41** Determine the value of the coefficient of correlation, $r$, for the following data.

| X | 4 | 6 | 7 | 11 | 14 | 17 | 21 |
|---|---|---|---|----|----|----|----|
| Y | 18 | 12 | 13 | 8 | 7 | 7 | 4 |

**3.42** Determine the value of $r$ for the following data.

| X | 158 | 296 | 87 | 110 | 436 |
|---|-----|-----|----|-----|-----|
| Y | 349 | 510 | 301 | 322 | 550 |

**3.43** In an effort to determine whether any correlation exists between the price of stocks of airlines, an analyst sampled six days of activity of the stock market. Using the following prices of Delta stock and Southwest stock, compute the coefficient of correlation. Stock prices have been rounded off to the nearest tenth for ease of computation.

| Delta | Southwest |
|-------|-----------|
| 47.6 | 15.1 |
| 46.3 | 15.4 |
| 50.6 | 15.9 |
| 52.6 | 15.6 |
| 52.4 | 16.4 |
| 52.7 | 18.1 |

**3.44** The following data are the claims (in $ millions) for BlueCross BlueShield benefits for nine states, along with the surplus (in $ millions) that the company had in assets in those states.

| State | Claims | Surplus |
|-------|--------|---------|
| Alabama | $1425 | $277 |
| Colorado | 273 | 100 |
| Florida | 915 | 120 |
| Illinois | 1687 | 259 |
| Maine | 234 | 40 |
| Montana | 142 | 25 |
| North Dakota | 259 | 57 |
| Oklahoma | 258 | 31 |
| Texas | 894 | 141 |

Use the data to compute a correlation coefficient, $r$, to determine the correlation between claims and surplus.

**3.45** The National Safety Council released the following data on the incidence rates for fatal or lost-worktime injuries per 100 employees for several industries in three recent years.

| Industry | Year 1 | Year 2 | Year 3 |
|---|---|---|---|
| Textile | .46 | .48 | .69 |
| Chemical | .52 | .62 | .63 |
| Communication | .90 | .72 | .81 |
| Machinery | 1.50 | 1.74 | 2.10 |
| Services | 2.89 | 2.03 | 2.46 |
| Nonferrous metals | 1.80 | 1.92 | 2.00 |
| Food | 3.29 | 3.18 | 3.17 |
| Government | 5.73 | 4.43 | 4.00 |

Compute $r$ for each pair of years and determine which years are most highly correlated.

## 3.6 DESCRIPTIVE STATISTICS ON THE COMPUTER

Both MINITAB and Excel yield extensive descriptive statistics. Even though each computer package can compute individual statistics such as a mean or a standard deviation, they can also produce multiple descriptive statistics at one time. Figure 3.17 displays a MINITAB output for the descriptive statistics associated with the computer production data presented earlier in this section. The MINITAB output contains, among other things, the mean, the median, the sample standard deviation, the minimum and maximum (which can then be used to compute the range), and $Q_1$ and $Q_3$ (from which the interquartile range can be computed). Excel's descriptive statistics output for the same computer production data is displayed in Figure 3.18. The Excel output contains the mean, the median, the mode, the sample standard deviation, the sample variance, and the range. The descriptive statistics feature on either of these computer packages yields a lot of useful information about a data set. MINITAB and Excel also have the capability of computing the correlation coefficient, $r$.

**FIGURE 3.17**

MINITAB Output for the Computer Production Problem

DESCRIPTIVE STATISTICS

| Variable | N | Mean | Median | TrMean | StDev | SE Mean |
|---|---|---|---|---|---|---|
| Computer | 5 | 13.00 | 16.00 | 13.00 | 5.70 | 2.55 |

| Variable | Minimum | Maximum | $Q_1$ | $Q_3$ |
|---|---|---|---|---|
| Computer | 5.00 | 18.00 | 7.00 | 17.50 |

**FIGURE 3.18**

Excel Output for the Computer Production Problem

COMPUTER PRODUCTION DATA

| | A | B |
|---|---|---|
| 1 | Mean | 13 |
| 2 | Standard error | 2.5495 |
| 3 | Median | 16 |
| 4 | Mode | N/A |
| 5 | Standard deviation | 5.7009 |
| 6 | Sample variance | 32.5 |
| 7 | Kurtosis | −1.7112 |
| 8 | Skewness | −0.8096 |
| 9 | Range | 13 |
| 10 | Minimum | 5 |
| 11 | Maximum | 18 |
| 12 | Sum | 65 |
| 13 | Count | 5 |

# Laundry Statistics

The descriptive statistics presented in this chapter are excellent for summarizing and presenting data sets in more concise formats. For example, question 1 of the managerial and statistical questions in the Decision Dilemma reports water measurements for 50 U.S. households. Using Excel and/or MINITAB, many of the descriptive statistics presented in this chapter can be applied to these data. The results are shown in Figures 3.19 and 3.20.

These computer outputs show that the average water usage is 15.48 gallons with a standard deviation of about 1.233 gallons. The median is 16 gallons with a range of 6 gallons (12 to 18). The first quartile is 15 gallons and the third quartile is 16 gallons. The mode is also 16 gallons. The MINITAB graph and the skewness measures show that the data are slightly skewed to the left. Applying Chebyshev's Theorem to the mean and standard deviation shows that at least 88.9% of the measurements should fall between 11.78 gallons and 19.18 gallons. An examination of the data and the minimum and maximum reveals that 100% of the data actually fall within these limits.

## FIGURE 3.19

Excel Descriptive Statistics

WATER USAGE

|   | A | B |
|---|---|---|
| 1 | Mean | 15.48 |
| 2 | Standard error | 0.174 |
| 3 | Median | 16 |
| 4 | Mode | 16 |
| 5 | Standard deviation | 1.233 |
| 6 | Sample variance | 1.52 |
| 7 | Kurtosis | 0.264 |
| 8 | Skewness | −0.531 |
| 9 | Range | 6 |
| 10 | Minimum | 12 |
| 11 | Maximum | 18 |
| 12 | Sum | 774 |
| 13 | Count | 50 |

According to the Decision Dilemma, the mean wash cycle time is 35 minutes with a standard deviation of 5 minutes. If the wash cycle times are approximately normally distributed, we can apply the empirical rule. According to the empirical rule, 68% of the times would fall within 30 and 40 minutes, 95% of the times would fall within 25 and 45 minutes, and 99.7% of the wash times would fall within 20 and 50 minutes. If the data are not normally distributed, Chebyshev's theorem reveals that at least 75% of the times should fall between 25 and 45 minutes and 88.9% should fall between 20 and 50 minutes.

Is amount of laundry correlated to household income? If a correlation coefficient is computed on the data from the Decision Dilemma, an $r$ of .723 is found. This result indicates that some correlation is likely between the two sets of data. However, it is not a perfect correlation nor is it a very strong correlation. The tendency appears to be that households with higher incomes do larger amounts of laundry. However, in some cases households with lower incomes still do relatively large amounts of laundry and households with higher incomes sometimes do less laundry.

## FIGURE 3.20

MINITAB Descriptive Statistics

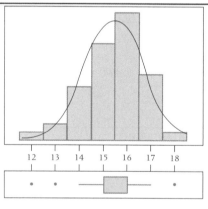

Variable: Water Usage

Anderson-Darling Normality Test
| A-Squared | 1.598 |
| P-Value | 0.000 |

| Mean | 15.4800 |
| St Dev | 1.2329 |
| Variance | 1.52 |
| Skewness | −5.3E−01 |
| Kurtosis | 0.263785 |
| N | 50 |

| Minimum | 12.0000 |
| 1st Quartile | 15.0000 |
| Median | 16.0000 |
| 3rd Quartile | 16.0000 |
| Maximum | 18.0000 |

95% Confidence Interval for Mu
| 15.1296 | 15.8304 |

95% Confidence Interval for Sigma
| 1.0299 | 1.5363 |

95% Confidence Interval for Median
| 15.0000 | 16.0000 |

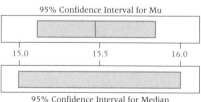

95% Confidence Interval for Mu

95% Confidence Interval for Median

## ETHICAL CONSIDERATIONS

In describing a body of data to an audience, it is best to use whatever measures it takes to present a "full" picture of the data. By limiting the descriptive measures used, the business researcher may give the audience only part of the picture and can skew the way the receiver understands the data. For example, if a researcher presents only the mean, the audience will have no insight into the variability of the data; in addition, the mean might be inordinately large or small because of extreme values. Likewise, the choice of the median precludes a picture that includes the extreme values. Using the mode can cause the receiver of the information to focus only on values that occur often.

At least one measure of variability is usually needed with at least one measure of central tendency for the audience to begin to understand what the data look like. Unethical researchers might be tempted to present only the descriptive measure that will convey the picture of the data that they wants the audience to see. Ethical researchers will instead use any and all methods that will present the fullest, most informative picture possible from the data.

A strong correlation does not necessarily indicate cause and effect. It is unprofessional and unethical to draw cause-and-effect conclusions just because two variables are related. For example, suppose the number of moving vans leased is shown to increase with temperature. Some decision makers might believe that the hotter the day, the more people tend to move. The reality might be that people tend to move after school is out for the year in order to be less disruptive of their children's schooling. School is usually out during the summer in most of the country when the temperatures are hotter. Hence, it may be the school schedule that actually drives the moves, not the temperature. A hot spell in January therefore does not necessarily generate a lot of moves.

Former governor of Colorado Richard Lamm has been quoted as having said that "Demographers are academics who can statistically prove that the average person in Miami is born Cuban and dies Jewish...."* People are more likely to reach this type of conclusion if incomplete or misleading descriptive statistics are provided by researchers.

*Alan L. Otten. "People Patterns/Odds and Ends," *The Wall Street Journal*, 29 June 1992, p. B1. Reprinted by permission of *The Wall Street Journal* © 1992, Dow Jones & Company, Inc. All Rights Reserved Worldwide.

## SUMMARY

Statistical descriptive measures include measures of central tendency, measures of variability, and measures of shape. Measures of central tendency and measures of variability are computed differently for ungrouped and grouped data. Measures of central tendency are useful in describing data because they communicate information about the more central portions of the data. The most common measures of central tendency are the three Ms: mode, median, and mean. In addition, percentiles and quartiles are measures of central tendency.

The mode is the most frequently occurring value in a set of data. If two values tie for the mode, the data are bimodal. Data sets can be multimodal. Among other things, the mode is used in business for determining sizes.

The median is the middle term in an ordered array of numbers containing an odd number of terms. For an array with an even number of terms, the median is the average of the two middle terms. The formula $(n + 1)/2$ specifies the location of the median. A median is unaffected by the magnitude of extreme values. This characteristic makes the median a most useful and appropriate measure of location in reporting such things as income, age, and prices of houses.

The arithmetic mean is widely used and is usually what researchers are referring to when they use the word *mean*. The arithmetic mean is the average. The population mean and the sample mean are computed in the same way but are denoted by different symbols. The arithmetic mean is affected by every value and can be inordinately influenced by extreme values.

Percentiles divide a set of data into 100 groups, which means 99 percentiles are needed. Quartiles divide data into four groups. The three quartiles are $Q_1$, which is the lower quartile; $Q_2$, which is the middle quartile and equals the median; and $Q_3$, which is the upper quartile.

Measures of variability are statistical tools used in combination with measures of central tendency to describe data. Measures of variability provide a description of data that measures of central tendency cannot give: information about the spread of the data values. These measures include the range, mean absolute deviation, variance, standard deviation, interquartile range, and coefficient of variation for ungrouped data.

One of the most elementary measures of variability is the range. It is the difference between the largest and smallest values. Although the range is easy to compute, it has limited usefulness. The interquartile range is the difference between the third and first quartile. It equals the range of the middle 50% of the data.

The mean absolute deviation (MAD) is computed by averaging the absolute values of the deviations from the mean. The mean absolute deviation provides the magnitude of the average deviation but without specifying its direction. The mean absolute deviation has limited usage in statistics, but interest is growing for the use of MAD in the field of forecasting.

Variance is widely used as a tool in statistics but is used little as a stand-alone measure of variability. The variance is the average of the squared deviations about the mean.

The square root of the variance is the standard deviation. It also is a widely used tool in statistics. It is used more often than the variance as a stand-alone measure. The standard deviation is best understood by examining its applications in determining where data are in relation to the mean. The empirical rule and Chebyshev's theorem are statements about the proportions of data values that are within various numbers of standard deviations from the mean.

The empirical rule reveals the percentage of values that are within one, two, or three standard deviations of the mean for a set of data. The empirical rule applies only if the data are in a bell-shaped distribution. According to the empirical rule, approximately 68% of all values of a normal distribution are within plus or minus one standard deviation of the mean. Ninety-five percent of all values are within two standard deviations either side of the mean, and virtually all values are within three standard deviations of the mean.

Chebyshev's theorem also delineates the proportion of values that are within a given number of standard deviations from the mean. However, it applies to any distribution. According to Chebyshev's theorem, at least $1 - 1/k^2$ values are within $k$ standard deviations of the mean. The $z$ score represents the number of standard deviations a value is from the mean for normally distributed data.

The coefficient of variation is a ratio of a standard deviation to its mean, given as a percentage. It is especially useful in comparing standard deviations or variances that represent data with different means.

Some measures of central tendency and some measures of variability are presented for grouped data. These measures include mean, mode, variance, and standard deviation. Generally, these measures are only approximate for grouped data because the values of the actual raw data are unknown.

Two measures of shape are skewness and kurtosis. Skewness is the lack of symmetry in a distribution. If a distribution is skewed, it is stretched in one direction or the other. The skewed part of a graph is its long, thin portion. One measure of skewness is the Pearsonian coefficient of skewness.

Kurtosis is the degree of peakedness of a distribution. A tall, thin distribution is referred to as leptokurtic. A flat distribution is platykurtic, and a distribution with a more normal peakedness is said to be mesokurtic.

A box and whisker plot is a graphical depiction of a distribution. The plot is constructed by using the median, the lower quartile, and the upper quartile. It can yield information about skewness and outliers.

Bivariate correlation can be accomplished with several different measures. In this chapter, only one coefficient of correlation is presented: the Pearson product-moment coefficient of correlation, $r$. This value ranges from −1 to 0 to +1. An $r$ value of +1 is perfect positive correlation, and an $r$ value of −1 is a perfect negative correlation. Negative correlation means that as one variable increases in value, the other variable tends to decrease. For $r$ values near zero, little or no correlation is present.

## KEY TERMS

| | | | |
|---|---|---|---|
| arithmetic mean | deviation from the mean | measures of shape | quartiles |
| bimodal | empirical rule | measures of variability | range |
| box and whisker plot | interquartile range | median | skewness |
| Chebyshev's theorem | kurtosis | mesokurtic | standard deviation |
| coefficient of correlation (r) | leptokurtic | mode | sum of squares of x |
| coefficient of skewness | mean absolute deviation | multimodal | variance |
| coefficient of variation (CV) | (MAD) | percentiles | z score |
| correlation | measures of central tendency | platykurtic | |

# FORMULAS

Population mean (ungrouped)

$$\mu = \frac{\Sigma x}{N}$$

Sample mean (ungrouped)

$$\bar{x} = \frac{\Sigma x}{n}$$

Mean absolute deviation

$$MAD = \frac{\Sigma |x - \mu|}{N}$$

Population variance (ungrouped)

$$\sigma^2 = \frac{\Sigma(x - \mu)^2}{N}$$

$$\sigma^2 = \frac{\Sigma x^2 - \frac{(\Sigma x)^2}{N}}{N}$$

$$\sigma^2 = \frac{\Sigma x^2 - N\mu^2}{N}$$

Population standard deviation (ungrouped)

$$\sigma = \sqrt{\sigma^2}$$

$$\sigma = \sqrt{\frac{\Sigma(x - \mu)^2}{N}}$$

$$\sigma = \sqrt{\frac{\Sigma x^2 - \frac{(\Sigma x)^2}{N}}{N}}$$

$$\sigma = \sqrt{\frac{\Sigma x^2 - N\mu^2}{N}}$$

Grouped mean

$$\mu_{grouped} = \frac{\Sigma fM}{N}$$

Population variance (grouped)

$$\sigma^2 = \frac{\Sigma f(M - \mu)^2}{N} = \frac{\Sigma fM^2 - \frac{(\Sigma fM)^2}{N}}{N}$$

Population standard deviation (grouped)

$$\sigma = \sqrt{\frac{\Sigma f(M - \mu)^2}{N}} = \sqrt{\frac{\Sigma fM^2 - \frac{(\Sigma fM)^2}{N}}{N}}$$

Sample variance

$$s^2 = \frac{\Sigma(x - \bar{x})^2}{n - 1}$$

$$s^2 = \frac{\Sigma x^2 - \frac{(\Sigma x)^2}{n}}{n - 1}$$

$$s^2 = \frac{\Sigma x^2 - n(\bar{x})^2}{n - 1}$$

Sample standard deviation

$$s = \sqrt{s^2}$$

$$s = \sqrt{\frac{\Sigma(x - \bar{x})^2}{n - 1}}$$

$$s = \sqrt{\frac{\Sigma x^2 - \frac{(\Sigma x)^2}{n}}{n - 1}}$$

$$s = \sqrt{\frac{\Sigma x^2 - n(\bar{x})^2}{n - 1}}$$

Chebyshev's theorem

$$1 - \frac{1}{k^2}$$

z score

$$z = \frac{x - \mu}{\sigma}$$

Coefficient of variation

$$CV = \frac{\sigma}{\mu}(100)$$

Interquartile range

$$IQR = Q_3 - Q_1$$

Sample variance (grouped)

$$s^2 = \frac{\Sigma f(M - \bar{x})^2}{n - 1} = \frac{\Sigma fM^2 - \frac{(\Sigma fM)^2}{n}}{n - 1}$$

Sample standard deviation (grouped)

$$s = \sqrt{\frac{\Sigma f(M - \bar{x})^2}{n - 1}} = \sqrt{\frac{\Sigma fM^2 - \frac{(\Sigma fM)^2}{n}}{n - 1}}$$

Pearsonian coefficient of skewness

$$S_k = \frac{3(\mu - M_d)}{\sigma}$$

Pearson's product-moment correlation coefficient

$$r = \frac{\Sigma(x - \bar{x})(y - \bar{y})}{\sqrt{\Sigma(x - \bar{x})^2 \Sigma(y - \bar{y})^2}} = \frac{\Sigma xy - \frac{(\Sigma x \Sigma y)}{n}}{\sqrt{\left[\Sigma x^2 - \frac{(\Sigma x)^2}{n}\right]\left[\Sigma y^2 - \frac{(\Sigma y)^2}{n}\right]}}$$

## SUPPLEMENTARY PROBLEMS

### CALCULATING THE STATISTICS

**3.46** The 2000 U.S. Census asked every household to report information on each person living there. Suppose for a sample of 30 households selected, the number of persons living in each was reported as follows.

2  3  1  2  6  4  2  1  5  3  2  3  1  2  2
1  3  1  2  2  4  2  1  2  8  3  2  1  1  3

Compute the mean, median, mode, range, lower and upper quartiles, and interquartile range for these data.

**3.47** The 2000 U.S. Census also asked for each person's age. Suppose that a sample of 40 households taken from the census data showed the age of the first person recorded on the census form to be as follows.

42  29  31  38  55  27  28
33  49  70  25  21  38  47
63  22  38  52  50  41  19
22  29  81  52  26  35  38
29  31  48  26  33  42  58
40  32  24  34  25

Compute $P_{10}$, $P_{80}$, $Q_1$, $Q_3$, the interquartile range, and the range for these data.

**3.48** According to the National Association of Investment Clubs, PepsiCo is the most popular stock with investment clubs with 11,388 clubs holding PepsiCo stock. Intel is a close second, followed by Motorola. For the following list of the most popular stocks with investment clubs, compute the mean, median, $P_{30}$, $P_{60}$, $P_{90}$, $Q_1$, $Q_3$, range, and interquartile range.

| Company | Number of Clubs Holding Stock |
|---|---|
| PepsiCo | 11,388 |
| Intel | 11,019 |
| Motorola | 9,863 |
| Tricon Global Restaurants | 9,168 |
| Merck & Co. | 8,687 |
| AFLAC | 6,796 |
| Diebold | 6,552 |
| McDonald's | 6,498 |
| Coca-Cola | 6,101 |
| Lucent Technologies | 5,563 |
| Home Depot | 5,414 |
| Clayton Homes | 5,390 |
| RPM | 5,033 |
| Cisco Systems | 4,541 |
| General Electric | 4,507 |
| Johnson & Johnson | 4,464 |
| Microsoft | 4,152 |
| Wendy's International | 4,150 |
| Walt Disney | 3,999 |
| AT&T | 3,619 |

**3.49** *Editor & Publisher International Yearbook* published a listing of the top 10 daily newspapers in the United States, as shown here. Use these population data to compute a mean and a standard deviation. The figures are given in average daily circulation from Monday through Friday. Because the numbers are large, it may save you some effort to recode the data. One way to recode these data is to move the decimal point six places to the left (e.g., 1,774,880 becomes 1.77488). If you recode the data this way, the resulting mean and standard deviation will be correct for the recoded data. To rewrite the answers so that they are correct for the original data, move the decimal point back to the right six places in the answers.

| Newspaper | Average Daily Circulation |
|---|---|
| Wall Street Journal | 1,762,751 |
| USA Today | 1,692,666 |
| New York Times | 1,097,180 |
| Los Angeles Times | 1,033,399 |
| Washington Post | 762,009 |
| (New York) Daily News | 704,463 |
| Chicago Tribune | 661,699 |
| Long Island Newsday | 576,345 |
| Houston Chronicle | 546,799 |
| Dallas Morning News | 495,597 |

**3.50** We show the companies with the largest oil refining capacity in the world according to the *Petroleum Intelligence Weekly*. Use these population data and answer the questions.

| Company | Capacity (barrels per day in 1,000s) |
|---|---|
| ExxonMobil | 6,300 |
| Royal Dutch/Shell | 3,791 |
| China Petrochemical | 2,867 |
| Petroleos de Venezuela | 2,437 |
| Saudi Arabian Oil | 1,970 |
| BP Amoco | 1,965 |
| Chevron | 1,661 |
| Petrobras | 1,540 |
| Texaco | 1,532 |
| Petroleos Mexicanos (Pemex) | 1,520 |
| National Iranian Oil | 1,092 |

a. What are the values of the mean and the median? Compare the answers and state which you prefer as a measure of location for these data and why.
b. What are the values of the range and interquartile range? How do they differ?
c. What are the values of variance and standard deviation for these data?
d. What is the z score for Texaco? What is the z score for ExxonMobil? Interpret these z scores.

e. Calculate the Pearsonian coefficient of skewness and comment on the skewness of this distribution.

**3.51** The U.S. Department of the Interior releases figures on mineral production. Following are the 10 leading states in nonfuel mineral production in the United States.

| State | Value ($ millions) |
|---|---|
| California | 3,350 |
| Nevada | 2,800 |
| Arizona | 2,550 |
| Texas | 2,050 |
| Florida | 1,920 |
| Michigan | 1,670 |
| Georgia | 1,660 |
| Minnesota | 1,570 |
| Utah | 1,420 |
| Missouri | 1,320 |

a. Calculate the mean, median, and mode.
b. Calculate the range, interquartile range, mean absolute deviation, sample variance, and sample standard deviation.
c. Compute the Pearsonian coefficient of skewness for these data.
d. Sketch a box and whisker plot.

**3.52** The radio music listener market is diverse. Listener formats might include adult contemporary, album rock, top 40, oldies, rap, country and western, classical, and jazz. In targeting audiences, market researchers need to be concerned about the ages of the listeners attracted to particular formats. Suppose a market researcher surveyed a sample of 170 listeners of oldies stations and obtained the following age distribution.

| Age | Frequency |
|---|---|
| 15–under 20 | 9 |
| 20–under 25 | 16 |
| 25–under 30 | 27 |
| 30–under 35 | 44 |
| 35–under 40 | 42 |
| 40–under 45 | 23 |
| 45–under 50 | 7 |
| 50–under 55 | 2 |

a. What are the mean and modal ages of oldies listeners?
b. What are the variance and standard deviation of the ages of oldies listeners?

**3.53** A research agency administers a demographic survey to 90 telemarketing companies to determine the size of their operations. When asked to report how many employees now work in their telemarketing operation, the companies gave responses ranging from 1 to 100. The agency's analyst organizes the figures into a frequency distribution.

| Number of Employees Working in Telemarketing | Number of Companies |
|---|---|
| 0–under 20 | 32 |
| 20–under 40 | 16 |
| 40–under 60 | 13 |
| 60–under 80 | 10 |
| 80–under 100 | 19 |

a. Compute the mean and mode for this distribution.
b. Compute the standard deviation for these data.

**3.54** Determine the Pearson product-moment correlation coefficient for the following data.

| $X$ | 1 | 10 | 9 | 6 | 5 | 3 | 2 |
|---|---|---|---|---|---|---|---|
| $Y$ | 8 | 4 | 4 | 5 | 7 | 7 | 9 |

### TESTING YOUR UNDERSTANDING

**3.55** Financial analysts like to use the standard deviation as a measure of risk for a stock. The greater the deviation in a stock price over time, the more risky it is to invest in the stock. However, the average prices of some stocks are considerably higher than the average price of others, allowing for the potential of a greater standard deviation of price. For example, a standard deviation of $5.00 on a $10.00 stock is considerably different from a $5.00 standard deviation on a $40.00 stock. In this situation, a coefficient of variation might provide insight into risk. Suppose stock X costs an average of $32.00 per share and showed a standard deviation of $3.45 for the past 60 days. Suppose stock Y costs an average of $84.00 per share and showed a standard deviation of $5.40 for the past 60 days. Use the coefficient of variation to determine the variability for each stock.

**3.56** The Polk Company reported that the average age of a car on U.S. roads in a recent year was 7.5 years. Suppose the distribution of ages of cars on U.S. roads is approximately bell-shaped. If 99.7% of the ages are between 1 year and 14 years, what is the standard deviation of car age? Suppose the standard deviation is 1.7 years and the mean is 7.5 years. Between what two values would 95% of the car ages fall?

**3.57** According to a *Human Resources* report, a worker in the industrial countries spends on average 419 minutes a day on the job. Suppose the standard deviation of time spent on the job is 27 minutes.

a. If the distribution of time spent on the job is approximately bell shaped, between what two times would 68% of the figures be? 95%? 99.7%?
b. If the shape of the distribution of times is unknown, approximately what percentage of the times would be between 359 and 479 minutes?
c. Suppose a worker spent 400 minutes on the job. What would that worker's $Z$ score be and what would it tell the researcher?

**3.58** During the 1990s, businesses were expected to show a lot of interest in Central and Eastern European countries. As new markets began to open, American business people needed a better understanding of the market potential there. The following are the per capita GDP figures for eight of these European countries published by the *World Almanac*.

| Country | Per Capita GDP (U.S. $) |
|---|---|
| Albania | 1,650 |
| Bulgaria | 4,300 |
| Croatia | 5,100 |
| Germany | 22,700 |
| Hungary | 7,800 |
| Poland | 7,200 |
| Romania | 3,900 |
| Bosnia/Herzegovina | 1,770 |

a. Compute the mean and standard deviation for Albania, Bulgaria, Croatia, and Germany.
b. Compute the mean and standard deviation for Hungary, Poland, Romania, and Bosnia/Herzegovina.
c. Use a coefficient of variation to compare the two standard deviations. Treat the data as population data.

**3.59** According to the Bureau of Labor Statistics, the average annual salary of a worker in Detroit, Michigan, is $35,748. Suppose the median annual salary for a worker in this group is $31,369 and the mode is $29,500. Is the distribution of salaries for this group skewed? If so, how and why? Which of these measures of central tendency would you use to describe these data? Why?

**3.60** How strong is the correlation between the inflation rate and 30-year treasury yields? The following data published by Fuji Securities are given as pairs of inflation rates and treasury yields for selected years over a 35-year period.

| Inflation Rate | 30-Year Treasury Yield |
|---|---|
| 1.57% | 3.05% |
| 2.23 | 3.93 |
| 2.17 | 4.68 |
| 4.53 | 6.57 |
| 7.25 | 8.27 |
| 9.25 | 12.01 |
| 5.00 | 10.27 |
| 4.62 | 8.45 |

Compute the Pearson product-moment correlation coefficient to determine the strength of the correlation between these two variables. Comment on the strength and direction of the correlation.

**3.61** According to the U.S. Army Corps of Engineers, the top 20 U.S. ports, ranked by total tonnage (in million tons), were as follows.

| Port | Total Tonnage |
|---|---|
| South Louisiana, LA | 214.2 |
| Houston, TX | 158.8 |
| New York, NY and NJ | 133.7 |
| New Orleans, LA | 87.5 |
| Corpus Christi, TX | 78.0 |
| Beaumont, TX | 69.4 |
| Baton Rouge, LA | 63.7 |
| Port of Plaquemines, LA | 62.5 |
| Long Beach, CA | 60.9 |
| Valdez, AK | 53.4 |
| Pittsburgh, PA | 52.9 |
| Tampa, FL | 51.5 |
| Lake Charles, LA | 50.7 |
| Texas City, TX | 49.5 |
| Mobile, AL | 45.4 |
| Duluth-Superior, MN and WI | 42.3 |
| Los Angeles, CA | 42.3 |
| Norfolk Harbor, VA | 40.8 |
| Philadelphia, PA | 39.3 |
| Baltimore, MD | 37.3 |

a. Construct a box and whisker plot for these data.
b. Discuss the shape of the distribution from the plot.
c. Are there outliers?
d. What are they and why do you think they are outliers?

**3.62** *Runzheimer International* publishes data on overseas business travel costs. They report that the average per diem total for a business traveler in Paris, France, is $349. Suppose the shape of the distribution of the per diem costs of a business traveler to Paris is unknown, but that 53% of the per diem figures are between $317 and $381. What is the value of the standard deviation? The average per diem total for a business traveler in Moscow is $415. If the shape of the distribution of per diem costs of a business traveler in Moscow is unknown and if 83% of the per diem costs in Moscow lie between $371 and $459, what is the standard deviation?

**INTERPRETING THE OUTPUT**

**3.63** *American Banker* compiled a list of the top 100 banking companies in the world according to total assets. Leading the list is the Bank of Tokyo–Mitsubishi, followed by the Deutsche Bank. The following Excel descriptive statistics output lists the variable total assets ($ millions) for these 100 banks. Study the output and describe in your own words what you can learn about the assets of these top 100 world banks.

|    | A | B |
|----|---|---|
| 1  | **Top World Banks** | |
| 2  | Mean | 213496.77 |
| 3  | Standard error | 12972.00 |
| 4  | Median | 164573 |
| 5  | Mode | N/A |
| 6  | Standard deviation | 129720 |
| 7  | Sample variance | 16827278273 |
| 8  | Kurtosis | 1.05 |
| 9  | Skewness | 1.18 |
| 10 | Range | 615029 |
| 11 | Minimum | 76891 |
| 12 | Maximum | 691920 |
| 13 | Sum | 21349677 |
| 14 | Count | 100 |

**3.64** *Hispanic Business, Inc.*, compiled a list of the top advertisers cultivating the Hispanic market. These data ($ millions) were entered into a MINITAB spreadsheet and analyzed using the graphical descriptive statistics feature. Study the output and describe the expenditures of these top Hispanic market advertisers.

Variable: Media Expenditures

| Mean | 7.8560 |
|------|--------|
| Standard deviation | 5.8860 |
| Variance | 34.6455 |
| Skewness | 3.6214 |
| Kurtosis | 17.7851 |
| N | 50 |
| Minimum | 3.25 |
| 1st Quartile | 4.50 |
| Median | 5.75 |
| 3rd Quartile | 8.625 |
| Maximum | 40.00 |

95% Confidence Interval for Mu

| 6.1832 | 9.5288 |
|--------|--------|

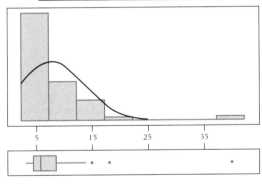

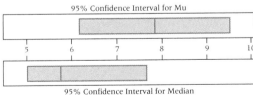

95% Confidence Interval for Mu

95% Confidence Interval for Median

**3.65** Many large companies are located around the world. The number of employees for 46 of the largest employers with headquarters outside the United States were analyzed with Excel's descriptive statistics feature. The data follow. Summarize what you have learned about the number of employees for these companies by studying this output.

|    | A | B |
|----|---|---|
| 1  | **Large Employers Outside of the United States** | |
| 2  | Mean | 183327.1304 |
| 3  | Standard error | 9480.8850 |
| 4  | Median | 157670 |
| 5  | Mode | 135000 |
| 6  | Standard deviation | 64302.4905 |
| 7  | Sample variance | 4134810279 |
| 8  | Kurtosis | 0.8266 |
| 9  | Skewness | 1.2996 |
| 10 | Range | 256106 |
| 11 | Minimum | 125894 |
| 12 | Maximum | 382000 |
| 13 | Sum | 8433048 |
| 14 | Count | 46 |

**3.66** The Competitive Media Reporting and Publishers Information Bureau compiled a list of the top 25 advertisers in the United States for a recent year. The total advertising expenditures for each company ($1,000s) were analyzed using MINITAB's numerical descriptive statistics feature and its box plot feature, both of which are displayed. Study this output and summarize the expenditures of the top 25 advertisers in your own words.

Descriptive Statistics

| Variable | N | Mean | Median | TrMean | StDev | SE Mean |
|----------|---|------|--------|--------|-------|---------|
| Top 25 A | 25 | 772702 | 613823 | 723681 | 436067 | 87213 |

| Variable | Minimum | Maximum | $Q_1$ | $Q_3$ |
|----------|---------|---------|-------|-------|
| Top 25 A | 445958 | 2226934 | 484600 | 788256 |

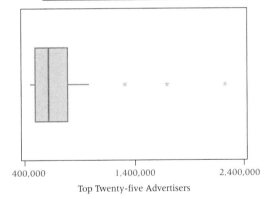

Top Twenty-five Advertisers

## ANALYZING THE DATABASES

*see* **www.wiley.com/college/black**

1. Use the manufacturing database. What is the mean amount of New Capital Expenditures? What is the median amount of New Capital Expenditures? What does the comparison of the mean and the median tell you about the data?

2. For the stock market database "describe" the Dollar Value variable. Include measures of central tendency, variability, and skewness. What did you find?

3. Using the financial database study Earnings per Share for Type 2 and Type 7 (chemical companies and petrochemical companies). Compute a coefficient of variation for Type 2 and for Type 7. Compare the two coefficients and comment. Use the hospital database. Construct a box and whisker plot for Births. Thinking about hospitals and birthing facilities, comment on why the box and whiskers plot may look the way it does.

4. Produce a correlation matrix for the variables Beds, Admissions, Census, Outpatient Visits, Births, Total Expenditures, Payroll Expenditures, and Personnel for the hospital database. Which variables are most highly correlated? Which variables are least correlated?

## CASE: COCA-COLA GOES SMALL IN RUSSIA

The Coca-Cola Company is the number-one seller of soft drinks in the world. Every day an average of more than 1 billion servings of Coca-Cola, Diet Coke, Sprite, Fanta, and other products of Coca-Cola are enjoyed around the world. The company has the world's largest production and distribution system for soft drinks and sells more than twice as many soft drinks as its nearest competitor. Coca-Cola products are sold in more than 200 countries around the globe.

For several reasons, the company believes it will continue to grow internationally. One reason is that disposable income is rising. Another is that outside the United States and Europe, the world is getting younger. In addition, reaching world markets is becoming easier as political barriers fall and transportation difficulties are overcome. Still another reason is that the sharing of ideas, cultures, and news around the world creates market opportunities. Part of the company mission is for Coca-Cola to maintain the world's most powerful trademark and effectively utilize the world's most effective and pervasive distribution system.

In June 1999 Coca-Cola Russia introduced a 200-milliliter (about 6.8 oz.) Coke bottle in Volgograd, Russia, in a campaign to market Coke to its poorest customers. This strategy was successful for Coca-Cola in other countries, such as India. The bottle sells for 12 cents, making it affordable to almost everyone. In 2001, Coca-Cola enjoyed a 25% volume growth in Russia including an 18% increase in unit case sales of Coca-Cola.

### Discussion

1. Because of the variability of bottling machinery, it is likely that every 200-milliliter bottle of Coca-Cola does not contain exactly 200 milliliters of fluid. Some bottles may contain more fluid and others less. Because 200-milliliter bottle fills are somewhat unusual, a production engineer wants to test some of the bottles from the first production runs to determine how close they are to the 200-milliliter specification. Suppose the following data are the fill measurements from a random sample of 50 bottles. Use the techniques presented in this chapter to describe the sample. Consider measures of central tendency, variability, and skewness. Based on this analysis, how is the bottling process working?

| | | | | |
|---|---|---|---|---|
| 200.1 | 199.9 | 200.2 | 200.2 | 200.0 |
| 200.1 | 200.9 | 200.1 | 200.3 | 200.5 |
| 199.7 | 200.4 | 200.3 | 199.8 | 199.3 |
| 200.1 | 199.4 | 199.6 | 199.2 | 200.2 |
| 200.4 | 199.8 | 199.9 | 200.2 | 199.6 |
| 199.6 | 200.4 | 200.4 | 200.6 | 200.6 |
| 200.1 | 200.8 | 199.9 | 200.0 | 199.9 |
| 200.3 | 200.5 | 199.9 | 201.1 | 199.7 |
| 200.2 | 200.5 | 200.2 | 199.7 | 200.9 |
| 200.2 | 199.5 | 200.6 | 200.3 | 199.8 |

2. Suppose that at another plant Coca-Cola is filling bottles with the more traditional 20 ounces of fluid. A lab randomly samples 150 bottles and tests the bottles for fill volume. The descriptive statistics are given in both MINITAB and Excel computer output. Write a brief report to supervisors summarizing what this output is saying about the process.

**Descriptive Statistics: Bottle Fills**

| Variable | N | Mean | Median | TrMean | StDev | SE Mean |
|---|---|---|---|---|---|---|
| Bottle F | 150 | 20.003 | 20.005 | 20.003 | 0.027 | 0.002 |

| Variable | Minimum | Maximum | $Q_1$ | $Q_3$ | |
|---|---|---|---|---|---|
| Bottle F | 19.920 | 20.090 | 19.985 | 20.021 | |

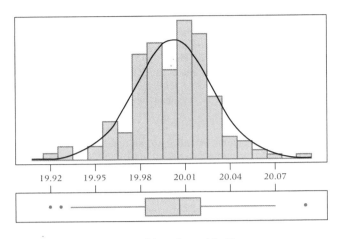

### Variable: Bottle Fills

Anderson-Darling Normality Test

| | |
|---|---|
| A-Squared | 0.588 |
| P-Value | 0.123 |
| | |
| Mean | 20.0028 |
| St Dev | 0.0266 |
| Variance | 7.09E−04 |
| Skewness | −8.6E−02 |
| Kurtosis | 1.01598 |
| $N$ | 150 |
| | |
| Minimum | 19.9200 |
| 1st Quartile | 19.9851 |
| Median | 20.0046 |
| 3rd Quartile | 20.0208 |
| Maximum | 20.0896 |

95% Confidence Interval for Mu

| | |
|---|---|
| 19.9985 | 20.0071 |

95% Confidence Interval for Sigma

| | |
|---|---|
| 0.0239 | 0.0300 |

95% Confidence Interval for Median

| | |
|---|---|
| 19.9977 | 20.0091 |

95% Confidence Interval for Mu

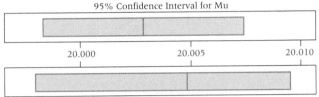

95% Confidence Interval for Median

### Excel Output

| | A | B |
|---|---|---|
| 1 | **Bottle Fills** | |
| 2 | Mean | 20.003 |
| 3 | Standard error | 0.002 |
| 4 | Median | 20.005 |
| 5 | Mode | 20.004 |
| 6 | Standard deviation | 0.027 |
| 7 | Sample variance | 0.001 |
| 8 | Kurtosis | 1.015 |
| 9 | Skewness | −0.085 |
| 10 | Range | 0.170 |
| 11 | Minimum | 19.92 |
| 12 | Maximum | 20.090 |
| 13 | Sum | 3000.416 |
| 14 | Count | 150 |

*Source*: Adapted from "Coke, Avis Adjust in Russia," *Advertising Age*, 5 July 1999, p. 25; Coca-Cola Web site at http://www.coca-cola.com/home.html. The Coca-Cola company's 2001 annual report found at: http://www2.coca-cola.com/investors/annualreport/2001/index.html.

## USING THE COMPUTER

### EXCEL

Excel can analyze data by using several of the techniques presented in this chapter. It has one particularly powerful command that generates many descriptive statistics.

Descriptive Statistics

Several of the descriptive statistics presented in this chapter can be accessed by Excel through the use of the Descriptive Statistics command. Begin by selecting **Tools** on the Excel menu bar. On the pull-down menu select **Data Analysis**. In the data analysis dialog box, select the option **Descriptive Statistics**. Input the range of the data to be described. Check whether the data are grouped by column or row. Check for labels in the first row. Of particular importance is to check the box at the bottom left entitled **Summary statistics**. Checking this box tells Excel to include a wide range of descriptive measures.

The output includes mean, median, mode, standard deviation, sample variance, a measure of kurtosis, a measure of skewness, range, minimum, maximum, sum, and count.

### Rank and Percentile

Excel has a command called Rank and Percentile that orders the data, assigns ranks to the data, and outputs the percentiles of the data. To access this command, select **Tools** from the menu bar of Excel. On the pull-down menu that appears, select **Data Analysis**. The data analysis dialog box will appear. Select **Rank and Percentile**. A rank and percentile dialog box will appear. Input the range of data. Check whether the data are in columns or rows and for labels in the first row.

### MINITAB

MINITAB Windows is capable of performing many of the tasks presented in this chapter, including descriptive statistics and box plots.

### Descriptive Statistics

Through the use of the Descriptive Statistics command, MINITAB yields a considerable number of the statistical techniques mentioned in this chapter. The process begins with the selection of **Stat** on the menu bar.

From the pull-down menu, select **Basic Statistics**. From the basic statistics pull-down menu, select **Display Descriptive Statistics** and a dialog box appears. Input the column(s) to be analyzed. If you click on **OK**, then your output will include the sample size, mean, median, standard deviation, minimum, maximum, the first quartile, and the third quartile. However, if you select the option, **Graph...**, you will have several other output options that are relatively self-explanatory. The options include **Histogram of data**, **Histogram of data with normal curve, Dotplot of data, Boxplot of data,** and **Graphical summary**. If you select **Graphical summary**, you will get output like that shown in the Case as "Bottle Fills." This output includes the features mentioned under tabular output plus a histogram of the data overlaid with a normal curve, a box plot, and other output that will be explained later in the text.

### Column Statistics

Column statistics can be obtained by selecting the command **Calc** on the MINITAB Windows menu bar. From the pull-down menu, select the **Column Statistics** command. The column statistics dialog box will appear. Check off the statistics you would like to calculate. Input the column with the data. The output will include the items you asked for.

A **Row Statistics** item can also be found on the **Calc** pull-down menu. Use it if your data are located in a row. You will get a row statistics dialog box that is virtually identical to the column statistics dialog box. Follow the same steps as those used with column statistics to get output on row data.

### Box and Whisker Plot

A box and whisker plot can be produced by selecting **Graph** on the menu bar. On the graph pull-down menu that appears, select **Boxplot** from the menu and a box plot dialog box will appear. Enter the variable location in **Y**. Select **IQRange Box** under Display. Several graphical options such as adding a title are given at the bottom of the dialog box. One particularly useful option is transposing the graph so that the whiskers parallel the $X$ axis. To do this, select **Options** at the bottom of the dialog box. You will then have the opportunity to check a box denoting that you want to transpose $X$ and $Y$. The resulting output is a box and whisker plot with an asterisk representing outliers.

# CHAPTER 9

# Statistical Inference: Hypothesis Testing for Single Populations

### LEARNING OBJECTIVES

The main objective of Chapter 9 is to help you to learn how to test hypotheses on single populations, thereby enabling you to:

1. Understand the logic of hypothesis testing and know how to establish null and alternative hypotheses.
2. Understand Type I and Type II errors and know how to solve for Type II errors.
3. Know how to implement the HTAB system to test hypotheses.
4. Test hypotheses about a single population mean when $\sigma$ is known.
5. Test hypotheses about a single population mean when $\sigma$ is unknown.
6. Test hypotheses about a single population proportion.
7. Test hypotheses about a single population variance.

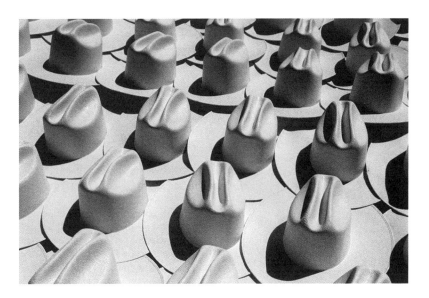

*Business Statistics For Contemporary Decision Making 4th Edition Update,*
Ken Black . ISBN-10 0-471-70563-2 ©2006 John Wiley & Sons, Inc.

Word-of-mouth information about products and services is exchanged on a daily basis by millions of consumers. Many of us seek out such advice because we want to obtain product information from a third party to assist us in the market decision-making process. What we receive is often subjective opinion that is flavored by other consumer's experiences or information they gathered from other sources. An underlying factor in the reliance on such word-of-mouth information is a trust in the source. It is important for businesses to understand the impact of such "business referrals."

The White House Office of Consumer Affairs determined in a study that at least 90% of unhappy customers will not do business with the offending company again. In addition, each unhappy customer will share his/her displeasure with at least nine other people. According to a study by Mediamark Research of New York City, about 50% of all Americans often seek the advice of others before buying services or products. In addition, almost 40% say that others seek out their advice before purchasing. Maritz Marketing Research of Fenton, Missouri, studied adults in an effort to determine for which products or services they seek advice. Forty-six percent seek advice when selecting a physician, 44% for a mechanic, and 42% for legal advice. In looking for a restaurant in which to celebrate a special occasion, 38% of all consumers seek out advice and information from others.

Some advice givers are referred to as *influentials*. Influentials are "trendsetting opinion leaders whose activism and expertise make them the natural source for word-of-mouth referrals." This group represents about 10% of all adult Americans. A report issued by Roper Starch Worldwide and cosponsored by *The Atlantic Monthly* stated that influentials tend to be among the first to try new products. They are looking for new restaurants and vacation spots to try, are activists on the job and in their community, and are self-indulgent. Businesses would do well to seek out such influentials and win them over to the company's products, thereby tapping into the word-of-mouth pipeline. On average, an influential recommends restaurants to 5.0 people a year. The following chart shows the average number of recommendations made by influentials per year on other items. These data were compiled and released by Roper Starch Worldwide.

| Product or Service | Average Number of Recommendations |
|---|---|
| Office equipment | 5.8 |
| Vacation destination | 5.1 |
| TV show | 4.9 |
| Retail store | 4.7 |
| Clothing | 4.5 |
| Consumer electronics | 4.5 |
| Car | 4.1 |
| Stocks, mutual funds, CDs, etc. | 3.4 |

## Managerial and Statistical Questions

1. Each of the figures enumerated in this Decision Dilemma were derived by studies conducted on samples and published as fact. If we want to challenge these figures by conducting surveys of our own, then how would we go about testing these results? Are these studies dated now? Do they apply to all market segments (geographically, economically, etc.)? How could we test to determine whether these results apply to our market segment today?

289

2. The Roper Starch Worldwide study listed the mean number of recommendations made by influentials per year for different products or services. If these figures become accepted by industry users, how can we conduct our own tests to determine whether they are actually true? If we randomly sampled some influentials and our mean figures did not match these figures, then could we automatically conclude that their figures are not true? How much difference would we have to obtain to reject their claims? Is there a possibility that we could make an error in conducting such research?

3. The studies by the White House Office of Consumer Affairs, Mediamark Research, and Maritz Marketing Research produced a variety of proportions about word-of-mouth advertising and advice seeking. Are these figures necessarily true? Since these figures are based on sample information and are probably point estimates, could there be error in the estimations? How can we test to determine whether these figures that become accepted in the media as population parameters are actually true? Could there be differences in various population subgroups?

4. Suppose you have theories regarding word-of-mouth advertising, business referrals, or influentials. How would you test the theories to determine whether they are true?

*Source:* Adapted from Chip Walker, "Word of Mouth," *American Demographics* (July 1995), pp. 38–45.

A foremost statistical mechanism for decision making is the hypothesis test. The concept of hypothesis testing lies at the heart of inferential statistics, and the use of statistics to "prove" or "disprove" claims hinges on it. With **hypothesis testing,** business researchers are able *to structure problems in such a way that they can use statistical evidence to test various theories about business phenomena.* Business applications of statistical hypothesis testing run the gamut from determining whether a production line process is out of control to providing conclusive evidence that a new management leadership approach is significantly more effective than an old one.

## 9.1 INTRODUCTION TO HYPOTHESIS TESTING

In the field of business, decision makers are continually attempting to find answers to questions such as the following:

- What container shape is most economical and reliable for shipping a product?
- Which management approach best motivates employees in the retail industry?
- How can the company's retirement investment financial portfolio be diversified for optimum performance?
- What is the best way to link client databases for fast retrieval of useful information?
- Which indicator best predicts the general state of the economy in the next six months?
- What is the most effective means of advertising in a business-to-business setting?

Business researchers are often called upon to provide insights and information to decision makers to assist them in answering such questions. In searching for answers to questions and in attempting to find explanations for business phenomena, business researchers often develop "hypotheses" that can be studied and explored. **Hypotheses** are *tentative explanations of a principle operating in nature.** In this text, we will explore various types of hypotheses, how to test them, and how to interpret the results of such tests so that useful information can be brought to bear on the business decision-making process.

---

* Paraphrasing of definition published in *Merriam Webster's Collegiate Dictionary*, 10th ed. (Springfield, MA: Merriam Webster, Inc., 1993).

## Types of Hypotheses

Three types of hypotheses that will be explored here:

1. *Research* hypotheses
2. *Statistical* hypotheses
3. *Substantive* hypotheses

Although much of the focus will be on testing statistical hypotheses, it is also important for business decision makers to have an understanding of both research and substantive hypotheses.

## Research Hypotheses

Research hypotheses are most nearly like hypotheses defined earlier. A **research hypothesis** is *a statement of what the researcher believes will be the outcome of an experiment or a study.* Before studies are undertaken, business researchers often have some idea or theory based on experience or previous work as to how the study will turn out. These ideas, theories, or notions established before an experiment or study is conducted are research hypotheses. Some examples of research hypotheses in business might include:

- Older workers are more loyal to a company.
- Companies with more than $1 billion in assets spend a higher percentage of their annual budget on advertising than do companies with less than $1 billion in assets.
- The implementation of a Six Sigma quality approach in manufacturing will result in greater productivity.
- The price of scrap metal is a good indicator of the industrial production index six months later.
- Airline company stock prices are positively correlated with the volume of OPEC oil production.

Virtually all inquisitive, thinking businesspeople have similar research hypotheses concerning relationships, approaches, and techniques in business. Such hypotheses can lead decision makers to new and better ways to accomplish business goals. However, to formally test research hypotheses, it is generally best to state them as statistical hypotheses.

## Statistical Hypotheses

In order to scientifically test research hypotheses, a more formal hypothesis structure needs to be set up using **statistical hypotheses.** Suppose business researchers want to "prove" the research hypothesis that older workers are more loyal to a company. A "loyalty" survey instrument is either developed or obtained. If this instrument is administered to both older and younger workers, how much higher do older workers have to score on the "loyalty" instrument (assuming higher scores indicate more loyal) than younger workers to prove the research hypothesis? What is the "proof threshold"? Instead of attempting to prove or disprove research hypotheses directly in this manner, business researchers convert their research hypotheses to statistical hypotheses and then test the statistical hypotheses using standard procedures.

All statistical hypotheses consist of two parts, a null hypothesis and an alternative hypothesis. These two parts are constructed to contain all possible outcomes of the experiment or study. Generally, the **null hypothesis** *states that the "null" condition exists; that is, there is nothing new happening, the old theory is still true, the old standard is correct, and the system is in control.* The **alternative hypothesis,** on the other hand, *states that the new theory is true, there are new standards, the system is out-of-control, and/or something is happening.* As an example, suppose flour packaged by a manufacturer is sold by weight; and a particular size of package is supposed to average 40 ounces. Suppose the manufacturer wants to test to determine whether their packaging process is out-of-control as determined by the weight of the flour packages. The null hypothesis for this experiment is that the average weight of the flour packages is 40 ounces (no problem). The alternative hypothesis is that the average is not 40 ounces (process is out-of-control).

It is common symbolism to represent the null hypothesis as $H_0$ and the alternative hypothesis as $H_a$. The null and alternative hypotheses for the flour example can be restated using these symbols and $\mu$ for the population mean as:

$$H_0: \mu = 40 \text{ oz.}$$

$$H_a: \mu \neq 40 \text{ oz.}$$

As another example, suppose a company has held an 18% share of the market. However, because of an increased marketing effort, company officials believe the company's market share is now greater than 18%, and the officials would like to prove it. The null hypothesis is that the market share is still 18% or perhaps it has even dropped below 18%. Converting the 18% to a proportion and using $p$ to represent the population proportion, results in the following null hypothesis:

$$H_0: p \leq .18$$

The alternative hypothesis is that the population proportion is now greater than .18:

$$H_a: p > .18$$

Note that the "new idea" or "new theory" that company officials want to "prove" is stated in the alternative hypothesis. The null hypothesis states that the old market share of 18% is still true.

Generally speaking, new hypotheses that business researchers want to "prove" are stated in the alternative hypothesis. Because many business researchers only undertake an experiment to determine whether their new hypothesis is correct, they are hoping that the alternative hypothesis will be "proven" true. However, if a manufacturer is testing to determine whether his process is out-of-control as shown in the flour-packaging example, then he is most likely hoping that the alternative hypothesis is not "proven" true thereby demonstrating that the process is still in control.

Note in the market share example that the null hypothesis also contains the less than case ($<$) because between the two hypotheses (null and alternative), all possible outcomes must be included ($<$, $>$, and $=$). One could say that the null and alternative hypotheses are mutually exclusive (no overlap) and collectively exhaustive (all cases included). Thus, whenever a decision is made about which hypothesis is true, logically either one is true or the other but not both. Even though the company officials are not interested in "proving" that their market share is less than 18%, logically, it should be included as a possibility. On the other hand, many researchers and statisticians leave out the "less than" ($<$) portion of the null hypothesis on the market share problem because company officials are only interested in "proving" that the market share has increased and the inclusion of the "less than" sign in the null hypothesis is confusing. This approach can be justified in the way that statistical hypotheses are tested. If the equal part of the null hypothesis is rejected because the market share is seemingly greater, then certainly the "less than" portion of the null hypothesis is also rejected because it is further away from "greater than" than is "equal." Using this logic, the null hypothesis for the market share problem can be written as

$$H_0: p = .18$$

rather than

$$H_0: p \leq .18$$

Thus, in this form, the statistical hypotheses for the market share problem can be written as

$$H_0: p = .18$$
$$H_a: p > .18$$

Even though the "less than" sign, $<$, is not included in the null hypothesis, it is implied that it is there. We will adopt such an approach in this book; and thus, all *null* hypotheses presented in this book will be written with an equal sign only ($=$) rather than with a directional sign ($\leq$) or ($\geq$).

Statistical hypotheses are written so that they will produce either a one-tailed or a two-tailed test. The hypotheses shown already for the flour package manufacturing problem are two-tailed:

$$H_0: \mu = 40 \text{ oz.}$$

$$H_a: \mu \neq 40 \text{ oz.}$$

**Two-tailed tests** always use = and ≠ in the statistical hypotheses and are directionless in that the alternative hypothesis allows for either the greater than (>) or less than (<) possibility. In this particular example, if the process is "out-of-control," plant officials might not know whether machines are overfilling or underfilling packages and are interested in testing for either possibility.

The hypotheses shown for the market share problem are one-tailed:

$$H_0: p = .18$$

$$H_a: p > .18$$

**One-tailed tests** are always directional, and the alternative hypothesis uses either the greater than (>) or the less than (<) sign. A one-tailed test should only be used when the researcher knows for certain that the outcome of an experiment is going to occur only in one direction or the researcher is only interested in one direction of the experiment as in the case of the market share problem. In one-tailed problems, the researcher is trying to "prove" that something is older, younger, higher, lower, more, less, greater, and so on. These words are considered "directional" words in that they indicate the direction of the focus of the research. Without these words, the alternative hypothesis of a one-tailed test cannot be established.

In business research, the conservative approach is to conduct a two-tailed test because sometimes study results can be obtained that are in opposition to the direction that researchers thought would occur. For example, in the market share problem, it might turn out that the company had actually lost market share; and even though company officials were not interested in "proving" such a case, they may need to know that it is true. It is recommended that, if in doubt, business researchers should use a two-tailed test.

## Substantive Hypotheses

In testing a statistical hypothesis, a business researcher reaches a conclusion based on the data obtained in the study. If the null hypothesis is rejected and therefore the alternative hypothesis is accepted, it is common to say that a statistically significant result has been obtained. For example, in the market share problem, if the null hypothesis is rejected, the result is that the market share is "significantly greater" than 18%. The word, *significant,* to statisticians and business researchers merely means that the result of the experiment is unlikely due to chance and a decision has been made to reject the null hypothesis. However, in everyday business life, the word, *significant,* is more likely to connote "important" or "a large amount." One problem that can arise in testing statistical hypotheses is that particular characteristics of the data can result in a statistically significant outcome that is not a significant business outcome.

As an example, consider the market share study. Suppose a large sample of potential customers is taken, and a sample market share of 18.2% is obtained. Suppose further that a statistical analysis of these data results in statistical significance. We would conclude statistically that the market share is significantly higher than 18%. This finding actually means that it is unlikely that the difference between the sample proportion and the population proportion of .18 is due just to chance. However, to the business decision maker, a market share of 18.2% might not be significantly higher than 18%. Because of the way the word *significant* is used to denote rejection of the null hypothesis rather than an important business difference, business decision makers need to exercise caution in interpreting the outcomes of statistical tests.

In addition to understanding a statistically significant result, business decision makers need to determine what, to them, is a *substantive* result. A **substantive result** is when *the outcome of a statistical study produces results that are important to the decision maker.* The importance to the researcher will vary from study to study. As an example, in a recent year, one healthcare administrator was excited because patient satisfaction had significantly increased (statistically) from one year to the next. However, an examination of the data revealed that on a five-point scale, their satisfaction ratings had gone up from 3.61 to only 3.63. Is going from a 3.61 rating to a 3.63 rating in one year really a substantive increase? On the other hand, increasing the average purchase at a large, high-volume store from $55.45 to $55.50 might be substantive as well as significant if volume is large enough to drive profits higher. Both business researchers and decision makers should be aware that statistically significant results are not always substantive results.

## Using the HTAB System to Test Hypotheses

In conducting business research, the process of testing hypotheses involves four major tasks:

- Task 1. Establishing the hypotheses
- Task 2. Conducting the test
- Task 3. Taking statistical action
- Task 4. Determining the business implications

This process, depicted in Figure 9.1, is referred to here as the HTAB system where HTAB is an acronym for **H**ypothesize, **T**est, **A**ction, **B**usiness.

Task 1, establishing the hypotheses, encompasses all activities that lead up to the establishment of the statistical hypotheses being tested. These activities might include investigating a business opportunity or problem, developing theories about possible solutions, and establishing research hypotheses. Task 2, conducting the test, involves the selection of the proper statistical test, setting the value of alpha, establishing a decision rule, gathering sample data, and computing the statistical analysis. Task 3, taking statistical action, is making a statistical decision about whether or not to reject the null hypothesis based on the outcome of the statistical test. Task 4, determining the business implications, is deciding what the statistical action means in business terms, that is, interpreting the statistical outcome in terms of business decision making.

Typically, statisticians and researchers present the hypothesis testing process in terms of an eight-step approach. These eight steps are as follows:

- Step 1. Establish a null and alternative hypothesis.
- Step 2. Determine the appropriate statistical test.
- Step 3. Set the value of alpha, the Type I error rate.
- Step 4. Establish the decision rule.
- Step 5. Gather sample data.
- Step 6. Analyze the data.
- Step 7. Reach a statistical conclusion.
- Step 8. Make a business decision.

**FIGURE 9.1**

HTAB System of
Testing Hypotheses

These eight steps fit nicely into the four HTAB tasks as a part of the HTAB paradigm. Figure 9.2 presents the HTAB paradigm incorporating the eight steps into the four HTAB tasks.

Task 1 of the HTAB system, hypothesizing, includes step 1, which is establishing a null and alternative hypothesis. In establishing the null and alternative hypotheses, it is important that the business researcher clearly identify what is being tested and whether the hypotheses are one-tailed or two-tailed. In hypothesis testing process, it is *always assumed that the null hypothesis is true* at the beginning of the study. In other words, it is assumed that the process is in control (no problem), that the market share has not increased, that older workers are not more loyal to a company than younger workers, and so on. This process is analogous to the U.S. trial system in which the accused is presumed innocent at the beginning of the trial.

Task 2 of the HTAB system, testing, includes steps 2 through 6. Step 2 is to select the most appropriate statistical test to use for the analysis. In selecting such a test, the business researcher needs to consider the type, number, and level of data being used in the study along with the statistic used in the analysis (mean, proportion, variance, etc.). In addition,

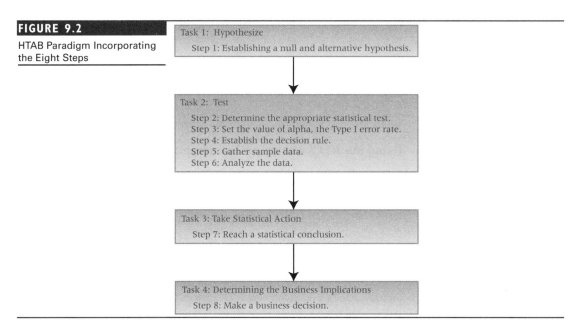

**FIGURE 9.2**

HTAB Paradigm Incorporating
the Eight Steps

Task 1:  Hypothesize

    Step 1: Establishing a null and alternative hypothesis.

Task 2:  Test

    Step 2: Determine the appropriate statistical test.
    Step 3: Set the value of alpha, the Type I error rate.
    Step 4: Establish the decision rule.
    Step 5: Gather sample data.
    Step 6: Analyze the data.

Task 3: Take Statistical Action

    Step 7: Reach a statistical conclusion.

Task 4: Determining the Business Implications

    Step 8: Make a business decision.

business researchers should consider the assumptions underlying certain statistical tests and determine whether they can be met in the study before using such tests.

At step 3, the value of alpha is set. Alpha is the probability of committing a Type I error and will be discussed later. Common values of alpha include .05, .01, .10, and .001.

A decision rule should be established before the study is undertaken (step 4). Using alpha and the test statistic, critical values can be determined. These **critical values** are *used at the decision step to determine whether the null hypothesis is rejected* or not. If the *p*-value method (discussed later) is used, the value of alpha is used as a critical probability value. The process begins by assuming that the null hypothesis is true. Data are gathered and statistics computed. If the evidence is away from the null hypothesis, the business researcher begins to doubt that the null hypothesis is really true. If the evidence is far enough away from the null hypothesis that the critical value is surpassed, the business researcher will reject the null hypothesis and declare that a statistically significant result has been attained. Here again, it is analogous to the U.S. court of law system. Initially, a defendant is assumed to be innocent. Prosecuting attorneys present evidence against the defendant (analogous to data gathered and analyzed in a study). At some point, if enough evidence is presented against the defendant such that the jury no longer believes the defendant is innocent, a critical level of evidence has been reached and the jury finds the defendant guilty. The first four steps in testing hypotheses should *always* be completed *before* the study is undertaken. It is not sound research to gather data first and then try to determine what to do with the data.

Step 5 is to gather sample data. This step might include the construction and implementation of a survey, conducting focus groups, randomly sampling items from an assembly line, or even sampling from secondary data sources (e.g., financial databases). In gathering data, the business researcher is cautioned to recall the proper techniques of random sampling (presented in Chapter 7). Care should be taken in establishing a frame, determining the sampling technique, and constructing the measurement device. A strong effort should be made to avoid all nonsampling errors. After the data are sampled, the test statistic can be calculated (step 6).

Task 3 of the HTAB system, take statistical action, includes step 7. Using the previously established decision rule (in step 4) and the value of the test statistic, the business researcher can draw a statistical conclusion. In *all* hypothesis tests, the business researcher needs to conclude whether the null hypothesis is rejected or is not rejected (step 7).

Task 4 of the HTAB system, determining the business implications, incorporates step 8. After a statistical decision is made, the business researcher or decision maker decides what business implications the study results contain (step 8). For example, if the hypothesis-testing procedure results in a conclusion that train passengers are significantly older today than they were in the past, the manager may decide to cater to these older customers or to draw up a strategy to make ridership more appealing to younger people. It is at this step that the business decision maker must decide whether a statistically significant result is really a substantive result.

## Rejection and Nonrejection Regions

Using the critical values established at step 4 of the hypothesis testing process, the possible statistical outcomes of a study can be divided into two groups:

1.  Those that cause the rejection of the null hypothesis
2.  Those that do not cause the rejection of the null hypothesis.

Conceptually and graphically, statistical outcomes that result in the rejection of the null hypothesis lie in what is termed the **rejection region.** Statistical outcomes that fail to result in the rejection of the null hypothesis lie in what is termed the **nonrejection region.**

As an example, consider the flour-packaging manufacturing example. The null hypothesis is that the average fill for the population of packages is 40 ounces. Suppose a sample of 100 such packages is randomly selected, and a sample mean of 40.01 ounces is obtained. Because this mean is not 40 ounces, should the business researcher decide to reject the null hypothesis? In the hypothesis test process we are using sample statistics (in this case, the sample mean of 40.1 ounces) to make decisions about population parameters (in this case, the population mean of 40 ounces). It makes sense that in taking random samples from a population with a mean of 40 ounces not all sample means will equal 40 ounces. In fact, the central limit theorem (see Chapter 7) states that for large sample sizes, sample means are normally distributed around the population mean. Thus, even when the population mean is 40 ounces, a sample mean might still be 40.1, 38.6, or even 44.2. However, suppose a sample mean of 50 ounces is obtained for 100 packages. This sample mean may be so far from what is reasonable to expect for a population with a mean of 40 ounces that the decision is made to reject the null hypothesis. This begs the question: when is the sample mean so far away from the population mean that the null hypothesis is rejected? The critical values established at step 4 of the hypothesis testing process are used to divide the means that lead to the rejection of the null hypothesis from those that do not. Figure 9.3 displays a normal distribution of sample means around a population mean of 40 ounces. Note the critical values in each end (tail) of the distribution. In each direction beyond the critical values lie the rejection regions. Any sample mean that falls in that region will lead the business researcher to reject the null hypothesis. Sample means that fall between the two critical values are close enough to the population mean that the business researcher will decide not to reject the null hypothesis. These means are in the nonrejection region.

---

**FIGURE 9.3**

Rejection and
Nonrejection Regions

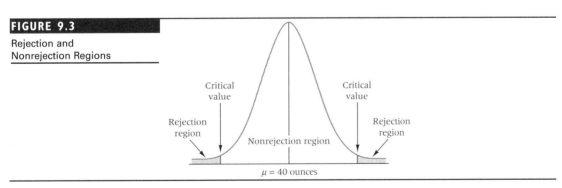

## Type I and Type II Errors

Because the hypothesis testing process uses sample statistics calculated from random data to reach conclusions about population parameters, it is possible to make an incorrect decision about the null hypothesis. In particular, two types of errors can be made in testing hypotheses: Type I error and Type II error.

A **Type I error** is committed by *rejecting a true null hypothesis*. With a Type I error, the null hypothesis is true, but the business researcher decides that it is not. As an example, suppose the flour-packaging process actually is "in control" and is averaging 40 ounces of flour per package. Suppose also that a business researcher randomly selects 100 packages, weighs the contents of each, and computes a sample mean. It is possible, by chance, to randomly select 100 of the more extreme packages (mostly heavy weighted or mostly light weighted) resulting in a mean that falls in the rejection region. The decision is to reject the null hypothesis even though the population mean is actually 40 ounces. In this case, the business researcher has committed a Type I error.

The notion of a Type I error can be used outside the realm of statistical hypothesis testing in the business world. For example, if a manager fires an employee because some evidence indicates that she is stealing from the company and if she really is not stealing from the company, then the manager has committed a Type I error. As another example, suppose a worker on the assembly line of a large manufacturer hears an unusual sound and decides to shut the line down (reject the null hypothesis). If the sound turns out not to be related to the assembly line and no problems are occurring with the assembly line, then the worker has committed a Type I error. In U.S. industries in the 1950s, 1960s, and 1970s when U.S. products were in great demand, workers were strongly discouraged from making such Type I errors because the production downtime was so expensive. An analogous courtroom example of a Type I error is when an innocent person is sent to jail.

In Figure 9.3, the rejection regions represent the possibility of committing a Type I error. Means that fall beyond the critical values will be considered so extreme that the business researcher chooses to reject the null hypothesis. However, if the null hypothesis is true, any mean that falls in a rejection region will result in a decision that produces a Type I error. The *probability of committing a Type I error* is called **alpha** ($\alpha$) or **level of significance.** Alpha equals the area under the curve that is in the rejection region beyond the critical value(s). The value of alpha is always set before the experiment or study is undertaken. As mentioned previously, common values of alpha are .05, .01, .10, and .001.

A **Type II error** is committed when a business researcher *fails to reject a false null hypothesis.* In this case, the null hypothesis is false, but a decision is made to not reject it. Suppose in the case of the flour problem that the packaging process is actually producing a population mean of 41 ounces even though the null hypothesis is 40 ounces. A sample of 100 packages yields a sample mean of 40.2 ounces, which falls in the nonrejection region. The business decision maker decides not to reject the null hypothesis. A Type II error has been committed. The packaging procedure is out-of-control and the hypothesis testing process does not identify it.

Suppose in the business world an employee is stealing from the company. A manager sees some evidence that the stealing is occurring but lacks enough evidence to conclude that the employee is stealing from the company. The manager decides not to fire the employee based on theft. The manager has committed a Type II error. Consider the manufacturing line with the noise. Suppose the worker decides not enough noise is heard to shut the line down, but in actuality, one of the cords on the line is unraveling, creating a dangerous situation. The worker is committing a Type II error. Beginning in the 1980s, U.S. manufacturers started protecting more against Type II errors. They found that in many cases, it was more costly to produce bad product (e.g., scrap/rework costs and loss of market share due to poor quality) than it was to make it right the first time. They encouraged workers to "shut down" the line if the quality of work was seemingly not what it should be (risking a Type I error) rather than allowing poor quality product to be shipped. In a court-of-law, a Type II error is committed when a guilty person is declared innocent.

The probability of committing a Type II error is **beta** ($\beta$). Unlike alpha, beta is not usually stated at the beginning of the hypothesis testing procedure. Actually, because beta occurs only when the null hypothesis is not true, the computation of beta varies with the many possible alternative parameters that might occur. For example, in the flour-packaging problem, if the population mean is not 40 ounces, then what is it? It could be 41, 38, or 42 ounces. A value of beta is associated with each of these alternative means.

How are alpha and beta related? First of all, because alpha can only be committed when the null hypothesis is rejected and beta can only be committed when the null hypothesis is not rejected, a business researcher cannot commit both a Type I error and a Type II error at the same time on the same hypothesis test. Generally, alpha and beta are inversely related. If alpha is reduced, then beta is increased, and vice versa. If the rejection regions displayed in Figure 9.3 are reduced, making it harder to reject the 40-ounce weight, it will be easier to not discern when the packaging process is out-of-control. In terms of the manufacturing assembly line, if management makes it harder for workers to shut down the assembly line (reduce Type I error), then there is a greater chance that bad product will be made or that a serious problem with the line will arise (increase Type II error). Legally, if the courts make it harder to send innocent people to jail, then they have made it easier let guilty people go free. One way to reduce both errors is to increase the sample size. If a larger sample is taken, it is more likely that the sample is representative of the population; which translates into a better chance that a business researcher will make the correct choice. Figure 9.4 shows the relationship between the two types of error. The "state of nature" is how things actually are and the "action" is the decision that the business researcher actually makes. Note that each action alternative contains only one of the errors along with the possibility that a correct decision has been made. **Power,** which is equal to $1 - \beta$, is *the probability of a test rejecting the null hypothesis when the null hypothesis is false.* Figure 9.4 shows the relationship between $\alpha$, $\beta$, and power.

## 9.2 TESTING HYPOTHESES ABOUT A POPULATION MEAN USING THE $z$ STATISTIC ($\sigma$ KNOWN)

One of the most basic hypothesis tests is a test about a population mean. A business researcher might be interested in testing to determine whether an established or accepted mean value for an industry is still true or in testing a hypothesized mean value for a new theory or product. As an example, a computer products company sets up a telephone service to assist customers by providing technical support. The average wait time during weekday hours is 37 minutes. However, a recent hiring effort added technical consultants to the system, and management believes that the average wait time decreased, and they want to prove it. Other business scenarios resulting in hypothesis tests of a single mean might include the following:

- A financial investment firm wants to test to determine whether the average hourly change in the Dow Jones Average over a 10-year period is +0.25.

- A manufacturing company wants to test to determine whether the average thickness of a plastic bottle is 2.4 millimeters.

| FIGURE 9.4 | | | State of nature | |
|---|---|---|---|---|
| Alpha, Beta, and Power | | | Null true | Null false |
| | | Fail to reject null | Correct decision | Type II error ($\beta$) |
| | Action | | | |
| | | Reject null | Type I error ($\alpha$) | Correct decision (power) |

■  A retail store wants to test to determine whether the average age of its customers is less than 40 years.

Formula (9.1) can be used to test hypotheses about a single population mean if the sample size is large ($n \geq 30$) for any population and for small samples ($n < 30$) if $x$ is known to be normally distributed.

| | |
|---|---|
| $z$ TEST FOR A SINGLE MEAN (9.1) | $$z = \dfrac{\bar{x} - \mu}{\dfrac{\sigma}{\sqrt{n}}}$$ |

A survey of CPAs across the United States found that the average net income for sole proprietor CPAs is \$74,914.* Because this survey is now more than ten years old, an accounting researcher wants to test this figure by taking a random sample of 112 sole proprietor accountants in the United States to determine whether the net income figure changed. The researcher could use the eight steps of hypothesis testing to do so. Assume the population standard deviation of net incomes for sole proprietor CPAs is \$14,530.

HYPOTHESIZE:

At step 1, the hypotheses must be established. Because the researcher is testing to determine whether the figure has changed, the alternative hypothesis is that the mean net income is not \$74,914. The null hypothesis is that the mean still equals \$74,914. These hypotheses follow.

$$H_0: \mu = \$74,914$$

$$H_a: \mu \neq \$74,914$$

TEST:

Step 2 is to determine the appropriate statistical test and sampling distribution. Because sample size is large ($n = 112$) and the researcher is using the sample mean as the statistic, the $z$ test in formula (9.1) is the appropriate test statistic.

$$z = \frac{\bar{x} - \mu}{\dfrac{\sigma}{\sqrt{n}}}$$

Step 3 is to specify the Type I error rate, or alpha, which is .05 in this problem. Step 4 is to state the decision rule. Because the test is two-tailed and alpha is .05, there is $\alpha/2$ or .025 area in each of the tails of the distribution. Thus, the rejection region is in the two ends of the distribution with 2.5% of the area in each. There is a .4750 area between the mean and each of the critical values that separate the tails of the distribution (the rejection region) from the nonrejection region. By using this .4750 area and Table A.5, the critical $z$ value can be obtained.

$$z_{\alpha/2} = \pm 1.96$$

Figure 9.5 displays the problem with the rejection regions and the critical values of $z$. The decision rule is that if the data gathered produce a $z$ value greater than 1.96 or less than −1.96, the test statistic is in one of the rejection regions and the decision is to reject the null hypothesis. If the $z$ value calculated from the data is between −1.96 and +1.96, the decision is to not reject the null hypothesis because the calculated $z$ value is in the nonrejection region.

Step 5 is to gather the data. Suppose the 112 CPAs who respond produce a sample mean of \$78,695. At step 6, the value of the test statistic is calculated by using $\bar{x} = \$78,695$, $n = 112$, $\sigma = \$14,530$, and a hypothesized $\mu = \$74,914$:

$$z = \frac{78,695 - 74,914}{\dfrac{14,530}{\sqrt{112}}} = 2.75$$

---

*Adapted from Daniel J. Flaherty, Raymond A. Zimmerman, and Mary Ann Murray, "Benchmarking Against the Best," *Journal of Accountancy* (July 1995), pp. 85–88.

**FIGURE 9.5**

CPA Net Income Example

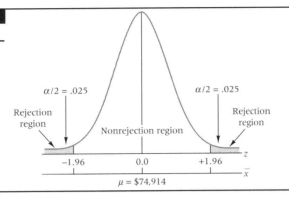

ACTION:

Because this test statistic, $z = 2.75$, is greater than the critical value of $z$ in the upper tail of the distribution, $z = +1.96$, the statistical conclusion reached at step 7 of the hypothesis-testing process is to reject the null hypothesis. *The calculated test statistic* is often referred to as the **observed value.** Thus, the observed value of $z$ for this problem is 2.75 and the critical value of $z$ for this problem is 1.96.

BUSINESS IMPLICATION:

Step 8 is to make a managerial decision. What does this result mean? Statistically, the researcher has enough evidence to reject the figure of $74,914 as the true national average net income for sole proprietor CPAs. Although the researcher conducted a two-tailed test, the evidence gathered indicates that the national average may have increased. The sample mean of $78,695 is $3,781 higher than the national mean being tested. The researcher can conclude that the national average is more than before, but because the $78,695 is only a sample mean, it offers no guarantee that the national average for all sole proprietor CPAs is $3,781 more. If a confidence interval were constructed with the sample data, $78,695 would be the point estimate. Other samples might produce different sample means. Managerially, this statistical finding may mean that CPAs will be more expensive to hire either as full-time employees or as consultants. It may mean that consulting services have gone up in price. For new accountants, it may mean the potential for greater earning power. If the sample mean of $78,695 is the actual new population average for the year 2005, it would represent an increase of $3,781 over a ten-year period. This increase may or may not be substantive depending on one's point of view.

## Testing the Mean with a Finite Population

If the hypothesis test for the population mean is being conducted with a known finite population, the population information can be incorporated into the hypothesis-testing formula. Doing so can increase the potential for rejecting the null hypothesis. However, remember from Chapter 7 that if the sample size is less than 5% of the population, the finite correction factor does not significantly alter the solution. Formula (9.1) can be amended to include the population information.

| FORMULA TO TEST HYPOTHESES ABOUT $\mu$ WITH A FINITE POPULATION (9.2) | $z = \dfrac{\bar{x} - \mu}{\dfrac{\sigma}{\sqrt{n}} \sqrt{\dfrac{N-n}{N-1}}}$ |
|---|---|

In the CPA net income example, suppose only 600 sole proprietor CPAs practice in the United States. A sample of 112 CPAs taken from a population of only 600 CPAs is

18.67% of the population and therefore is much more likely to be representative of the population than a sample of 112 CPAs taken from a population of 20,000 CPAs (.56% of the population). The finite correction factor takes this difference into consideration and allows for an increase in the observed value of $z$. The observed $z$ value would change to

$$z = \frac{\bar{x} - \mu}{\frac{\sigma}{\sqrt{n}}\sqrt{\frac{N-n}{N-1}}} = \frac{78{,}695 - 74{,}914}{\frac{14{,}530}{\sqrt{112}}\sqrt{\frac{600-112}{600-1}}} = \frac{3{,}781}{1{,}239.2} = 3.05$$

Use of the finite correction factor increased the observed $z$ value from 2.75 to 3.05. The decision to reject the null hypothesis does not change with this new information. However, on occasion, the finite correction factor can make the difference between rejecting and failing to reject the null hypothesis.

## Using the *p*-Value to Test Hypotheses

Another way to reach a statistical conclusion in hypothesis testing problems is by using the **p-value,** sometimes referred to as **observed significance level.** The $p$-value is growing in importance with the increasing use of statistical computer packages to test hypotheses. No preset value of $\alpha$ is given in the $p$-value method. Instead, the probability of getting a test statistic at least as extreme as the observed test statistic (computed from the data) is computed under the assumption that the null hypothesis is true. Virtually every statistical computer program yields this probability ($p$-value). The $p$-value defines the smallest value of alpha for which the null hypothesis can be rejected. For example, if the $p$-value of a test is .038, the null hypothesis cannot be rejected at $\alpha = .01$ because .038 is the smallest value of alpha for which the null hypothesis can be rejected. However, the null hypothesis can be rejected for $\alpha = .05$.

Suppose a researcher is conducting a one-tailed test with a rejection region in the upper tail and obtains an observed test statistic of $z = 2.04$ from the sample data. Using the standard normal table, Table A.5, we find that the probability of randomly obtaining a $z$ value this great or greater by chance is .5000 − .4793 = .0207. The $p$ value is .0207. Using this information, the researcher would reject the null hypothesis for $\alpha = .05$ or .10 or any value more than .0207. The researcher would not reject the null hypothesis for any alpha value less than or equal to .0207 (in particular, $\alpha = .01, .001$, etc.).

For a two-tailed test, recall that we split alpha to determine the critical value of the test statistic. With the $p$-value, the probability of getting a test statistic at least as extreme as the observed value is computed. This $p$-value is then compared to $\alpha/2$ for two-tailed tests to determine statistical significance. The business researcher should be cautioned that some statistical computer packages are programmed to double the observed probability and report that value as the $p$-value when the user signifies that a two-tailed test is being requested. The researcher then compares this $p$-value to alpha values to decide whether to reject the null hypothesis. In other words, rather than the researcher splitting alpha, the probability of the observed test statistic is doubled. The researcher must be sure she understands what the computer software package does to the $p$-value for a two-tailed test before she reaches a statistical conclusion.

As an example of using $p$-values with a two-tailed test, consider the CPA net income problem. The observed test statistic for this problem is $z = 2.75$. Using Table A.5, we know that the probability of obtaining a test statistic at least this extreme if the null hypothesis is true is .5000 − .4970 = .0030. Observe that in the MINITAB output in Figure 9.6 the $p$-value is .0060. MINITAB doubles the $p$-value on a two-tailed test so that the researcher can compare the $p$-value to $\alpha$ to reach a statistical conclusion. On the other hand, when Excel yields a $p$-value in its output, it always gives the one-tailed value, which in this case is .003 (see output in Figure 9.6). To reach a statistical conclusion from an Excel produced $p$-value when doing a two-tailed test, the researcher must either compare the $p$-value to $\alpha/2$ or double it and compare it to $\alpha$.

| **FIGURE 9.6** |
|---|
| MINITAB and Excel Output with *p* Values |

**MINITAB Output**

```
                        Z-TEST
```

Test of mu=74914 vs mu not=74914
The assumed sigma=14530

| Variable | N | Mean | StDev | SE Mean | Z | p |
|---|---|---|---|---|---|---|
| Net Income | 112 | 78695 | 14543 | 1373 | 2.75 | 0.0060 |

**Excel Output**

| | A | B |
|---|---|---|
| 1 | Sample Mean | 78695 |
| 2 | Standard Error | 1374 |
| 3 | Standard Deviation | 14543 |
| 4 | Count (n) | 112 |
| 5 | Hypothesized Value of Mu | 74914 |
| 6 | P-value | 0.003 |

## Using the Critical Value Method to Test Hypotheses

Another method of testing hypotheses is the critical value method. In the CPA income example, the null hypothesis was rejected because the computed value of *z* was in the rejection zone. What mean income would it take to cause the observed *z* value to be in the rejection zone? The **critical value method** *determines the critical mean value required for z to be in the rejection region and uses it to test the hypotheses.*

This method also uses formula (9.1). However, instead of an observed *z*, a critical $\bar{x}$ value, $\bar{x}_C$, is determined. The critical table value of $z_c$ is inserted into the formula, along with $\mu$ and $\sigma$. Thus,

$$z_c = \frac{\bar{x}_c - \mu}{\frac{\sigma}{\sqrt{n}}}$$

Substituting values from the CPA income example gives

$$\pm 1.96 = \frac{\bar{x}_c - 74{,}914}{\frac{14{,}530}{\sqrt{112}}}$$

or

$$\bar{x}_c = 74{,}914 \pm 1.96 \frac{14{,}530}{\sqrt{112}} = 74{,}914 \pm 2{,}691$$

lower $\bar{x}_c = 72{,}223$ and upper $\bar{x}_c = 77{,}605$.

Figure 9.7 depicts graphically the rejection and nonrejection regions in terms of means instead of *z* scores.

With the critical value method, most of the computational work is done ahead of time. In this problem, before the sample means are computed, the analyst knows that a sample mean value of greater than $77,605 or less than $72,223 must be attained to reject the hypothesized population mean. Because the sample mean for this problem was $78,695, which is greater than $77,605, the analyst rejects the null hypothesis. This method is particularly attractive in industrial settings where standards can be set ahead of time and then quality control technicians can gather data and compare actual measurements of products to specifications.

**FIGURE 9.7**

Rejection and Nonrejection
Regions for Critical
Value Method

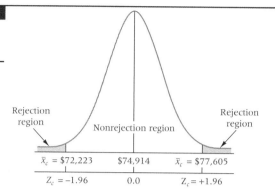

| Rejection region | Nonrejection region | Rejection region |
|---|---|---|
| $\bar{x}_c = \$72{,}223$ | $\$74{,}914$ | $\bar{x}_c = \$77{,}605$ |
| $Z_c = -1.96$ | $0.0$ | $Z_c = +1.96$ |

**DEMONSTRATION PROBLEM 9.1**

In an attempt to determine why customer service is important to managers in the United Kingdom, researchers surveyed managing directors of manufacturing plants in Scotland.* One of the reasons proposed was that customer service is a means of retaining customers. On a scale from 1 to 5, with 1 being low and 5 being high, the survey respondents rated this reason more highly than any of the others, with a mean response of 4.30. Suppose U.S. researchers believe American manufacturing managers would not rate this reason as highly and conduct a hypothesis test to prove their theory. Alpha is set at .05. Data are gathered and the following results are obtained. Use these data and the eight steps of hypothesis testing to determine whether U.S. managers rate this reason significantly lower than the 4.30 mean ascertained in the United Kingdom. Assume from previous studies that the population standard deviation is 0.574.

| 3 | 4 | 5 | 5 | 4 | 5 | 5 | 4 | 4 | 4 | 4 |
|---|---|---|---|---|---|---|---|---|---|---|
| 4 | 4 | 4 | 4 | 5 | 4 | 4 | 4 | 3 | 4 | 4 |
| 4 | 3 | 5 | 4 | 4 | 5 | 4 | 4 | 4 | 5 | |

*Solution*

**H**YPOTHESIZE:

STEP 1. Establish hypotheses. Because the U.S. researchers are interested only in "proving" that the mean figure is lower in the United States, the test is one-tailed. The alternative hypothesis is that the population mean is lower than 4.30. The null hypothesis states the equality case.

$$H_0: \mu = 4.30$$
$$H_a: \mu < 4.30$$

**T**EST:

STEP 2. Determine the appropriate statistical test. The test statistic is

$$z = \frac{\bar{x} - \mu}{\dfrac{\sigma}{\sqrt{n}}}$$

STEP 3. Specify the Type I error rate.

$$\alpha = .05$$

---

* William G. Donaldson, "Manufacturers Need to Show Greater Commitment to Customer Service," *Industrial Marketing Management*, vol. 24 (October 1995), pp. 421–430. The 1-to-5 scale has been reversed here for clarity of presentation.

STEP 4. State the decision rule. Because this test is a one-tailed test, the critical $z$ value is found by looking up $.5000 - .0500 = .4500$ as the area in Table A.5. The critical value of the test statistic is $z_{.05} = -1.645$. An observed test statistic must be less than $-1.645$ to reject the null hypothesis. The rejection region and critical value can be depicted as in the following diagram.

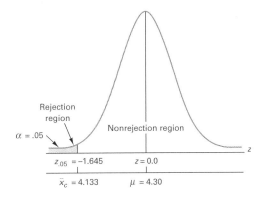

STEP 5. Gather the sample data. The data are shown.
STEP 6. Calculate the value of the test statistic.

$$\bar{x} = 4.156 \qquad \sigma = .574$$

$$z = \frac{4.156 - 4.30}{\frac{.574}{\sqrt{32}}} = -1.42$$

**A**CTION:

STEP 7. State the statistical conclusion. Because the observed test statistic is not less than the critical value and is not in the rejection region, the statistical conclusion is that the null hypothesis cannot be rejected.

**B**USINESS IMPLICATION:

STEP 8. Make a managerial decision. The test does not result in enough evidence to conclude that U.S. managers think it is less important to use customer service as a means of retaining customers than do U.K. managers. Customer service is an important tool for retaining customers in both countries according to managers.

*Using the p-value:* The observed test statistic is $z = -1.42$. From Table A.5, the probability of getting a $z$ value at least this extreme when the null hypothesis is true is $.5000 - .4222 = .0778$. Hence, the null hypothesis cannot be rejected at $\alpha = .05$ because the smallest value of alpha for which the null hypothesis can be rejected is .0778.

*Using the critical value method:* For what sample mean (or more extreme) value would the null hypothesis be rejected? This critical sample mean can be determined by using the critical $z$ value associated with alpha, $z_{.05} = -1.645$.

$$z_c = \frac{\bar{x}_c - \mu}{\frac{\sigma}{\sqrt{n}}}$$

$$-1.645 = \frac{\bar{x}_c - 4.30}{\frac{.574}{\sqrt{32}}}$$

$$\bar{x}_c = 4.133$$

The decision rule is that a sample mean less than 4.133 would be necessary to reject the null hypothesis. Because the mean obtained from the sample data is 4.156, the researchers fail to reject the null hypothesis. The preceding diagram includes a scale with the critical sample mean and the rejection region for the critical value method.

Managing Information with Technology    111

| FIGURE 9.8 |
|---|

MINITAB and Excel Output for
Demonstration Problem 9.1

**MINITAB Output**

```
One-Sample Z: Ratings

Test of mu = 4.3 vs mu < 4.3
The assumed sigma = 0.574

Variable   N    Mean   StDev   SE Mean
Ratings    32   4.156  0.574   0.101

Variable   95.0% Upper Bound    Z      P
Ratings          4.323        -1.42   0.078
```

**Excel Output**

| | A |
|---|---|
| 1 | |
| 2 | The p-value for the ratings problem is **0.078339** |
| 3 | |

## Using the Computer to Test Hypotheses About a Population Mean Using the $z$ Statistic

Both MINITAB and Excel can be used to test hypotheses about a single population mean using the $z$ statistic. Figure 9.8 contains output from both MINITAB and Excel for Demonstration Problem 9.1. For $z$ tests, MINITAB requires knowledge of the population standard deviation. Note that the standard MINITAB output includes a statement of the one-tailed hypothesis, the observed $z$ value, and the $p$-value. Because this test is a one-tailed test, the $p$-value was not doubled. The Excel output contains only the right-tailed $p$-value of the $z$ statistic. With a negative observed $z$ for Demonstration Problem 9.1, the $p$-value was calculated by taking $1 - $ (Excel's answer).

## 9.2 PROBLEMS

9.1   **a.**  Use the data given to test the following hypotheses.

$$H_0: \mu = 25 \qquad H_a: \mu \neq 25$$
$$\bar{x} = 28.1, n = 57, \sigma = 8.46, \alpha = .01$$

    **b.**  Use the $p$-value to reach a statistical conclusion

    **c.**  Using the critical value method, what are the critical sample mean values?

9.2   Use the data given to test the following hypotheses. Assume the data are normally distributed in the population.

$$H_0: \mu = 7.48 \qquad H_a: \mu < 7.48$$
$$\bar{x} = 6.91, n = 24, \sigma = 1.21, \alpha = .01$$

9.3   **a.**  Use the data given to test the following hypotheses.

$$H_0: \mu = 1200 \qquad H_a: \mu \geq 1200$$
$$\bar{x} = 1215, n = 113, \sigma = 100, \alpha = .10$$

    **b.**  Use the $p$-value to obtain the results.

    **c.**  Solve for the critical value required to reject the mean.

9.4   The Environmental Protection Agency releases figures on urban air soot in selected cities in the United States. For the city of St. Louis, the EPA claims that the average number of micrograms of suspended particles per cubic meter of air is 82. Suppose St. Louis officials have been working with businesses, commuters, and industries to reduce this figure. These city officials hire an environmental company to take random measures of air soot over a period of several weeks. The resulting data follow. Assume that the population standard deviation is 9.184. Use these data to determine whether the urban air soot in St. Louis is significantly lower than it was when the EPA conducted its measurements. Let $\alpha = .01$. If the null hypothesis is rejected, discuss the substantive hypothesis.

| 81.6 | 66.6 | 70.9 | 82.5 | 58.3 | 71.6 | 72.4 |
| 96.6 | 78.6 | 76.1 | 80.0 | 73.2 | 85.5 | 73.2 |
| 68.6 | 74.0 | 68.7 | 83.0 | 86.9 | 94.9 | 75.6 |
| 77.3 | 86.6 | 71.7 | 88.5 | 87.0 | 72.5 | 83.0 |
| 85.8 | 74.9 | 61.7 | 92.2 | | | |

9.5 According to the U.S. Bureau of Labor Statistics, the average weekly earnings of a production worker in 1997 were $424.20. Suppose a labor researcher wants to test to determine whether this figure is still accurate today. The researcher randomly selects 54 production workers from across the United States and obtains a representative earnings statement for one week from each. The resulting sample average is $432.69. Assuming a population standard deviation of $33.90, and a 5% level of significance, determine whether the mean weekly earnings of a production worker have changed.

9.6 According to a study several years ago by the Personal Communications Industry Association, the average wireless phone user earns $62,600 per year. Suppose a researcher believes that the average annual earnings of a wireless phone user are lower now, and he sets up a study in an attempt to prove his theory. He randomly samples 18 wireless phone users and finds out that the average annual salary for this sample is $58,974, with a population standard deviation of $7,810. Use $\alpha = .01$ to test the researcher's theory. Assume wages in this industry are normally distributed.

9.7 A manufacturing company produces valves in various sizes and shapes. One particular valve plate is supposed to have a tensile strength of 5 pounds per millimeter (lbs/mm). The company tests a random sample of 42 such valve plates from a lot of 650 valve plates. The sample mean is a tensile strength of 5.0611 lbs/mm, and the population standard deviation is .2803 lbs/mm. Use $\alpha = .10$ and test to determine whether the lot of valve plates has an average tensile strength of 5 lbs/mm.

9.8 A manufacturing firm has been averaging 18.2 orders per week for several years. However, during a recession, orders appeared to slow. Suppose the firm's production manager randomly samples 32 weeks and finds a sample mean of 15.6 orders. The population standard deviation is 2.3 orders. Test to determine whether the average number of orders is down by using $\alpha = .10$.

9.9 A study conducted by Runzheimer International showed that Paris is the most expensive place to live of the 12 European Union cities. Paris ranks second in housing expense, with a rental unit of six to nine rooms costing an average of $4,292 a month. Suppose a company's CEO believes this figure is too high and decides to conduct her own survey. Her assistant contacts the owners of 55 randomly selected rental units of six to nine rooms and finds that the sample average cost is $4,008. Assume that the population standard deviation is $386. Using the sample results and $\alpha = .01$, test to determine whether the figure published by Runzheimer International is too high. If the null hypothesis is rejected, discuss whether the results are substantive.

9.10 The American Water Works Association estimates that the average person in the United States uses 123 gallons of water per day. Suppose some researchers believe that more water is being used now and want to test to determine whether it is so. They randomly select a sample of Americans and carefully keep track of the water used by each sample member for a day, then analyze the results by using a statistical computer software package. The output is given here. Assume $\alpha = .05$.

How many people were sampled? What was the sample mean? Was this a one- or two-tailed test? What was the result of the study? What decision could be stated about the null hypothesis from these results?

```
              One-Sample Z: Wateruse
Test of mu = 123 vs mu > 123
The assumed sigma = 27.68

Variable   N    Mean    StDev   SE Mean
Wateruse   40   132.36  27.68   4.38

Variable   95.0% Lower Bound    Z      P
Wateruse        125.16          2.14   0.016
```

## 9.3 TESTING HYPOTHESES ABOUT A POPULATION MEAN USING THE *t* STATISTIC (*σ* UNKNOWN)

Very often when a business researcher is gathering data to test hypotheses about a single population mean, the value of the population standard deviation is unknown and the researcher must use the sample standard deviation as an estimate of it. In such cases, the *z* test cannot be used.

Chapter 8 presented the *t* distribution, which can be used to analyze hypotheses about a single population mean when *σ* is unknown if the population is normally distributed for the measurement being studied. In this section, we will examine the *t* test for a single population mean. In general, this *t* test is applicable whenever the researcher is drawing a single random sample to test the value of a population mean (*μ*), the population standard deviation is unknown, and the population is normally distributed for the measurement of interest. Recall from Chapter 8 that the assumption that the data be normally distributed in the population is rather robust.

The formula for testing such hypotheses follows.

| *t* TEST FOR *μ* (9.3) | $$t = \frac{\bar{x} - \mu}{\frac{s}{\sqrt{n}}}$$ $$df = n - 1$$ |
|---|---|

The U.S. Farmers' Production Company builds large harvesters. For a harvester to be properly balanced when operating, a 25-pound plate is installed on its side. The machine that produces these plates is set to yield plates that average 25 pounds. The distribution of plates produced from the machine is normal. However, the shop supervisor is worried that the machine is out of adjustment and is producing plates that do not average 25 pounds. To test this concern, he randomly selects 20 of the plates produced the day before and weighs them. Table 9.1 shows the weights obtained, along with the computed sample mean and sample standard deviation.

The test is to determine whether the machine is out of control, and the shop supervisor has not specified whether he believes the machine is producing plates that are too heavy or too light. Thus a two-tailed test is appropriate. The following hypotheses are tested.

$$H_0: \mu = 25 \text{ pounds}$$
$$H_a: \mu \neq 25 \text{ pounds}$$

An *α* of .05 is used. Figure 9.9 shows the rejection regions.

Because *n* = 20, the degrees of freedom for this test are 19 (20 − 1). The *t* distribution table is a one-tailed table but the test for this problem is two-tailed, so alpha must be split, which yields *α*/2 = .025, the value in each tail. (To obtain the table *t* value when conducting

**TABLE 9.1**

Weights in Pounds of a Sample of 20 Plates

| | | | | |
|---|---|---|---|---|
| 22.6 | 22.2 | 23.2 | 27.4 | 24.5 |
| 27.0 | 26.6 | 28.1 | 26.9 | 24.9 |
| 26.2 | 25.3 | 23.1 | 24.2 | 26.1 |
| 25.8 | 30.4 | 28.6 | 23.5 | 23.6 |

$\bar{x} = 25.51$, $s = 2.1933$, n = 20

## FIGURE 9.9

Rejection Regions for the
Machine Plate Example

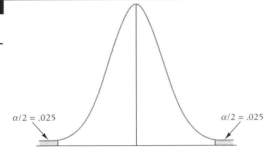

## FIGURE 9.10

Graph of Observed and Critical
*t* Values for the Machine Plate
Example

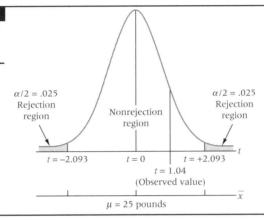

## FIGURE 9.11

MINITAB and Excel Output for
the Machine Plate Example

**MINITAB Output**

One-Sample T: Weight

Test of mu = 25 vs mu not = 25

| Variable | N | Mean | StDev | SE Mean |
|---|---|---|---|---|
| Weight | 20 | 25.510 | 2.193 | 0.490 |

| Variable | 95.0% CI | | T | P |
|---|---|---|---|---|
| Weight | ( 24.484, | 26.536) | 1.04 | 0.311 |

**Excel Output**

| | A | B |
|---|---|---|
| 1 | Mean | 25.51 |
| 2 | Variance | 4.810 |
| 3 | df | 19 |
| 4 | t Stat | 1.04 |
| 5 | P (T<=t) one-tail | 0.1557 |
| 6 | t Critical one-tail | 1.73 |
| 7 | P (T<=t) two-tail | 0.3114 |
| 8 | t Critical two-tail | 2.09 |

a two-tailed test, always split alpha and use $\alpha/2$.) The table *t* value for this example is 2.093.
Table values such as this one are often written in the following form:

$$t_{.025,19} = 2.093$$

Figure 9.10 depicts the *t* distribution for this example, along with the critical values,
the observed *t* value, and the rejection regions. In this case, the decision rule is to reject the

null hypothesis if the observed value of $t$ is less than $-2.093$ or greater than $+2.093$ (in the tails of the distribution). Computation of the test statistic yields

$$t = \frac{\bar{x} - \mu}{\frac{s}{\sqrt{n}}} = \frac{25.51 - 25.00}{\frac{2.1933}{\sqrt{20}}} = 1.04 \text{ (observed } t \text{ value)}$$

Because the observed $t$ value is $+1.04$, the null hypothesis is not rejected. Not enough evidence is found in this sample to reject the hypothesis that the population mean is 25 pounds.

Figure 9.11 shows MINITAB and Excel output for this example. Note that the MINITAB output includes the observed $t$ value (1.04) and the $p$-value (.311). Since this test is a two-tailed test, MINITAB has doubled the one-tailed $p$-value for $t = 1.04$. Thus the $p$-value of .311 can be compared directly to $\alpha = .05$ to reach the conclusion to fail to reject the null hypothesis.

The Excel output contains the observed $t$ value (1.04) plus the $p$-value and the critical table $t$ value for both a one-tailed and a two-tailed test. Since this test is a two-tailed test, the $p$-value of .3114 is used to compare to $\alpha = .05$. Excel also gives the table value of $t = 2.09$ for a two-tailed test, which allows one to verify that the statistical conclusion is to fail to reject the null hypothesis because the observed $t$ value is only 1.04, which is less than 2.09.

---

**DEMONSTRATION PROBLEM 9.2**

Figures released by the U.S. Department of Agriculture show that the average size of farms has increased since 1940. In 1940, the mean size of a farm was 174 acres; by 1997, the average size was 471 acres. Between those years, the number of farms decreased but the amount of tillable land remained relatively constant, so now farms are bigger. This trend might be explained, in part, by the inability of small farms to compete with the prices and costs of large-scale operations and to produce a level of income necessary to support the farmers' desired standard of living. Suppose an agribusiness researcher believes the average size of farms increased from the 1997 mean figure of 471 acres. To test this notion, she randomly sampled 23 farms across the United States and ascertained the size of each farm from county records. The data she gathered follow. Use a 5% level of significance to test her hypothesis.

| 445 | 489 | 474 | 505 | 553 | 477 | 454 | 463 | 466 |
|-----|-----|-----|-----|-----|-----|-----|-----|-----|
| 557 | 502 | 449 | 438 | 500 | 466 | 477 | 557 | 433 |
| 545 | 511 | 590 | 561 | 560 | | | | |

**Solution**

**H**YPOTHESIZE:

STEP 1. The researcher's hypothesis is that the average size of a U.S. farm is more than 471 acres. Because this theory is unproven, it is the alternate hypothesis. The null hypothesis is that the mean is still 471 acres.

$$H_0: \mu = 471$$
$$H_a: \mu > 471$$

**T**EST:

STEP 2. The statistical test to be used is

$$t = \frac{\bar{x} - \mu}{\frac{s}{\sqrt{n}}}$$

STEP 3. The value of alpha is .05.

STEP 4. With 23 data points, df $= n - 1 = 23 - 1 = 22$. This test is one-tailed, and the critical table $t$ value is

$$t_{.05,22} = 1.717$$

The decision rule is to reject the null hypothesis if the observed test statistic is greater than 1.717.

STEP 5. The gathered data are shown.

STEP 6. The sample mean is 498.78 and the sample standard deviation is 46.94. The observed *t* value is

$$t = \frac{\bar{x} - \mu}{\frac{s}{\sqrt{n}}} = \frac{498.78 - 471}{\frac{46.94}{\sqrt{23}}} = 2.84$$

**A**CTION:

STEP 7. The observed *t* value of 2.84 is greater than the table *t* value of 1.717, so the business researcher rejects the null hypothesis. She accepts the alternative hypothesis and concludes that the average size of a U.S. farm is now more than 471 acres. The following graph represents this analysis pictorially.

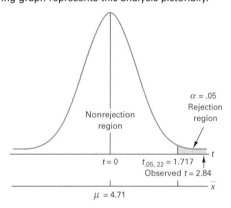

**B**USINESS IMPLICATIONS:

STEP 8. Agribusiness researchers can speculate about what it means to have larger farms. If the average size of a farm has increased from 471 acres to almost 500 acres, it may represent a substantive increase.

It could mean that small farms are not financially viable. It might mean that corporations are buying out small farms and that large company farms are on the increase. Such a trend might spark legislative movements to protect the small farm. Larger farm sizes might also affect commodity trading.

---

| FIGURE 9.12 |
| --- |
| MINITAB and Excel Output for Demonstration Problem 9.2 |

**MINITAB Output**

```
One-Sample T: Acres

Test of mu = 471 vs mu > 471
Variable    N     Mean    StDev   SE Mean
Acres       23   498.78   46.94     9.79

Variable   95.0% Lower Bound     T       P
Acres                481.97    2.84   0.005
```

**Excel Output**

| | A | B |
| --- | --- | --- |
| 1 | Mean | 498.78 |
| 2 | Variance | 2203.63 |
| 3 | Observations | 23 |
| 4 | df | 22 |
| 5 | t Stat | 2.84 |
| 6 | P (T<=t) one-tail | 0.0048 |
| 7 | t Critical one-tail | 1.72 |
| 8 | P (T<=t) two-tail | 0.0096 |
| 9 | t Critical two-tail | 2.07 |

### Using the Computer to Test Hypotheses About a Population Mean Using the *t* Test

MINITAB has the capability of computing a one-sample *t* test for means. Figure 9.12 contains MINITAB output for Demonstration Problem 9.2. The output contains the hypotheses being tested, the sample statistics, the observed *t* value (2.84), and the *p*-value (.005). Because the *p*-value is less than $\alpha = .05$, the decision is to reject the null hypothesis.

Excel does not have a one-sample *t* test function. However, by using the two-sample *t* test for means with unequal variances, the results for a one-sample test can be obtained. This is accomplished by inputting the sample data for the first sample and the value of the parameter being tested (in this case, $\mu = 471$) for the second sample. The output includes the observed *t* value (2.84) and both the table *t* values and *p*-values for one- and two-tailed tests. Because Demonstration Problem 9.2 was a one-tailed test, the *p*-value of .0048, which is the same value obtained using MINITAB, is used.

## 9.3 PROBLEMS

**9.11** A random sample of size 20 is taken, resulting in a sample mean of 16.45 and a sample standard deviation of 3.59. Assume *x* is normally distributed and use this information and $\alpha = .05$ to test the following hypotheses.

$$H_0: \mu = 16 \qquad H_a: \mu \neq 16$$

**9.12** A random sample of 51 items is taken, with $\bar{x} = 58.42$ and $s^2 = 25.68$. Use these data to test the following hypotheses, assuming you want to take only a 1% risk of committing a Type I error and that *x* is normally distributed.

$$H_0: \mu = 60 \qquad H_a: \mu < 60$$

**9.13** The following data were gathered from a random sample of 11 items.

| 1200 | 1175 | 1080 | 1275 | 1201 | 1387 |
|------|------|------|------|------|------|
| 1090 | 1280 | 1400 | 1287 | 1225 | |

Use these data and a 5% level of significance to test the following hypotheses, assuming that the data come from a normally distributed population.

$$H_0: \mu = 1160 \qquad H_a: \mu > 1160$$

**9.14** The following data (in pounds), which were selected randomly from a normally distributed population of values, represent measurements of a machine part that is supposed to weigh, on average, 8.3 pounds.

| 8.1 | 8.4 | 8.3 | 8.2 | 8.5 | 8.6 | 8.4 | 8.3 | 8.4 | 8.2 |
|-----|-----|-----|-----|-----|-----|-----|-----|-----|-----|
| 8.8 | 8.2 | 8.2 | 8.3 | 8.1 | 8.3 | 8.4 | 8.5 | 8.5 | 8.7 |

Use these data and $\alpha = .01$ to test the hypothesis that the parts average 8.3 pounds.

**9.15** A hole-punch machine is set to punch a hole 1.84 centimeters in diameter in a strip of sheet metal in a manufacturing process. The strip of metal is then creased and sent on to the next phase of production, where a metal rod is slipped through the hole. It is important that the hole be punched to the specified diameter of 1.84 cm. To test punching accuracy, technicians have randomly sampled 12 punched holes and measured the diameters. The data (in centimeters) follow. Use an alpha of .10 to determine whether the holes are being punched an average of 1.84 centimeters. Assume the punched holes are normally distributed in the population.

| 1.81 | 1.89 | 1.86 | 1.83 |
|------|------|------|------|
| 1.85 | 1.82 | 1.87 | 1.85 |
| 1.84 | 1.86 | 1.88 | 1.85 |

**9.16** Suppose a study reports that the average price for a gallon of self-serve regular unleaded gasoline is $1.16. You believe that the figure is higher in your area of the country. You decide to test this claim for your part of the United States by randomly calling gasoline stations. Your random survey of 25 stations produces the following prices.

| | | | | |
|---|---|---|---|---|
| $1.27 | $1.29 | $1.16 | $1.20 | $1.37 |
| 1.20 | 1.23 | 1.19 | 1.20 | 1.24 |
| 1.16 | 1.07 | 1.27 | 1.09 | 1.35 |
| 1.15 | 1.23 | 1.14 | 1.05 | 1.35 |
| 1.21 | 1.14 | 1.14 | 1.07 | 1.10 |

Assume gasoline prices for a region are normally distributed. Do the data you obtained provide enough evidence to reject the claim? Use a 1% level of significance.

9.17 Suppose that in past years the average price per square foot for warehouses in the United States has been $32.28. A national real estate investor wants to determine whether that figure has changed now. The investor hires a researcher who randomly samples 19 warehouses that are for sale across the United States and finds that the mean price per square foot is $31.67, with a standard deviation of $1.29. If the researcher uses a 5% level of significance, what statistical conclusion can be reached? What are the hypotheses?

9.18 According to a National Public Transportation survey, the average commuting time for people who commute to a city with a population of 1 to 3 million is 19.0 minutes. Suppose a researcher lives in a city with a population of 2.4 million and wants to test this claim in her city. She takes a random sample of commuters and gathers data. The data are analyzed using both MINITAB and Excel, and the output is shown here. What are the results of the study? What are the hypotheses?

**MINITAB Output:**

```
One-Sample T: Commute Time
Test of mu = 19 vs mu not = 19

Variable       N    Mean    StDev   SE Mean
Commute Time   26   19.534  4.100   0.804

Variable            95.0% CI           T     P
Commute Time   (17.878, 21.190)  0.66  0.513
```

**Excel Output:**

| | A | B |
|---|---|---|
| 1 | Mean | 19.534 |
| 2 | Variance | 16.813 |
| 3 | Observations | 26 |
| 4 | df | 25 |
| 5 | t Stat | 0.66 |
| 6 | P (T<=t) one-tail | 0.256 |
| 7 | t Critical one-tail | 1.71 |
| 8 | P (T<=t) two-tail | 0.513 |
| 9 | t Critical two-tail | 2.06 |

# 9.4 TESTING HYPOTHESES ABOUT A PROPORTION

Data analysis used in business decision making often contains proportions to describe such aspects as market share, consumer makeup, quality defects, on-time deliver rate, profitable stocks, and others. Business surveys often produce information expressed in proportion form such as .45 of all businesses offer flexible hours to employees or .88 of all businesses have Web sites. Business researchers conduct hypothesis tests about such proportions to determine whether they have changed in some way. As an example, suppose a company held a 26% or .26 share of the market for several years. Due to a massive marketing effort and improved product quality, company officials believe that the market share increased; and they want to prove it. Other examples of hypothesis testing about a single population proportion might include:

- A market researcher wants to test to determine whether the proportion of new car purchasers who are female has increased.
- A financial researcher wants to test to determine whether the proportion of companies that were profitable last year in the average investment officer's portfolio is .60.
- A quality manager for a large manufacturing firm wants to test to determine whether the proportion of defective items in a batch is less than .04.

Formula (9.4) for inferential analysis of a proportion was introduced in section 7.3 of Chapter 7. Based on the central limit theorem, this formula makes possible the testing of hypotheses about the population proportion in a manner similar to that of the formula used to test sample means. Recall that $\hat{p}$ denotes a sample proportion and $p$ denotes the population proportion. To validly use this test, the sample size must be large enough such that $n \cdot p \geq 5$ and $n \cdot q \geq 5$.

| | |
|---|---|
| **$z$ TEST OF A POPULATION PROPORTION (9.4)** | $$z = \dfrac{\hat{p} - p}{\sqrt{\dfrac{p \cdot q}{n}}}$$ |

where

$\hat{p}$ = sample proportion
$p$ = population proportion
$q$ = $1 - p$

A manufacturer believes exactly 8% of its products contain at least one minor flaw. Suppose a company researcher wants to test this belief. The null and alternative hypotheses are

$$H_0\colon p = .08$$

$$H_a\colon p \neq .08$$

This test is two-tailed because the hypothesis being tested is whether the proportion of products with at least one minor flaw is .08. Alpha is selected to be .10. Figure 9.13 shows the distribution, with the rejection regions and $z_{.05}$. Because $\alpha$ is divided for a two-tailed test, the table value for an area of $(1/2)(.10) = .05$ is $z_{.05} = \pm 1.645$.

---

**FIGURE 9.13**

Distribution with Rejection Regions for Flawed-Product Example

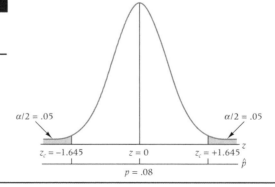

$\alpha/2 = .05$             $\alpha/2 = .05$

$z_c = -1.645$     $z = 0$     $z_c = +1.645$

$p = .08$

---

For the business researcher to reject the null hypothesis, the observed $z$ value must be greater than 1.645 or less than −1.645. The business researcher randomly selects a sample of 200 products, inspects each item for flaws, and determines that 33 items have at least one minor flaw. Calculating the sample proportion gives

$$\hat{p} = \frac{33}{200} = .165$$

The observed $z$ value is calculated as:

$$z = \frac{\hat{p} - p}{\sqrt{\dfrac{p \cdot q}{n}}} = \frac{.165 - .080}{\sqrt{\dfrac{(.08)(.92)}{200}}} = \frac{.085}{.019} = 4.43$$

Note that the denominator of the $z$ formula contains the population proportion. Although the business researcher does not actually know the population proportion, he is testing a population proportion value. Hence he uses the hypothesized population value in the denominator of the formula as well as in the numerator. This method contrasts with the confidence interval formula, where the sample proportion is used in the denominator.

The observed value of $z$ is in the rejection region (observed $z = 4.43 >$ table $z_{.05} = +1.645$), so the business researcher rejects the null hypothesis. He concludes that the proportion of items with at least one minor flaw in the population from which the sample of 200 was drawn is not .08. With $\alpha = .10$, the risk of committing a Type I error in this example is .10.

The observed value of $z = 4.43$ is outside the range of most values in virtually all $z$ tables. Thus if the researcher were using the $p$-value to arrive at a decision about the null hypothesis, the probability would be .0000, and he would reject the null hypothesis.

The MINITAB output shown in Figure 9.14 displays a $p$-value of .000 for this problem, underscoring the decision to reject the null hypothesis.

Suppose the researcher wanted to use the critical value method. He would enter the table value of $z_{.05} = 1.645$ in the $Z$ formula for single sample proportions, along with the hypothesized population proportion and $n$, and solve for the critical value of denoted as $\hat{p}_C$. The result is

$$z_{\alpha/2} = \frac{\hat{p}_c - p}{\sqrt{\dfrac{p \cdot q}{n}}}$$

$$\pm 1.645 = \frac{\hat{p}_c - .08}{\sqrt{\dfrac{(.08)(.92)}{200}}}$$

$$\hat{p}_c = .08 \pm 1.645 \sqrt{\dfrac{(.08)(.92)}{200}} = .08 \pm .032$$

$$= .048 \text{ and } .112$$

Examination of the sample proportion, $\hat{p} = .165$, and Figure 9.15 clearly show that the sample proportion is in the rejection region. The statistical conclusion is to reject the null hypothesis. The proportion of products with at least one flaw is not .08.

| **FIGURE 9.14** | TEST AND CI FOR ONE PROPORTION |
|---|---|

MINITAB Output for the
Flawed-Product Example

```
TEST AND CI FOR ONE PROPORTION

Test of p = 0.08 vs p not = 0.08
Sample   X    N   Sample p        90.0% CI         P-Value
1       33  200  0.165000  (0.123279, 0.214351)    0.000
```

**STATISTICS IN BUSINESS TODAY**

### Testing Hypotheses about Commuting

How do Americans commute to work? A National Public Transportation survey taken a few years ago indicated that almost 80% of U.S. commuters drive alone to work, more than 11% carpool, and approximately 5% use public transportation. Using hypothesis testing methodology presented in this chapter, researchers can test whether these proportions still hold true today as well as how these figures vary by region. For example, in New York City it is almost certain that the proportion of commuters using public transportation is much higher than 5%. In rural parts of the country where public transportation is unavailable, the proportion of commuters using public transportation would be zero.

What is the average travel time of a commute to work in the United States? According to the National Public Transportation Survey, travel time varies according to the type of transportation used. For example, the average travel time of a commute using a private vehicle is 20 minutes as compared to 42 minutes using public transportation. In part, this difference can be accounted for by the travel speed in miles per hour: private vehicles average 35 miles per hour over a commute compared to 19 miles per hour averaged by public transportation vehicles. It is possible to test any of these means using hypothesis testing techniques presented in this chapter to either validate the figures or to determine whether the figures are no longer true.

**FIGURE 9.15**

Distribution Using Critical Value Method for the Flawed-Product Example

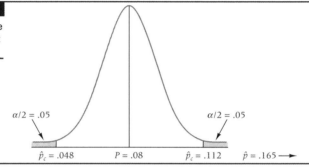

$\alpha/2 = .05$          $\alpha/2 = .05$

$\hat{p}_c = .048$     $P = .08$     $\hat{p}_c = .112$     $\hat{p} = .165 \longrightarrow$

---

**DEMONSTRATION PROBLEM 9.3**

A survey of the morning beverage market shows that the primary breakfast beverage for 17% of Americans is milk. A milk producer in Wisconsin, where milk is plentiful, believes the figure is higher for Wisconsin. To test this idea, she contacts a random sample of 550 Wisconsin residents and asks which primary beverage they consumed for breakfast that day. Suppose 115 replied that milk was the primary beverage. Using a level of significance of .05, test the idea that the milk figure is higher for Wisconsin.

#### Solution

**H**YPOTHESIZE:

STEP 1. The milk producer's theory is that the proportion of Wisconsin residents who drink milk for breakfast is higher than the national proportion, which is the alternative hypothesis. The null hypothesis is that the proportion in Wisconsin does not differ from the national average. The hypotheses for this problem are

$$H_0: p = .17$$
$$H_a: p > .17$$

**T**EST:

STEP 2. The test statistic is

$$z = \frac{\hat{p} - p}{\sqrt{\dfrac{p \cdot q}{n}}}$$

STEP 3. The Type I error rate is .05.

STEP 4. This test is a one-tailed test, and the table value is $z_{.05} = +1.645$. The sample results must yield an observed $z$ value greater than 1.645 for the milk producer to reject the null hypothesis. The following diagram shows $z_{.05}$ and the rejection region for this problem.

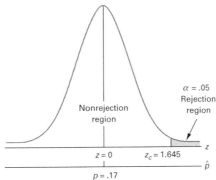

STEP 5.    $n = 550$ and $x = 115$

$$\hat{p} = \frac{115}{550} = .209$$

STEP 6.    $z = \dfrac{\hat{p} - p}{\sqrt{\dfrac{p \cdot q}{n}}} = \dfrac{.209 - .17}{\sqrt{\dfrac{(.17)(.83)}{550}}} = \dfrac{.039}{.016} = 2.44$

**A**CTION:

STEP 7. Because $z = 2.44$ is beyond $z_{.05} = 1.645$ in the rejection region, the milk producer rejects the null hypothesis. On the basis of the random sample, the producer is ready to conclude that the proportion of Wisconsin residents who drink milk as the primary beverage for breakfast is higher than the national proportion.

**B**USINESS IMPLICATIONS:

STEP 8. If the proportion of residents who drink milk for breakfast is higher in Wisconsin than in other parts of the United States, milk producers might have a market opportunity in Wisconsin that is not available in other parts of the country. Perhaps Wisconsin residents are being loyal to home-state products, in which case marketers of other Wisconsin products might be successful in appealing to residents to support their products. The fact that more milk is sold in Wisconsin might mean that if Wisconsin milk producers appealed to markets outside Wisconsin in the same way they do inside the state, they might increase their market share of the breakfast beverage market in other states. Is a proportion of almost .21 really a substantive increase over .17? Certainly in a market of any size at all, an increase of almost 4% of the market share could be worth millions of dollars and in such a case, would be substantive.

The probability of obtaining a $z \geq 2.44$ by chance is .0073. Because this probability is less than $\alpha = .05$, the null hypothesis is also rejected with the $p$-value.

A critical proportion can be solved for by

$$z_{.05} = \frac{\hat{p}_c - p}{\sqrt{\dfrac{p \cdot q}{n}}}$$

$$1.645 = \frac{\hat{p}_c - .17}{\sqrt{\dfrac{(.17)(.83)}{550}}}$$

$$\hat{p}_c = .17 + 1.645 \sqrt{\frac{(.17)(.83)}{550}} = .17 + .026 = .196$$

With the critical value method, a sample proportion greater than .196 must be obtained to reject the null hypothesis. The sample proportion for this problem is .209, so the null hypothesis is also rejected with the critical value method.

| FIGURE 9.16 | Test and CI for One Proportion |
|---|---|

MINITAB Output for
Demonstration Problem 9.3

```
Test of p = 0.17 vs p > 0.17

                                    Exact
Sample X    N     Sample p    90.0% Lower Bound    P-Value
1     115   550    0.209091    0.186770    0.010
```

## Using the Computer to Test Hypotheses About a Population Proportion

MINITAB has the capability of testing hypotheses about a population proportion. Figure 9.16 shows the MINITAB output for Demonstration Problem 9.3. Notice that the output includes a restatement of the hypotheses, the sample proportion, and the $p$-value. From this information, a decision regarding the null hypothesis can be made by comparing the $p$-value (.010) to $\alpha$ (.050). Because the $p$-value is less than $\alpha$, the decision is to reject the null hypothesis.

## 9.4 PROBLEMS

9.19 Suppose you are testing $H_0$: $p = .45$ versus $H_a$: $p > .45$. A random sample of 310 people produces a value of $\hat{p} = .465$. Use $\alpha = .05$ to test this hypothesis.

9.20 Suppose you are testing $H_0$: $p = .63$ versus $H_a$: $p < .63$. For a random sample of 100 people, $x = 55$, where x denotes the number in the sample that have the characteristic of interest. Use a .01 level of significance to test this hypothesis.

9.21 Suppose you are testing $H_0$: $p = .29$ versus $H_a$: $p \neq .29$. A random sample of 740 items shows that 207 have this characteristic. With a .05 probability of committing a Type I error, test the hypothesis. For the $p$-value method, what is the probability of the calculated $z$ value for this problem? If you had used the critical value method, what would the two critical values be? How do the sample results compare with the critical values?

9.22 The Independent Insurance Agents of America conducted a survey of insurance consumers and discovered that 48% of them always reread their insurance policies, 29% sometimes do, 16% rarely do, and 7% never do. Suppose a large insurance company invests considerable time and money in rewriting policies so that they will be more attractive and easy to read and understand. After using the new policies for a year, company managers want to determine whether rewriting the policies significantly changed the proportion of policyholders who always reread their insurance policy. They contact 380 of the company's insurance consumers who purchased a policy in the past year and ask them whether they always reread their insurance policies. One hundred and sixty-four respond that they do. Use a 1% level of significance to test the hypothesis.

9.23 A study by Hewitt Associates showed that 79% of companies offer employees flexible scheduling. Suppose a researcher believes that in accounting firms this figure is lower. The researcher randomly selects 415 accounting firms and through interviews determines that 303 of these firms have flexible scheduling. With a 1% level of significance, does the test show enough evidence to conclude that a significantly lower proportion of accounting firms offer employees flexible scheduling?

9.24 A survey was undertaken by Bruskin/Goldring Research for Quicken to determine how people plan to meet their financial goals in the next year. Respondents were allowed to select more than one way to meet their goals. Thirty-one percent said that they were using a financial planner to help them meet their goals. Twenty-four percent were using family/friends to help them meet their financial goals followed by broker/accountant (19%), computer software (17%), and books (14%). Suppose another researcher takes a similar survey of 600 people to test these results. If 200 people respond that they are going to use a financial planner to help them meet their goals, is this proportion enough evidence to reject the 31% figure generated in the Bruskin/Goldring survey using $\alpha = .10$? If 130 respond that they are going to use family/friends to help them meet their financial goals, is this result enough evidence to declare that the proportion is significantly lower than Bruskin/Goldring's figure of .24 if $\alpha = .05$?

9.25  Eighteen percent of U.S.-based multinational companies provide an allowance for personal long-distance calls for executives living overseas, according to the Institute for International Human Resources and the National Foreign Trade Council. Suppose a researcher thinks that U.S.-based multinational companies are having a more difficult time recruiting executives to live overseas and that an increasing number of these companies are providing an allowance for personal long-distance calls to these executives to ease the burden of living away from home. To test this hypothesis, a new study is conducted by contacting 376 multinational companies. Twenty-two percent of these surveyed companies are providing an allowance for personal long-distance calls to executives living overseas. Does the test show enough evidence to declare that a significantly higher proportion of multinational companies provide a long-distance call allowance? Let $\alpha = .01$.

9.26  A large manufacturing company investigated the service it received from suppliers and discovered that, in the past, 32% of all materials shipments were received late. However, the company recently installed a just-in-time system in which suppliers are linked more closely to the manufacturing process. A random sample of 118 deliveries since the just-in-time system was installed reveals that 22 deliveries were late. Use this sample information to test whether the proportion of late deliveries was reduced significantly. Let $\alpha = .05$.

9.27  Where do CFOs get their money news? According to Robert Half International, 47% get their money news from newspapers, 15% get it from communication/colleagues, 12% get it from television, 11% from the Internet, 9% from magazines, 5% from radio, and 1% don't know. Suppose a researcher wants to test these results. She randomly samples 67 CFOs and finds that 40 of them get their money news from newspapers. Does the test show enough evidence to reject the findings of Robert Half International? Use $\alpha = .05$.

## 9.5 TESTING HYPOTHESES ABOUT A VARIANCE

At times a researcher needs to test hypotheses about a population variance. For example, in the area of statistical quality control, manufacturers try to produce equipment and parts that are consistent in measurement. Suppose a company produces industrial wire that is specified to be a particular thickness. Because of the production process, the thickness of the wire will vary slightly from one end to the other and from lot to lot and batch to batch. Even if the average thickness of the wire as measured from lot to lot is on specification, the variance of the measurements might be too great to be acceptable. In other words, on the average the wire is the correct thickness, but some portions of the wire might be too thin and others unacceptably thick. By conducting hypothesis tests for the variance of the thickness measurements, the quality control people can monitor for variations in the process that are too great.

The procedure for testing hypotheses about a population variance is similar to the techniques presented in Chapter 8 for estimating a population variance from the sample variance. Formula (9.5) used to conduct these tests assumes a normally distributed population.

| FORMULA FOR TESTING HYPOTHESES ABOUT A POPULATION VARIANCE (9.5) | $\chi^2 = \dfrac{(n-1)s^2}{\sigma^2}$ <br> $\mathrm{df} = n-1$ |
|---|---|

**Note**: *As was mentioned in Chapter 8, the chi-square test of a population variance is extremely sensitive to violations of the assumption that the population is normally distributed.*

As an example, a manufacturing firm has been working diligently to implement a just-in-time inventory system for its production line. The final product requires the installation of a pneumatic tube at a particular station on the assembly line. With the just-in-time inventory system, the company's goal is to minimize the number of pneumatic tubes that are piled up at the station waiting to be installed. Ideally, the tubes would arrive just as the operator needs them. However, because of the supplier and the variables involved in getting the tubes to the line, most of the time there will be some buildup of tube inventory. The company expects that, on the average, about 20 pneumatic tubes will be at the station. However, the production superintendent does not want the variance of this inventory to be greater than 4. On a given day, the number of pneumatic tubes piled up at the workstation is determined eight different times and the following numbers of tubes are recorded.

$$23 \quad 17 \quad 20 \quad 29 \quad 21 \quad 14 \quad 19 \quad 24$$

Using these sample data, we can test to determine whether the variance is greater than 4. The hypothesis test is one-tailed. Assume the number of tubes is normally distributed. The null hypothesis is that the variance is acceptable with no problems—the variance is equal to 4. The alternative hypothesis is that the variance is greater than 4.

$$H_0: \sigma^2 = 4$$

$$H_a: \sigma^2 > 4$$

Suppose alpha is .05. Because the sample size is eight, the degrees of freedom for the critical table chi-square value are $8 - 1 = 7$. Using Table A.8, we find the critical chi-square value.

$$\chi^2_{.05, 7} = 14.0671$$

Because the alternative hypothesis is greater than 4, the rejection region is in the upper tail of the chi-square distribution. The sample variance is calculated from the sample data to be

$$s^2 = 20.9821$$

The observed chi-square value is calculated as

$$\chi^2 = \frac{(8-1)(20.9821)}{4} = 36.72$$

Because this observed chi-square value, $\chi^2 = 36.72$, is greater than the critical chi-square table value, $\chi^2_{.05, 7} = 14.0671$, the decision is to reject the null hypothesis. On the basis of this sample of eight data measurements, the population variance of inventory at this workstation is greater than 4. Company production personnel and managers might want to investigate further to determine whether they can find a cause for this unacceptable variance. Figure 9.17 shows a chi-square distribution with the critical value, the rejection region, the nonrejection region, the value of $\alpha$, and the observed chi-square value.

Using Excel, the *p*-value of the observed chi-square, 36.72, is determined to be .0000053. Because this value is less than $\alpha = .05$, the conclusion is to reject the null hypothesis using the *p*-value. In fact, using this *p*-value, the null hypothesis could be rejected for

$$\alpha = .00001$$

---

**FIGURE 9.17**

Hypothesis Test Distribution for Pneumatic Tube Example

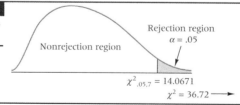

Nonrejection region

Rejection region
$\alpha = .05$

$\chi^2_{.05,7} = 14.0671$

$\chi^2 = 36.72 \longrightarrow$

---

This null hypothesis can also be tested by the critical value method. Instead of solving for an observed value of chi-square, the critical chi-square value for alpha is inserted into formula (9.5) along with the hypothesized value of $\sigma^2$ and the degrees of freedom $(n-1)$. Solving for $s^2$ yields a critical sample variance value, $s_c^2$.

$$\chi_c^2 = \frac{(n-1)s_c^2}{\sigma^2}$$

$$s_c^2 = \frac{\chi_c^2 \cdot \sigma^2}{(n-1)} = \frac{(14.0671)(4)}{7} = 8.038$$

The critical value of the sample variance is $s_C^2 = 8.038$. Because the observed sample variance actually was 20.9821, which is larger than the critical variance, the null hypothesis is rejected.

---

**DEMONSTRATION PROBLEM 9.4**

A small business has 37 employees. Because of the uncertain demand for its product, the company usually pays overtime on any given week. The company assumed that about 50 total hours of overtime per week is required and that the variance on this figure is about 25. Company officials want to know whether the variance of overtime hours has changed. Given here is a sample of 16 weeks of overtime data (in hours per week). Assume hours of overtime are normally distributed. Use these data to test the null hypothesis that the variance of overtime data is 25. Let $\alpha = .10$.

| | | | |
|---|---|---|---|
| 57 | 56 | 52 | 44 |
| 46 | 53 | 44 | 44 |
| 48 | 51 | 55 | 48 |
| 63 | 53 | 51 | 50 |

**Solution**

**H**YPOTHESIZE:

STEP 1. This test is a two-tailed test. The null and alternative hypotheses are

$$H_0: \sigma^2 = 25$$
$$H_a: \sigma^2 \neq 25$$

**T**EST:

STEP 2. The test statistic is

$$\chi^2 = \frac{(n-1)s^2}{\sigma^2}$$

STEP 3. Because this test is two-tailed, $\alpha = .10$ must be split: $\alpha/2 = .05$.

STEP 4. The degrees of freedom are $16 - 1 = 15$. The two critical chi-square values are

$$\chi_{(1-.05),15}^2 = \chi_{.95,15}^2 = 7.26094$$

$$\chi_{.05,15}^2 = 24.9958$$

The decision rule is to reject the null hypothesis if the observed value of the test statistic is less than 7.26094 or greater than 24.9958.

STEP 5. The data are as listed previously.

STEP 6. The sample variance is

$$s^2 = 28.1$$

The observed chi-square value is calculated as

$$\chi^2 = \frac{(n-1)s^2}{\sigma^2} = \frac{(15)(28.1)}{25} = 16.86$$

**A**CTION:

STEP 7. This observed chi-square value is in the nonrejection region because $\chi_{.95,15}^2 = 7.26094 < \chi_{observed}^2 = 16.86 < \chi_{.05,15}^2 = 24.9958$. The company fails to reject the null hypothesis. The population variance of overtime hours per week is 25.

BUSINESS IMPLICATIONS:

STEP 8. This result indicates to the company managers that the variance of weekly overtime hours is about what they expected.

## 9.5 PROBLEMS

9.28 Test each of the following hypotheses by using the given information. Assume the populations are normally distributed.

a. $H_0: \sigma^2 = 20$
$H_a: \sigma^2 > 20$
$\alpha = .05, n = 15, s^2 = 32$

b. $H_0: \sigma^2 = 8.5$
$H_a: \sigma^2 \neq 8.5$
$\alpha = .10, n = 22, s^2 = 17$

c. $H_0: \sigma^2 = 45$
$H_a: \sigma^2 < 45$
$\alpha = .01, n = 8, s = 4.12$

d. $H_0: \sigma^2 = 5$
$H_a: \sigma^2 \neq 5$
$\alpha = .05, n = 11, s^2 = 1.2$

9.29 Previous experience shows the variance of a given process to be 14. Researchers are testing to determine whether this value has changed. They gather the following dozen measurements of the process. Use these data and $\alpha = .05$ to test the null hypothesis about the variance. Assume the measurements are normally distributed.

| 52 | 44 | 51 | 58 | 48 | 49 |
|----|----|----|----|----|----|
| 38 | 49 | 50 | 42 | 55 | 51 |

9.30 A manufacturing company produces bearings. One line of bearings is specified to be 1.64 centimeters (cm) in diameter. A major customer requires that the variance of the bearings be no more than .001 cm². The producer is required to test the bearings before they are shipped, and so the diameters of 16 bearings are measured with a precise instrument, resulting in the following values. Assume bearing diameters are normally distributed. Use the data and $\alpha = .01$ to test the data to determine whether the population of these bearings is to be rejected because of too high a variance.

| 1.69 | 1.62 | 1.63 | 1.70 |
|------|------|------|------|
| 1.66 | 1.63 | 1.65 | 1.71 |
| 1.64 | 1.69 | 1.57 | 1.64 |
| 1.59 | 1.66 | 1.63 | 1.65 |

9.31 A savings and loan averages about $100,000 in deposits per week. However, because of the way pay periods fall, seasonality, and erratic fluctuations in the local economy, deposits are subject to a wide variability. In the past, the variance for weekly deposits has been about $199,996,164. In terms that make more sense to managers, the standard deviation of weekly deposits has been $14,142. Shown here are data from a random sample of 13 weekly deposits for a recent period. Assume weekly deposits are normally distributed. Use these data and $\alpha = .10$ to test to determine whether the variance for weekly deposits has changed.

| $93,000 | $135,000 | $112,000 |
|---------|----------|----------|
| 68,000 | 46,000 | 104,000 |
| 128,000 | 143,000 | 131,000 |
| 104,000 | 96,000 | 71,000 |
| 87,000 | | |

9.32 A company produces industrial wiring. One batch of wiring is specified to be 2.16 centimeters (cm) thick. A company inspects the wiring in seven locations and determines that, on the average, the wiring is about 2.16 cm thick. However, the measurements vary. It is unacceptable for the variance of the wiring to be more than .04 cm$^2$. The standard deviation of the seven measurements on this batch of wiring is .34 cm. Use $\alpha = .01$ to determine whether the variance on the sample wiring is too great to meet specifications. Assume wiring thickness is normally distributed.

## 9.6 SOLVING FOR TYPE II ERRORS

If a researcher reaches the statistical conclusion not to reject the null hypothesis, he makes either a correct decision or a Type II error. If the null hypothesis is true, the researcher makes a correct decision. If the null hypothesis is false, a Type II error results.

In business, failure to reject the null hypothesis may mean staying with the status quo, not implementing a new process, or not making adjustments. If a new process, product, theory, or adjustment is not significantly better than what is currently accepted practice, the decision maker makes a correct decision. However, if the new process, product, theory, or adjustment would significantly improve sales, the business climate, costs, or morale, the decision maker makes an error in judgment (Type II). In business, Type II errors can translate to lost opportunities, poor product quality (as a result of failure to discern a problem in the process), or failure to react to the marketplace. Sometimes the ability to react to changes, new developments, or new opportunities is what keeps a business moving and growing. The Type II error plays an important role in business statistical decision making.

Determining the probability of committing a Type II error is more complex than finding the probability of committing a Type I error. The probability of committing a Type I error either is given in a problem or is stated by the researcher before proceeding with the study. A Type II error, $\beta$, varies with possible values of the alternative parameter. For example, suppose a researcher is conducting a statistical test on the following hypotheses.

$$H_0: \mu = 12 \text{ ounces}$$

$$H_a: \mu < 12 \text{ ounces}$$

A Type II error can be committed only when the researcher fails to reject the null hypothesis and the null hypothesis is false. In these hypotheses, if the null hypothesis, $\mu = 12$ ounces, is false, what is the true value for the population mean? Is the mean really 11.99 or 11.90 or 11.5 or 10 ounces? For each of these possible values of the population mean, the researcher can compute the probability of committing a Type II error. Often, when the null hypothesis is false, the value of the alternative mean is unknown, so the researcher will compute the probability of committing Type II errors for several possible values. How can the probability of committing a Type II error be computed for a specific alternative value of the mean?

Suppose that, in testing the preceding hypotheses, a sample of 60 cans of beverage yields a sample mean of 11.985 ounces. Assume that the population standard deviation is 0.10 ounces. From $\alpha = .05$ and a one-tailed test, the table $z_{.05}$ value is $-1.645$. The observed $z$ value from sample data is

$$z = \frac{11.985 - 12.00}{\frac{.10}{\sqrt{60}}} = -1.16$$

From this observed value of $z$, the researcher determines not to reject the null hypothesis. By not rejecting the null hypothesis, the researcher either makes a correct decision or commits a Type II error. What is the probability of committing a Type II error in this problem if the population mean actually is 11.99?

The first step in determining the probability of a Type II error is to calculate a critical value for the sample mean, $\bar{x}_c$. In testing the null hypothesis by the critical value method, this value is used as the cutoff for the nonrejection region. For any sample mean obtained that is less than $\bar{x}_c$ (or greater for an upper-tail rejection region), the null hypothesis is rejected. Any sample mean greater than $\bar{x}_c$ (or less for an upper-tail rejection region) causes the researcher to fail to reject the null hypothesis. Solving for the critical value of the mean gives

$$z_c = \frac{\bar{x}_c - \mu}{\frac{\sigma}{\sqrt{n}}}$$

$$-1.645 = \frac{\bar{x}_c - 12}{\frac{.10}{\sqrt{60}}}$$

$$\bar{x}_c = 11.979$$

Figure 9.18(a) shows the distribution of values when the null hypothesis is true. It contains a critical value of the mean, $\bar{x}_c = 11.979$ ounces, below which the null hypothesis will be rejected. Figure 9.18(b) shows the distribution when the alternative mean, $\mu_1 = 11.99$ ounces, is true. How often will the business researcher fail to reject the top distribution as true when, in reality, the bottom distribution is true? If the null hypothesis is false, the researcher will fail to reject the null hypotheses whenever $\bar{x}$ is in the nonrejection region, $\bar{x}_c \geq 11.979$ ounces. If $\mu$ actually equals 11.99 ounces, what is the probability of failing to reject $\mu = 12$ ounces when 11.979 ounces is the critical value? The business researcher calculates this probability by extending the critical value ($\bar{x}_c = 11.979$ ounces) from distribution (a) to distribution (b) and solving for the area to the right of $\bar{x}_c = 11.979$.

$$z_1 = \frac{\bar{x}_c - \mu_1}{\frac{\sigma}{\sqrt{n}}} = \frac{11.979 - 11.99}{\frac{.10}{\sqrt{60}}} = -0.85$$

**FIGURE 9.18**

Type II Error for Soft Drink Example with Alternative Mean = 11.99 Ounces

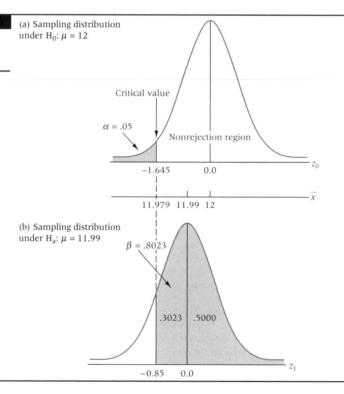

(a) Sampling distribution under $H_0$: $\mu = 12$

Critical value

$\alpha = .05$

Nonrejection region

−1.645          0.0                    $z_0$

11.979  11.99  12                     $\bar{x}$

(b) Sampling distribution under $H_a$: $\mu = 11.99$

$\beta = .8023$

.3023  .5000

−0.85     0.0                          $z_1$

This value of $z$ yields an area of .3023. The probability of committing a Type II error is all the area to the right of $\bar{x}_c = 11.979$ in distribution (b), or $.3023 + .5000 = .8023$. Hence there is an 80.23% chance of committing a Type II error if the alternative mean is 11.99 ounces.

| DEMONSTRATION PROBLEM 9.5 | Recompute the probability of committing a Type II error for the soft drink example if the alternative mean is 11.96 ounces. |

**Solution**

Everything in distribution (a) of Figure 9.18 stays the same. The null hypothesized mean is still 12 ounces, the critical value is still 11.979 ounces, and $n = 60$. However, distribution (b) of Figure 9.18 changes with $\mu_1 = 11.96$ ounces, as the following diagram shows.

The $z$ formula used to solve for the area of distribution (b), $\mu_1 = 11.96$, to the right of 11.979 is

$$z_1 = \frac{\bar{x}_c - \mu_1}{\frac{\sigma}{\sqrt{n}}} = \frac{11.979 - 11.96}{\frac{.10}{\sqrt{60}}} = 1.47$$

From Table A.5, only .0708 of the area is to the right of the critical value. Thus the probability of committing a Type II error is only .0708, as illustrated in the following diagram.

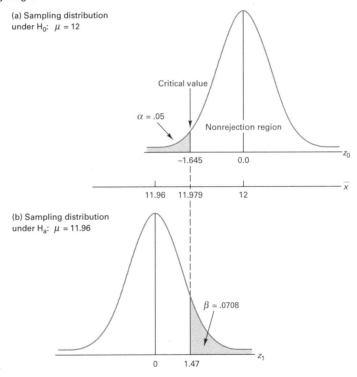

(a) Sampling distribution under $H_0$: $\mu = 12$

Critical value

$\alpha = .05$

Nonrejection region

$-1.645$    0.0    $z_0$

11.96   11.979   12   $\bar{x}$

(b) Sampling distribution under $H_a$: $\mu = 11.96$

$\beta = .0708$

0   1.47   $z_1$

| DEMONSTRATION PROBLEM 9.6 | Suppose you are conducting a two-tailed hypothesis test of proportions. The null hypothesis is that the population proportion is .40. The alternative hypothesis is that the population proportion is not .40. A random sample of 250 produces a sample proportion of .44. With alpha of .05, the table $z$ value for $\alpha/2$ is 1.96. The observed $z$ from the sample information is |

$$z = \frac{\hat{p} - p}{\sqrt{\dfrac{p \cdot q}{n}}} = \frac{.44 - .40}{.031} = 1.29$$

Thus the null hypothesis is not rejected. Either a correct decision is made or a Type II error is committed. Suppose the alternative population proportion really is .36. What is the probability of committing a Type II error?

**Solution**

Solve for the critical value of the proportion.

$$z_c = \frac{\hat{p}_c - p}{\sqrt{\dfrac{p \cdot q}{n}}}$$

$$\pm 1.96 = \frac{\hat{p}_c - .40}{\sqrt{\dfrac{(.40)(.60)}{250}}}$$

$$\hat{p}_c = .40 \pm .06$$

The critical values are .34 on the lower end and .46 on the upper end. The alternative population proportion is .36. The following diagram illustrates these results and the remainder of the solution to this problem.

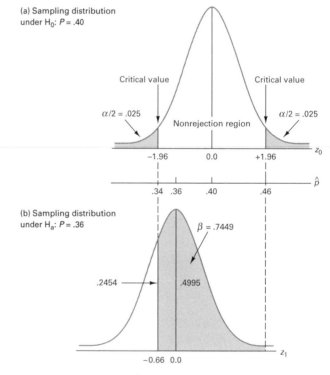

(a) Sampling distribution under $H_0$: $P = .40$

(b) Sampling distribution under $H_a$: $P = .36$

Solving for the area between $\hat{p}_c = .34$ and $p_1 = .36$ yields

$$z_1 = \frac{.34 - .36}{\sqrt{\dfrac{(.36)(.64)}{250}}} = -0.66$$

The area associated with $z_1 = -0.66$ is .2454.

The area between .36 and .46 of the sampling distribution under $H_a$: $p = .36$ (graph (b)) can be solved for by using the following z value.

$$z = \frac{.46 - .36}{\sqrt{\frac{(.36)(.64)}{250}}} = 3.29$$

The area from Table A.5 associated with $z = 3.29$ is .4995. Combining this value with the .2454 obtained from the left side of the distribution in graph (b) yields the total probability of committing a Type II error:

$$.2454 + .4995 = .7449$$

With two-tailed tests, both tails of the distribution contain rejection regions. The area between the two tails is the nonrejection region and the region where Type II errors can occur. If the alternative hypothesis is true, the area of the sampling distribution under $H_a$ between the locations where the critical values from $H_0$ are located is $\beta$. In theory, both tails of the sampling distribution under $H_a$ would be non-$\beta$ area. However, in this problem, the right critical value is so far away from the alternative proportion ($p_1 = .36$) that the area between the right critical value and the alternative proportion is near .5000 (.4995) and virtually no area falls in the upper right tail of the distribution (.0005).

## Some Observations About Type II Errors

Type II errors are committed only when the researcher fails to reject the null hypothesis but the alternative hypothesis is true. If the alternative mean or proportion is close to the hypothesized value, the probability of committing a Type II error is high. If the alternative value is relatively far away from the hypothesized value, as in the problem with $\mu = 12$ ounces and $\mu_a = 11.96$ ounces, the probability of committing a Type II error is small. The implication is that when a value is being tested as a null hypothesis against a true alternative value that is relatively far away, the sample statistic obtained is likely to show clearly which hypothesis is true. For example, suppose a researcher is testing to determine whether a company really is filling 2-liter bottles of cola with an average of 2 liters. If the company decides to underfill the bottles by filling them with only 1 liter, a sample of 50 bottles is likely to average a quantity near the 1-liter fill rather than near the 2-liter fill. Committing a Type II error is highly unlikely. Even a customer probably could see by looking at the bottles on the shelf that they are underfilled. However, if the company fills 2-liter bottles with 1.99 liters, the bottles are close in fill volume to those filled with 2.00 liters. In this case, the probability of committing a Type II error is much greater. A customer probably could not catch the underfill just by looking.

In general, if the alternative value is relatively far from the hypothesized value, the probability of committing a Type II error is smaller than it is when the alternative value is close to the hypothesized value. The probability of committing a Type II error decreases as alternative values of the hypothesized parameter move farther away from the hypothesized value. This situation is shown graphically in operating characteristic curves and power curves.

## Operating Characteristic and Power Curves

Because the probability of committing a Type II error changes for each different value of the alternative parameter, it is best in managerial decision making to examine a series of possible alternative values. For example, Table 9.2 shows the probabilities of committing a Type II error ($\beta$) for several different possible alternative means for the soft drink example discussed in Demonstration Problem 9.5, in which the null hypothesis was $H_0$: $\mu = 12$ ounces and $\alpha = .05$.

As previously mentioned, power is the probability of rejecting the null hypothesis when it is false and represents the correct decision of selecting the alternative hypothesis when it is true. Power is equal to $1 - \beta$. Note that Table 9.2 also contains the power values for the alternative means and that the $\beta$ and power probabilities sum to 1 in each case.

These values can be displayed graphically as shown in Figures 9.19 and 9.20. Figure 9.19 is a MINITAB-generated **operating characteristic (OC) curve** *constructed by plotting the $\beta$ values against the various values of the alternative hypothesis.* Notice that when the alternative means are near the value of the null hypothesis, $\mu = 12$, the probability of committing a Type II error is high because it is difficult to discriminate between a distribution with a mean of 12 and a distribution with a mean of 11.999. However, as the values of the alternative means move away from the hypothesized value, $\mu = 12$, the values of $\beta$ drop. This visual representation underscores the notion that it is easier to discriminate between a distribution with $\mu = 12$ and a distribution with $\mu = 11.95$ than between distributions with $\mu = 12$ and $\mu = 11.999$.

Figure 9.20 is an Excel **power curve** constructed by *plotting the power values $(1 - \beta)$ against the various values of the alternative hypotheses.* Note that the power increases as the alternative mean moves away from the value of $\mu$ in the null hypotheses. This relationship makes sense. As the alternative mean moves farther and farther away from the null hypothesized mean, a correct decision to reject the null hypothesis becomes more likely.

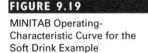

**TABLE 9.2**

$\beta$ Values and Power Values for the Soft Drink Example

| Alternative Mean | Probability of Committing A Type II Error, $\beta$ | Power |
|---|---|---|
| $\mu_a = 11.999$ | .94 | .06 |
| $\mu_a = 11.995$ | .89 | .11 |
| $\mu_a = 11.99$ | .80 | .20 |
| $\mu_a = 11.98$ | .53 | .47 |
| $\mu_a = 11.97$ | .24 | .76 |
| $\mu_a = 11.96$ | .07 | .93 |
| $\mu_a = 11.95$ | .01 | .99 |

**FIGURE 9.19**

MINITAB Operating-Characteristic Curve for the Soft Drink Example

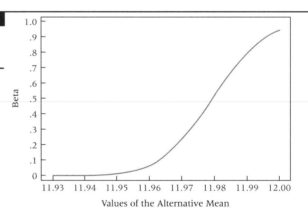

**FIGURE 9.20**

Excel Power Curve for the Soft Drink Example

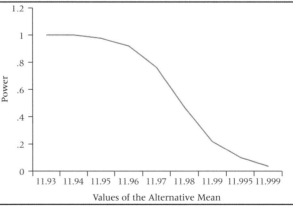

## Effect of Increasing Sample Size on the Rejection Limits

The size of the sample affects the location of the rejection limits. Consider the soft drink example in which we were testing the following hypotheses.

$$H_0: \mu = 12.00 \text{ ounces}$$

$$H_a: \mu < 12.00 \text{ ounces}$$

Sample size was 60 ($n = 60$) and the standard deviation was .10 ($\sigma = .10$). With $\alpha = .05$, the critical value of the test statistic was $z_{.05} = -1.645$. From this information, a critical raw score value was computed:

$$z_c = \frac{\bar{x}_c - \mu}{\frac{\sigma}{\sqrt{n}}}$$

$$-1.645 = \frac{\bar{x}_c - 12}{\frac{.10}{\sqrt{60}}}$$

$$\bar{x}_c = 11.979$$

Any sample mean obtained in the hypothesis-testing process that is less than 11.979 will result in a decision to reject the null hypothesis.

Suppose the sample size is increased to 100. The critical raw score value is

$$-1.645 = \frac{\bar{x}_c - 12}{\frac{.10}{\sqrt{100}}}$$

$$\bar{x}_c = 11.984$$

**FIGURE 9.21**

Type II Error for Soft Drink Example with *n* Increased to 100

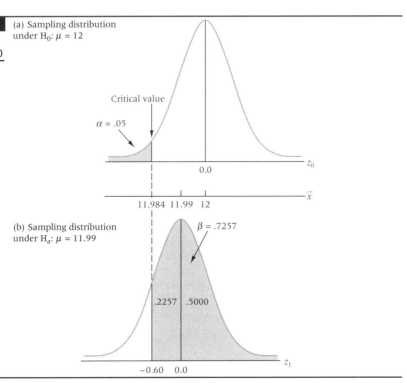

(a) Sampling distribution under $H_0: \mu = 12$

(b) Sampling distribution under $H_a: \mu = 11.99$

Notice that the critical raw score value is nearer to the hypothesized value ($\mu = 12$) for the larger sample size than it was for a sample size of 60. Because $n$ is in the denominator of the standard error of the mean ($\sigma/\sqrt{n}$), an increase in $n$ results in a decrease in the standard error of the mean, which when multiplied by the critical value of the test statistic ($z_{\alpha/2}$) results in a critical raw score that is closer to the hypothesized value. For $n = 500$, the critical raw score value for this problem is 11.993.

Increased sample size not only affects the distance of the critical raw score value from the hypothesized value of the distribution, but also can result in reducing $\beta$ for a given value of $\alpha$. Examine Figure 9.18. Note that the critical raw score value is 11.979 with alpha equal to .05 for $n = 60$. The value of $\beta$ for an alternative mean of 11.99 is .8023. Suppose the sample size is 100. The critical raw score value (already solved) is 11.984. The value of $\beta$ is now .7257. The computation is

$$z = \frac{11.984 - 11.99}{\dfrac{.10}{\sqrt{100}}} = -0.60$$

The area under the standard normal curve for $z = -0.60$ is .2257. Adding .2257 + .5000 (from the right half of the $H_a$ sampling distribution) results in a $\beta$ of .7257. Figure 9.21 shows the sampling distributions with $\alpha$ and $\beta$ for this problem. In addition, by increasing sample size a business researcher could reduce alpha without necessarily increasing beta. It is possible to reduce the probabilities of committing Type I and Type II errors simultaneously by increasing sample size.

## 9.6 PROBLEMS

9.33  Suppose a null hypothesis is that the population mean is greater than or equal to 100. Suppose further that a random sample of 48 items is taken and the population standard deviation is 14. For each of the following $\alpha$ values, compute the probability of committing a Type II error if the population mean actually is 99.

   a.  $\alpha = .10$

   b.  $\alpha = .05$

   c.  $\alpha = .01$

   d.  Based on the answers to parts (a), (b), and (c), what happens to the value of $\beta$ as $\alpha$ gets smaller?

9.34  For Problem 9.33, use $\alpha = .05$ and solve for the probability of committing a Type II error for the following possible true alternative means.

   a.  $\mu_a = 98.5$

   b.  $\mu_a = 98$

   c.  $\mu_a = 97$

   d.  $\mu_a = 96$

   e.  What happens to the probability of committing a Type II error as the alternative value of the mean gets farther from the null hypothesized value of 100?

9.35  Suppose a hypothesis states that the mean is exactly 50. If a random sample of 35 items is taken to test this hypothesis, what is the value of $\beta$ if the population standard deviation is 7 and the alternative mean is 53? Use $\alpha = .01$.

9.36  An alternative hypothesis is that $p < .65$. To test this hypothesis, a random sample of size 360 is taken. What is the probability of committing a Type II error if $\alpha = .05$ and the alternative proportion is as follows?

   a.  $p_a = .60$

   b.  $p_a = .55$

   c.  $p_a = .50$

9.37  The New York Stock Exchange recently reported that the average age of a female shareholder is 44 years. A broker in Chicago wants to know whether this figure is accurate for the female shareholders in Chicago. The broker secures a master list of shareholders in Chicago and takes a random sample of 58 women. Suppose the average age for shareholders in the sample is 45.1 years, with a population standard deviation of 8.7 years. Test to determine whether the broker's sample data differ significantly enough from the 44-years figure released by the New York Stock Exchange to declare that Chicago female shareholders are different in age from female shareholders in general. Use $\alpha = .05$. If no significant difference is noted, what is the broker's probability of committing a Type II error if the average age of a female Chicago shareholder is actually 45 years? 46 years? 47 years? 48 years? Construct an OC curve for these data. Construct a power curve for these data.

9.38 A Harris poll was taken to determine which of 13 major industries are doing a good job of serving their customers. Among the industries rated most highly by Americans for serving their customers were computer hardware and software companies, car manufacturers, and airlines. The industries rated lowest on serving their customers were tobacco companies, managed care providers, and health insurance companies. Seventy-one percent of those polled responded that airlines are doing a good job serving their customers. Suppose due to rising ticket prices, a researcher feels that this figure is now too high. He takes a poll of 463 Americans, and 324 say that the airlines are doing a good job of serving their customers. Does the survey show enough evidence to declare that the proportion of Americans saying that the airlines are doing a good job of serving their customers is significantly lower than stated in the Harris poll? Let alpha equal 10. If the researcher fails to reject the null hypothesis and if the figure is actually 69% now, what is the probability of committing a Type II error? What is the probability of committing a Type II error if the figure is really 66%? 60%?

## Business Referrals

In the Decision Dilemma, many data facts are reported from numerous surveys about consumers seeking advice from others before purchasing items or services. Most of the statistics are stated as though they are facts about the population. For example, one study reports that 46% of all consumers seek advice when selecting a physician. Suppose a business researcher believes that this figure is not true, has changed over time, is not true for a particular region of the country, or is different for a particular type of medicine. Using hypothesis techniques presented in Section 9.4 of this chapter, this figure (46%) can be tested as a population proportion. Because the figures presented in the Decision Dilemma have been published and widely disseminated, the researcher who wants to test them would likely place these figures in the null hypothesis (e.g., $H_0: p = .46$), gather a random sample from whichever population is to be studied, and conduct a hypothesis test.

It was reported by Roper Starch Worldwide that influentials make recommendations about office equipment an average of 5.8 times per year. These and any of the other means reported in this study could be tested. The researcher would need to scientifically identify influentials in the population and randomly select a sample. A research mechanism could be set up whereby the number of referrals by each influential could be recorded for a year and averaged thereby producing a sample mean and a sample standard deviation. Using a selected value of alpha, the sample mean could be statistically tested against the population mean (in this case, $H_0$: $\mu = 5.8$). The probability of falsely rejecting a true null would be alpha. If the null was actually false ($\mu \neq 5.8$), the probability ($\beta$) of failing to reject the false null hypothesis would depend upon what the true number of mean referrals per year was for influentials on office equipment.

If a researcher has theories on influentials and these research theories can be stated as statistical hypotheses, the theory should be formulated as an alternate hypothesis; and the null hypothesis should be that the theory is not true. Samples are randomly selected. If the statistic of choice is a mean, then a $z$ test or $t$ test for a population mean should be used in the analysis dependent on whether or not the population standard deviation is known or unknown. In many studies, the sample standard deviation is used in the analysis instead of the unknown population standard deviation. In these cases, a $t$ test should be used when the assumption that the population data are normally distributed can be made. If the statistic is a proportion, then the $z$ test for a population proportion is appropriate. Techniques presented in Chapter 8, Section 8.5, can be used to assist the researcher in determining how large a sample to take. Using alpha, a critical table $z$ value can be determined and inserted into the sample size determination formulas to determine sample size.

## ETHICAL CONSIDERATIONS

The process of hypothesis testing encompasses several areas that could potentially lead to unethical activity, beginning with the null and alternative hypotheses. In the hypothesis-testing approach, the preliminary assumption is that the null hypothesis is true. If a researcher has a new theory or idea that he or she is attempting to prove, it is somewhat unethical to express that theory or idea as the null hypothesis. In doing so, the researcher is assuming that what he or she is trying to prove is true and the burden of proof is on the data to reject this idea or theory. Statistical hypothesis testing is set up so that the new idea or theory is not assumed to be true; the burden of proof is on the researcher to demonstrate through the data and the rejection of the null hypothesis that the new idea or theory is true. The researcher must take great care not to assume that what he or she is attempting to prove is true.

The value of alpha should be established before the experiment is undertaken. Too many researchers "data snoop"—that is, they look at the data and the results of the data analysis and then decide what alpha could be used in order to reject the null hypothesis.

Hypothesis testing through random sampling opens up many possible unethical situations that can occur in sampling, such as identifying a frame that is favorable to the outcome the researcher is seeking or using nonrandom sampling techniques to test hypotheses. In addition, the researcher should be careful to use the proper test statistic for tests of a population mean, particularly when $\sigma$ is unknown. If $t$ tests are used, or in testing a population variance, the researcher should be careful to apply the techniques only when it can be shown with some confidence that the population is normally distributed. The chi-square test of a population variance has been shown to be extremely sensitive to the assumption that the population is normally distributed. Unethical usage of this technique occurs when the statistician does not carefully check the population distribution shape for compliance with this assumption. Failure to do so can easily result in the reporting of spurious conclusions.

It can be unethical from a business decision-making point of view to knowingly use the notion of statistical significance to claim business significance when the results are not substantive. Therefore, it is unethical to intentionally attempt to mislead the business user by inappropriately using the word *significance*.

## SUMMARY

Three types of hypotheses were presented in this chapter: research hypotheses, statistical hypotheses, and substantive hypotheses. Research hypotheses are statements of what the researcher believes will be the outcome of an experiment or study. In order to test hypotheses, business researchers formulate their research hypotheses into statistical hypotheses. All statistical hypotheses consist of two parts, a null hypothesis and an alternative hypothesis. The null and alternative hypotheses are structured so that either one or the other is true but not both. In testing hypotheses, the researcher assumes that the null hypothesis is true. By examining the sampled data, the researcher either rejects or does not reject the null hypothesis. If the sample data are significantly in opposition to the null hypothesis, the researcher rejects the null hypothesis and accepts the alternative hypothesis by default.

Hypothesis tests can be one-tailed or two-tailed. Two-tailed tests always utilize = and ≠ in the null and alternative hypotheses. These tests are nondirectional in that significant deviations from the hypothesized value that are either greater than or less than the value are in rejection regions. The one-tailed test is directional, and the alternative hypothesis contains < or > signs. In these tests, only one end or tail of the distribution contains a rejection region. In a one-tailed test, the researcher is interested only in deviations from the hypothesized value that are either greater than or less than the value but not both.

Not all statistically significant outcomes of studies are important business outcomes. A substantive result is when the outcome of a statistical study produces results that are important to the decision maker.

When a business researcher reaches a decision about the null hypothesis, the researcher either makes a correct decision or an error. If the null hypothesis is true, the researcher can make a Type I error by rejecting the null hypothesis. The probability of making a Type I error is alpha ($\alpha$). Alpha is usually set by the researcher when establishing the hypotheses. Another expression sometimes used for the value of $\alpha$ is level of significance.

If the null hypothesis is false and the researcher fails to reject it, a Type II error is committed. Beta ($\beta$) is the probability of committing a Type II error. Type II errors must be computed from the hypothesized value of the parameter, $\alpha$, and a specific alternative value of the parameter being examined. As many possible Type II errors in a problem exist as there are possible alternative statistical values.

If a null hypothesis is true and the researcher fails to reject it, no error is committed, and the researcher makes a correct decision. Similarly, if a null hypothesis is false and it is rejected, no error is committed. Power $(1 - \beta)$ is the probability of a statistical test rejecting the null hypothesis when the null hypothesis is false.

An operating characteristic (OC) curve is a graphical depiction of values of $\beta$ that can occur as various values of the alternative hypothesis are explored. This graph can be studied to determine what happens to $\beta$ as one moves away from the value of the null hypothesis. A power curve is used in conjunction with an operating characteristic curve. The power curve is a graphical depiction of the values of power as various values of the alternative hypothesis are examined. The researcher can view the increase in power as values of the alternative hypothesis diverge from the value of the null hypothesis.

Included in this chapter were hypothesis tests for a single mean when $\sigma$ is known and when $\sigma$ is unknown, a test of a single population proportion, and a test for a population variance. Three different analytic approaches were presented: (1) standard method, (2) *p*-value, and (3) critical value method.

## KEY TERMS

| | | | |
|---|---|---|---|
| alpha ($\alpha$) | level of significance | operating characteristic | statistical hypothesis |
| alternative hypothesis | nonrejection region | (OC) curve | substantive result |
| beta ($\beta$) | null hypothesis | *p*-value | two-tailed test |
| critical value | observed significance level | power | Type I error |
| critical value method | observed value | power curve | Type II error |
| hypothesis | one-tailed test | rejection region | |
| hypothesis testing | | research hypothesis | |

# FORMULAS

$z$ test for a single mean (9.1)

$$z = \frac{\bar{x} - \mu}{\frac{\sigma}{\sqrt{n}}}$$

Formula to test hypotheses about $\mu$ with a finite population (9.2)

$$z = \frac{\bar{x} - \mu}{\frac{\sigma}{\sqrt{n}} \sqrt{\frac{N-n}{N-1}}}$$

$t$ test for a single mean (9.3)

$$t = \frac{\bar{x} - \mu}{\frac{s}{\sqrt{n}}}$$
$$\text{df} = n - 1$$

$z$ test of a population proportion (9.4)

$$z = \frac{\hat{p} - p}{\sqrt{\frac{p \cdot q}{n}}}$$

Formula for testing hypotheses about a population variance (9.5)

$$\chi^2 = \frac{(n-1)s^2}{\sigma^2}$$
$$\text{df} = n - 1$$

# SUPPLEMENTARY PROBLEMS

## CALCULATING THE STATISTICS

**9.39** Use the information given and the HTAB system to test the hypotheses. Let $\alpha = .01$.

$H_0: \mu = 36$   $H_a: \mu \neq 36$   $n = 63$   $\bar{x} = 38.4$   $\sigma = 5.93$

**9.40** Use the information given and the HTAB system to test the hypotheses. Let $\alpha = .05$. Assume the population is normally distributed.

$H_0: \mu = 7.82$   $H_a: \mu < 7.82$   $n = 17$   $\bar{x} = 17.1$   $s = 1.69$

**9.41** For each of the following problems, test the hypotheses. Incorporate the HTAB system with its eight-step process.

**a.** $H_0: p = .28$   $H_a: p > .28$   $n = 783$   $x = 230$   $\alpha = .10$
**b.** $H_0: p = .61$   $H_a: p \neq .61$   $n = 401$   $\hat{p} = .56$   $\alpha = .05$

**9.42** Test the following hypotheses by using the information given and the HTAB system. Let alpha be .01. Assume the population is normally distributed.

$H_0: \sigma^2 = 15.4$   $H_a: \sigma^2 > 15.4$   $n = 18$   $s^2 = 29.6$

**9.43** Solve for the value of beta in each of the following problems.

**a.** $H_0: \mu = 130$   $H_a: \mu > 130$   $n = 75$   $\sigma = 12$   $\alpha = .01$.
The alternative mean is actually 135.
**b.** $H_0: p = .44$   $H_a: p < .44$   $n = 1095$   $\alpha = .05$.
The alternative proportion is actually .42.

## TESTING YOUR UNDERSTANDING

**9.44** According to a survey by ICR for Vienna Systems, a majority of American households have tried to cut long-distance phone bills. Of those who have tried to cut the bills, 32% have done so by switching long-distance companies. Suppose business researchers believe that this figure may be higher today. To test this theory, a researcher conducts another survey by randomly contacting 80 American households who have tried to cut long-distance phone bills. If 39% of the contacted households say they have tried to cut their long-distance phone bills by switching long-distance companies, is this result enough evidence to state that a significantly higher proportion of American households are trying to cut long-distance phone bills by switching companies? Let $\alpha = .01$.

**9.45** According to Zero Population Growth, the average urban U.S. resident consumes 3.3 pounds of food per day. Is this figure accurate for rural U.S. residents? Suppose 64 rural U.S. residents are identified by a random procedure and their average consumption per day is 3.45 pounds of food. Assume a population variance of 1.31 pounds of food per day. Use a 5% level of significance to determine whether the Zero Population Growth figure for urban U.S. residents also is true for rural U.S. residents on the basis of the sample data.

**9.46** Brokers generally agree that bonds are a better investment during times of low interest rates than during times of high interest rates. A survey of executives during a time of low interest rates showed that 57% of them had some retirement funds invested in bonds. Assume this percentage is constant for bond market investment by executives with retirement funds. Suppose interest rates have risen lately and the proportion of executives with retirement investment money in the bond market may have dropped. To test this idea, a researcher randomly samples 210 executives who have retirement funds. Of these, 93 now have retirement funds invested in bonds. For $\alpha = .10$, does the test show enough evidence to declare that the proportion of executives with retirement fund investments in the bond market is significantly lower than .57?

9.47 Highway engineers in Ohio are painting white stripes on a highway. The stripes are supposed to be approximately 10 feet long. However, because of the machine, the operator, and the motion of the vehicle carrying the equipment, considerable variation occurs among the stripe lengths. Engineers claim that the variance of stripes is not more than 16 inches. Use the sample lengths given here from 12 measured stripes to test the variance claim. Assume stripe length is normally distributed. Let $\alpha = .05$.

**Stripe Lengths in Feet**

| | | | |
|---|---|---|---|
| 10.3 | 9.4 | 9.8 | 10.1 |
| 9.2 | 10.4 | 10.7 | 9.9 |
| 9.3 | 9.8 | 10.5 | 10.4 |

9.48 A computer manufacturer estimates that its line of minicomputers has, on average, 8.4 days of downtime per year. To test this claim, a researcher contacts seven companies that own one of these computers and is allowed to access company computer records. It is determined that, for the sample, the average number of downtime days is 5.6, with a sample standard deviation of 1.3 days. Assuming that number of downtime days is normally distributed, test to determine whether these minicomputers actually average 8.4 days of downtime in the entire population. Let $\alpha = .01$.

9.49 A life insurance salesperson claims the average worker in the city of Cincinnati has no more than $25,000 of personal life insurance. To test this claim, you randomly sample 100 workers in Cincinnati. You find that this sample of workers averages $26,650 of personal life insurance. The population standard deviation is $12,000.

a. Determine whether the test shows enough evidence to reject the null hypothesis posed by the salesperson. Assume the probability of committing a Type I error is .05.

b. If the actual average for this population is $30,000, what is the probability of committing a Type II error?

9.50 A financial analyst has been watching a particular stock for several months. The price of this stock remained fairly stable during this time. In fact, the financial analyst claims that the variance of the price of this stock did not exceed $4 for the entire period. Recently, the market heated up, and the price of this stock appears more volatile. To determine whether it is more volatile, a sample of closing prices of this stock for 8 days is taken randomly. The sample mean price is $36.25, with a sample standard deviation of $7.80. Using a level of significance

of .10, test to determine whether the financial analyst's previous variance figure is now too low. Assume stock prices are normally distributed.

9.51 A study of MBA graduates by Universum for The American Graduate Survey 1999 revealed that MBA graduates have several expectations of prospective employers beyond their base pay. In particular, according to the study 46% expect a performance-related bonus, 46% expect stock options, 42% expect a signing bonus, 28% expect profit sharing, 27% expect extra vacation/personal days, 25% expect tuition reimbursement, 24% expect health benefits, and 19% expect guaranteed annual bonuses. Suppose a study is conducted in an ensuing year to see whether these expectations have changed. If 125 MBA graduates are randomly selected and if 66 expect stock options, does this result provide enough evidence to declare that a significantly higher proportion of MBAs expect stock options? Let $\alpha = .05$. If the proportion really is .50, what is the probability of committing a Type II error?

9.52 Suppose the number of beds filled per day in a medium-sized hospital is normally distributed. A hospital administrator tells the board of directors that, on the average, at least 185 beds are filled on any given day. One of the board members believes this figure is inflated, and she manages to secure a random sample of figures for 16 days. The data are shown here. Use $\alpha = .05$ and the sample data to test whether the hospital administrator's statement is false. Assume the number of filled beds per day is normally distributed in the population.

**Number of Beds Occupied per Day**

| | | | |
|---|---|---|---|
| 173 | 149 | 166 | 180 |
| 189 | 170 | 152 | 194 |
| 177 | 169 | 188 | 160 |
| 199 | 175 | 172 | 187 |

9.53 According to the International Data Corporation, Compaq Computers holds a 16% share of the personal computer market in the United States and a 12.7% share of the worldwide market. Suppose a market researcher believes that Compaq holds a higher share of the market in the southwestern region of the United States. To verify this theory, he randomly selects 428 people who purchased a personal computer in the last month in the southwestern region of the United States. Eighty-four of these purchases were Compaq Computers. Using a 1% level of significance, test the market researcher's theory. What is the probability of making a Type I error? If the market share is really .21 in the southwestern region of the United States, what is the probability of making a Type II error?

9.54 A national publication reported that a college student living away from home spends, on average, no more than $15 per month on laundry. You believe this figure is too low and want to disprove this claim. To conduct the test, you randomly select 35 college students and ask them to keep track of the amount of money they spend during a given month for laundry. The sample produces an average expenditure on laundry of $19.34, with a population standard deviation of $4.52. Use these sample data to conduct the hypothesis test. Assume you are willing to take a 10% risk of making a Type I error.

**9.55** A local company installs natural-gas grills. As part of the installation, a ditch is dug to lay a small natural-gas line from the grill to the main line. On the average, the depth of these lines seems to run about 1 foot. The company claims that the depth does not vary by more than 16 inches (the variance). To test this claim, a researcher randomly took 22 depth measurements at different locations. The sample average depth was 13.4 inches with a standard deviation of 6 inches. Is this enough evidence to reject the company's claim about the variance? Assume line depths are normally distributed. Let $\alpha = .05$.

**9.56** A study of pollutants showed that certain industrial emissions should not exceed 2.5 parts per million. You believe a particular company may be exceeding this average. To test this supposition, you randomly take a sample of nine air tests. The sample average is 3.4 parts per million, with a sample standard deviation of .6. Does this result provide enough evidence for you to conclude that the company is exceeding the safe limit? Use $\alpha = .01$. Assume emissions are normally distributed.

**9.57** The average cost per square foot for office rental space in the central business district of Philadelphia is $23.58, according to Cushman & Wakefield. A large real estate company wants to confirm this figure. The firm conducts a telephone survey of 95 offices in the central business district of Philadelphia and asks the office managers how much they pay in rent per square foot. Suppose the sample average is $22.83 per square foot. The population standard deviation is $5.11.

a. Conduct a hypothesis test using $\alpha = .05$ to determine whether the cost per square foot reported by Cushman & Wakefield should be rejected.

b. If the decision in part (a) is to fail to reject and if the actual average cost per square foot is $22.30, what is the probability of committing a Type II error?

**9.58** The American Water Works Association reports that, on average, men use between 10 and 15 gallons of water daily to shave when they leave the water running. Suppose the following data are the numbers of gallons of water used in a day to shave by 12 randomly selected men and the data come from a normal distribution of data. Use these data and a 5% level of significance to test to determine whether the population variance for such water usage is 2.5 gallons.

| 10 | 8 | 13 | 17 | 13 | 15 |
|----|---|----|----|----|----|
| 12 | 13 | 15 | 16 | 9 | 7 |

## INTERPRETING THE OUTPUT

**9.59** According to the U.S. Census Bureau, the average American generates 4.4 pounds of garbage per day. Suppose we believe that because of recycling and a greater emphasis on the environment, the figure is now lower. To test this notion, we take a random sample of Americans and have them keep a log of their garbage for a day. We record and analyze the results by using a statistical computer package. The output follows. Describe the sample. What statistical decisions can be made on the basis of this analysis? Let alpha be .05. Discuss any substantive results.

```
One-Sample T: Garbage

Test of mu = 4.4 vs mu < 4.4
Variable   N    Mean    StDev   SE Mean
Garbage    22   3.969   0.866   0.185
Variable   95.0% Upper Bound    T       P
Garbage          4.286         -2.34   0.015
```

**9.60** One survey conducted by RHI Management Resources determined that the Lexus is the favorite luxury car for 25% of CFOs. Suppose a financial management association conducts its own survey of CFOs in an effort to determine whether this figure is correct. They use an alpha of .05. Following is the MINITAB output with the results of the survey. Discuss the findings, including the hypotheses, one- or two-tailed tests, sample statistics, and the conclusion. Explain from the data why you reached the conclusion you did. Are these results substantive?

```
Test and CI for One Proportion

Test of p = 0.25 vs p not = 0.25
Sample  X    N    Sample p       95.0% CI           P-Value
1       79   384  0.205729  (0.166399, 0.249663)    0.045
```

**9.61** In a recent year, published statistics by the National Cattlemen's Beef Association claimed that the average retail beef price for USDA All Fresh beef was $2.51. Suppose a survey of retailers is conducted this year to determine whether the price of USDA All Fresh beef has increased. The Excel output of the results of the survey are shown here. Analyze the output and explain what it means in this study. An alpha of .05 was used in this analysis. Comment on any substantive results.

| | A | B |
|---|---|---|
| 1 | Mean | 2.55 |
| 2 | Variance | 0.0218 |
| 3 | Observations | 26 |
| 4 | df | 26 |
| 5 | t Stat | 1.51 |
| 6 | P (T<=t) one-tail | 0.072 |
| 7 | t Critical one-tail | 1.71 |
| 8 | P (T<=t) two-tail | 0.144 |
| 9 | t Critical two-tail | 2.06 |

**9.62** The American Express Retail Index states that the average U.S. household will spend $2,747 on home improvement projects this year. Suppose a large national home improvement company wants to test that figure in the West, theorizing that the average might be lower in the West. The research firm hired to conduct the study arrives at the results shown here. Analyze the data and explain the results. Comment on any substantive findings.

```
One-Sample Z: Home Improv

Test of mu = 2747 vs mu < 2747
The assumed sigma = 1557

  Variable    N    Mean   StDev  SE Mean
Home Improv   67   2349   1818     190

  Variable    95.0% Upper Bound    Z      P
Home Improv            2662      2.09  0.018
```

## ANALYZING THE DATABASES

see www.wiley.com/college/black

1. Suppose the average number of employees per industry group in the manufacturing database is believed to be less than 150 (1,000s). Test this belief as the alternative hypothesis by using the 140 SIC Code industries given in the database as the sample. Let $\alpha = .01$. Assume that the number of employees per industry group are normally distributed in the population. What did you decide and why?

2. Examine the hospital database. Suppose you want to "prove" that the average hospital in the United States averages more than 700 births per year. Use the hospital database as your sample and test this hypothesis. Let alpha be .01. On average, do hospitals in the United States employ fewer than 900 personnel? Use the hospital database as your sample and an alpha of .10 to test this figure as the alternative hypothesis. Assume that the number of births and number of employees in hospitals are normally distributed in the population.

3. Consider the financial database. Are the average earnings per share for companies in the stock market less than $2.50? Use the sample of companies represented by this database to test that hypothesis. Let $\alpha = .05$. Test to determine whether the average return on equity for all companies is equal to 21. Use this database as the sample and $\alpha = .10$. Assume that the earnings per share and return on equity are normally distributed in the population.

4. Fifteen years ago, the average production in the United States for green beans was 166,770 pounds per month. Use the 12 months in 1997 (the last 12 months in the database) in the agriculture database as a sample to test to determine whether the mean monthly production figure for green beans in the United States is now different from the old figure. Let $\alpha = .01$. Assume that the monthly production of beans is normally distributed in the population.

## CASE: FRITO-LAY TARGETS THE HISPANIC MARKET

Frito Company was founded in 1932 in San Antonio, Texas, by Elmer Doolin. H. W. Lay & Company was founded in Atlanta, Georgia, by Herman W. Lay in 1938. In 1961, the two companies merged to form Frito-Lay, Inc., with headquarters in Texas. Frito-Lay produced, distributed, and marketed snack foods with particular emphasis on various types of chips. In 1965, the company merged with Pepsi-Cola to form PepsiCo, Inc. Three decades later, Pepsi-Cola combined its domestic and international snack food operations into one business unit called Frito-Lay Company. According to data released by Information Resources, Frito-Lay brands account for more than 60% of the share of the snack chip market.

Despite its overall popularity, Frito-Lay faces a general lack of appeal in the Hispanic market, which is a growing segment of the U.S. population. In an effort to better penetrate that market, Frito-Lay hired various market researchers to determine why Hispanics do not purchase their products as often as company officials had hoped and what could be done about the problem.

Driving giant RVs through Hispanic neighborhoods and targeting Hispanic women (who tend to buy most of the groceries for their families), the researchers tested various brands and discovered several things. Hispanics thought Frito-Lay products were too bland, not spicy enough. Hispanics also were relatively unaware of Frito-Lay advertising. In addition, they tended to purchase snacks in small bags rather than in large family-style bags and at small local grocery stores rather than at large supermarkets.

After the "road test," focus groups composed of male teens and male young adults—a group that tends to consume a lot of chips—were formed. The researchers determined that even though many of the teens spoke English at school, they spoke Spanish at home with their family. From this discovery, it was concluded that Spanish advertisements would be needed to reach Hispanics. In addition, the use of Spanish rock music, a growing movement in the Hispanic youth culture, could be effective in some ads.

Researchers also found that using a "Happy Face" logo, which is an icon of Frito-Lay's sister company in Mexico, was effective. Because it reminded the 63% of all Hispanics in the

United States who are Mexican-American of snack foods from home, the logo increased product familiarity.

As a result of this research, Frito-Lay launched its first Hispanic products in San Antonio in 1997. Since that time, sales of the Doritos brand improved 32% in Hispanic areas and Doritos Salsa Verde sales have grown to represent 15% of all sales. Frito-Lay later expanded its line of products into other areas of the United States with large Hispanic populations.

### Discussion

In the research process for Frito-Lay Company, many different numerical questions were raised regarding Frito-Lay products, advertising techniques, and purchase patterns among Hispanics. In each of these areas, statistics—in particular, hypothesis testing—plays a central role. Using the case information and the concepts of statistical hypothesis testing, discuss the following:

1. Many proportions were generated in the focus groups and market research that were conducted for this project, including the proportion of the market that is Hispanic, the proportion of Hispanic grocery shoppers that are women, the proportion of chip purchasers that are teens, and so on. Use techniques presented in this chapter to analyze each of the following and discuss how the results might affect marketing decision makers regarding the Hispanic market.

   a. The case information stated that 63% of all U.S. Hispanics are Mexican-American. How might we test that figure? Suppose 850 U.S. Hispanics are randomly selected using U.S. Census Bureau information. Suppose 575 state that they are Mexican-Americans. Test the 63% percentage using an alpha of .05.

   b. Suppose that in the past 94% of all Hispanic grocery shoppers were women. Perhaps due to changing cultural values, we believe that more Hispanic men are now grocery shopping. We randomly sample 689 Hispanic grocery shoppers from around the United States and 606 are women. Does this result provide enough evidence to conclude that a lower proportion of Hispanic grocery shoppers now are women?

   c. What proportion of Hispanics listen primarily to advertisements in Spanish? Suppose one source says that in the past the proportion has been about .83. We want to test to determine whether this figure is true. A random sample of 438 Hispanics is selected, and the MINITAB results of testing this hypothesis are shown here. Discuss and explain this output and the implications of this study using $\alpha = .05$.

```
Test and CI for One Proportion
Test of p = 0.83 vs p not = 0.83
Sample   X    N   Sample p       95.0% CI         P-Value
1       347  438  0.792237  (0.751184, 0.829290)   0.042
```

2. The statistical mean can be used to measure various aspects of the Hispanic culture and the Hispanic market, including size of purchase, frequency of purchase, age of consumer, size of store, and so on. Use techniques presented in this chapter to analyze each of the following and discuss how the results might affect marketing decisions.

   a. What is the average age of a purchaser of Doritos Salsa Verde? Suppose initial tests indicate that the mean age is 31. Is this figure really correct? To test whether it is, a researcher randomly contacts 24 purchasers of Doritos Salsa Verde with results shown in the following Excel output. Discuss the output in terms of a hypothesis test to determine whether the mean age is actually 31. Let $\alpha$ be .01.

|   | A | B |
|---|---|---|
| 1 | Mean | 28.81 |
| 2 | Variance | 50.2651 |
| 3 | Observations | 24 |
| 4 | df | 23 |
| 5 | t Stat | −1.52 |
| 6 | P (T<=t) one-tail | 0.0716 |
| 7 | t Critical one-tail | 1.71 |
| 8 | P (T<=t) two-tail | 0.1431 |
| 9 | t Critical two-tail | 2.07 |

   b. What is the average expenditure of a Hispanic customer on chips per year? Suppose it is hypothesized that the figure is $45 per year. A researcher who knows the Hispanic market believes that this figure is too high and wants to prove her case. She randomly selects 18 Hispanics, has them keep a log of grocery purchases for one year, and obtains the following figures. Analyze the data using techniques from this chapter and an alpha of .05. Assume that expenditures per customer are normally distributed in the population.

| $55 | 37 | 59 | 57 | 27 | 28 |
|---|---|---|---|---|---|
| 16 | 46 | 34 | 62 | 9 | 34 |
| 4 | 25 | 38 | 58 | 3 | 50 |

*Source:* Adapted from "From Bland to Brand," *American Demographics* (March 1999), p. 57; Frito-Lay, available at http://www.fritolay.com; and Ronald J. Alsop, ed., *The Wall Street Journal Almanac 1999* (New York: Ballantine Books, 1998), p. 202.

# USING THE COMPUTER

## EXCEL

Excel has somewhat limited capability for doing hypothesis testing with single samples. It can compute $z$ tests for single population means by using the Paste Function. Begin by clicking on the Paste Function $f_x$ on the standard tool bar. The Paste Function dialog box will appear. From the **Function category** on the left, select **Statistical**. A menu of statistical techniques will appear on the right. Select **ZTEST** from this list. A dialog box will appear. This box requires the location of the data array in the first space beside **Array**. Place the hypothesized value of the mean in the second space beside **X**. Record the population standard deviation in the third line beside **Sigma**. The output is the right-tailed $p$-value for the test statistic. If the $z$ value is negative, subtract $1 -$ (Excel output) to obtain the $p$-value for the left tail.

A single-sample $t$ test can be computed in Excel by "fooling" the Excel dialog box for **t-Test: Two-Sample Assuming Unequal Variances**. First load the single-sample data in a column. Next, place the value of the hypothesized mean in another column in as many cells as there are data in the single-sample data column. Next, select **Tools** from the menu bar. Select **Data Analysis** from the pull-down menu. From the Data Analysis dialog box, select **t-Test: Two-Sample Assuming Unequal Variances**. In the dialog box that appears, place the location of the cells containing the single-sample data in **Variable 1 Range**. Place the location of the cells containing the repeated value of the hypothesized mean in **Variable 2 Range**. Place 0 in **Hypothesized Mean Difference**. Finally, fill in the labels and alpha information. The result will be the output for a single-sample $t$ test.

## MINITAB

MINITAB Windows conducts hypothesis tests by using the same commands, pull-down menus, and dialog boxes as those used to construct confidence intervals (discussed in Chapter 8). Begin by selecting **Stat** from the menu bar. From the pull-down menu that appears, select **Basic Statistics**. A second pull-down menu will appear. To conduct hypothesis tests in which the population standard deviation is known, select **1–sample Z**. To conduct hypothesis tests in which the population standard deviation is unknown, select **1–sample t**.

In the dialog boxes of each, enter the column location of the data being tested in the first space, **Variables**. (If a $z$ test is being conducted, enter the value of the known population standard deviation in the space labeled **Sigma**.) In the **Test Mean** space enter the hypothesized value of $\mu$. Select **Options**. From the Options dialog box enter the level of confidence if different from 95% and select whether the alternative hypothesis is **less than**, **greater than**, or **not equal**. The output includes a statement of the hypotheses, the sample size, the sample mean and standard deviation, the standard error of the mean, the $t$ statistics, and the $p$-value of the statistic.

MINITAB is able to test hypotheses about single proportions using the same process presented in Chapter 8. Begin the process by selecting **Stat** from the menu bar. From the pull-down menu, select **Basic Statistics**. From that pull-down menu, select **1 Proportion**. In the dialog box that appears, select either **Samples in columns** or **Summarized data**. If the data are in columns and if only one of two possible values is in each cell, then select **Samples in columns**. If you want to enter the summary data, select **Summarized data**. Using this option, place the size of the sample in the **Number of trials** space, and the number of items containing characteristic of interest, $x$, in the **Number of successes** space. To test a hypothesis, select **Options**. This command allows you to place the hypothesized proportion in **Test proportion**. Beside **Alternative** select the appropriate alternative hypothesis being tested. The resulting output includes a sample proportion, a confidence interval, and a $p$-value.

# APPENDIX B: ANSWERS TO SELECTED ODD-NUMBERED QUANTITATIVE PROBLEMS

## CHAPTER 1

1.5   a.   ratio
       b.   ratio
       c.   ordinal
       d.   nominal
       e.   ratio
       f.   ratio
       g.   nominal
       h.   ratio

1.7   a.   900 electric contractors
       b.   35 electric contractors
       c.   average score for 35 participants
       d.   average score for all 900 electric contractors

## CHAPTER 2

No answers given

## CHAPTER 3

3.1   4
3.3   294
3.5   −1
3.7   107, 127, 145, 114, 127.5, 143.5
3.9   624, 751, 486, 677, 775.5, 1096
3.11   a.   8
        b.   2.041
        c.   6.204

       d.   2.491
       e.   4
       f.   0.69, −0.92, −0.11, 1.89, −1.32, −0.52, 0.29

3.13   a.   4.598
        b.   4.598

3.15   58,631.359; 242.139

3.17   a.   .75
        b.   .84
        c.   .609
        d.   .902

3.19   a.   2.667
        b.   11.060
        c.   3.326
        d.   2.5
        e.   −0.85
        f.   37.65%

3.21   Between 113 and 137
       Between 101 and 149
       Between 89 and 161

3.23   2.236

3.25   95%, 2.5%, .15%, 16%

3.27   4.64, 1

3.29   185.694, 13.627

3.31   a.   44.9
        b.   39
        c.   187.2
        d.   13.7

3.33   a.   38
        b.   25

*Business Statistics For Contemporary Decision Making 4th Edition Update,*
Ken Black . ISBN-10  0-471-70563-2 ©2006 John Wiley & Sons, Inc.

c.  251

d.  15.843

3.35  skewed right

3.37  0.726

3.39  no outliers. negatively skewed

3.41  −0.927

3.43  0.645

3.45  0.975, 0.985, 0.957

3.47  23, 49.5, 27.5, 47.5, 20, 62

3.49  933, 290.8, 438, 789.2

3.51  a.  2031, 1795, no mode

b.  2030, 980, 525.2, 441387.78, 664.37

c.  1.066

d.  no outliers

3.53  a.  42.89, 10

b.  31.346

3.55  10.78%, 6.43%

3.57  a.  392 to 446, 365 to 473, 338 to 500

b.  79.7%

c.  −0.704

3.59  skewed right

3.61  $Q_1 = 43.85$, $Q_2 = 53.15$, $Q_3 = 73.7$, no outliers

# CHAPTER 4

4.1  15, .60

4.3  {4, 8, 10, 14, 16, 18, 20, 22, 26, 28, 30}

4.5  20, combinations, .60

4.7  38,760

4.9  a.  .7167

b.  .5000

c.  .65

d.  .5167

4.11  not solvable

4.13  a.  .86

b.  .31

c.  .14

4.15  a.  .2807

b.  .0526

c.  .0000

d.  .0000

4.17  a.  .0122

b.  .0144

4.19  a.  .57

b.  .3225

c.  .4775

d.  .5225

e.  .6775

f.  .0475

4.21  a.  .039

b.  .571

c.  .129

4.23  a.  .2286

b.  .2297

c.  .3231

d.  .0000

4.25  not independent

4.27  a.  .4054

b.  .3261

c.  .4074

d.  .32

4.29  a.  .03

b.  .2875

c.  .3354

d.  .9759

4.31  a.  .45

b.  .95

c.  .4743, .4269, .0988

d.  .2748, .4533, .2719

4.33  .65, .859, .6205

4.35  a.  .0897

b.  .0000

c.  .2821

d.  .0000

e.  .3636

f.  .3810

g.  .4615

h.  .2051

4.37  a.  .91

b.  .09

c.  .3462

d.  .13

4.39  a.  .042

b.  .034

c.  .2625

d.  .1976

e.  .525

4.41  a.  .43

b.  .189

c.  .6143

    **d.** $.5374 \leq p \leq .6446$

**8.49**  **a.**  827

    **b.**  196

    **c.**  849

    **d.**  897

**8.51**  722

**8.53**  $196.33 \leq \mu \leq 229.67$

**8.55**  196

**8.57**  $117.534 \leq \mu \leq 138.466, 20.932$

**8.59**  196

**8.61**  $.233 \leq p \leq .427$

**8.63**  $4.6736 \leq \mu \leq 4.9664$

**8.65**  $.28 \leq p \leq .38$

**8.67**  $1.69 \leq \mu \leq 2.51$

**8.69**  $1.209 \leq \mu \leq 1.379$

# CHAPTER 9

**9.1**  **a.**  $z = 2.77$, reject

    **b.**  .0028

    **c.**  22.115, 27.885

**9.3**  **a.**  $z = 1.59$, reject

    **b.**  .0559

    **c.**  1212.04

**9.5**  $z = 1.84$, fail to reject

**9.7**  $z = 1.41$, fail to reject

**9.9**  $z = -5.46$, reject

**9.11**  $t = 0.56$, fail to reject

**9.13**  $t = 2.44$, reject

**9.15**  $t = 1.59$, fail to reject

**9.17**  $t = -2.06$, fail to reject

**9.19**  $z = 0.53$, fail to reject

**9.21**  $z = -0.60$, fail to reject

    .2743, .257 and .323

**9.23**  $z = -3.00$, reject

**9.25**  $z = 2.02$, fail to reject

**9.27**  $z = 2.08$, reject

**9.29**  $\chi^2 = 23.64$, reject

**9.31**  $\chi^2 = 49.93$, reject

**9.33**  **a.**  .7852

    **b.**  .8749

    **c.**  .9671

**9.35**  .5160

**9.37**  $z = 0.96$, fail to reject, .8599, .5832, .2514, .0618

**9.39**  $z = 3.21$, reject

**9.41**  **a.**  $z = 0.85$, fail to reject

    **b.**  $z = -2.05$, reject

**9.43**  **a.**  $\beta = .1003$

    **b.**  $\beta = .6255$

**9.45**  $z = 1.05$, fail to reject

**9.47**  $\chi^2 = 24.63$, reject

**9.49**  **a.**  $z = 1.38$, fail to reject

    **b.**  $z = -2.52, \beta = .0059$

**9.51**  $z = 1.53$, fail to reject, .7704

**9.53**  $z = 2.05$, fail to reject, .01, .3300

**9.55**  $\chi^2 = 47.25$, reject

**9.57**  **a.**  $z = -1.43$, fail to reject

    **b.**  .3156

# CHAPTER 10

**10.1**  **a.**  $z = -1.02$, fail to reject

    **b.**  $\pm 3.08$

    **c.**  .1539

**10.3**  **a.**  $z = 5.48$, reject

    **b.**  $4.04 \leq \mu_1 - \mu_2 \leq 10.02$

**10.5**  $-1.86 \leq \mu_1 - \mu_2 \leq -0.54$

**10.7**  $z = -2.32$, fail to reject

**10.9**  $z = 2.27$, reject

**10.11**  $t = -1.05$, fail to reject

**10.13**  $t = 4.64$, reject

**10.15**  $1905.38 \leq \mu_1 - \mu_2 \leq 3894.62$

**10.17**  $t = 2.06$, fail to reject

**10.19**  $t = 4.95$, reject

**10.21**  $t = 3.31$, reject

**10.23**  $26.29 \leq D \leq 54.83$

**10.25**  $-3415.6 \leq D \leq 6021.2$

**10.27**  $6.58 \leq D \leq 49.60$

**10.29**  $63.71 \leq D \leq 86.29$

**10.31**  **a.**  $z = 0.75$, fail to reject

    **b.**  $z = 4.83$, reject

**10.33**  $z = -3.35$, reject

**10.35**  $z = -0.94$, fail to reject

**10.37**  $z = 2.35$, reject

**10.39**  $F = 1.80$, fail to reject

**10.41**  $F = 0.81$, fail to reject

**10.43**  $F = 1.53$, fail to reject

**10.45**  $z = -2.38$, reject

**10.47**  $t = 0.85$, fail to reject

**10.49**  $t = -5.26$, reject

# INDEX

# CHAPTER 2

# Preparation of data files

This chapter describes the process involved from data source to data file; that is, the conversion of raw source material to a usable data file. It focuses on defining variables, assigning appropriate numeric codes to alphanumeric data and dealing with missing data. These preparatory steps are desirable before data entry can begin. Other procedures such as applying variable definition attributes to other variables, entering data, inserting and deleting cases and variables, saving data and opening existing data files will also be addressed.

## Working example

You have developed a questionnaire that asks questions relating to an individual's shopping behaviour. The variables you have measured include: gender, age, desire for 24-hour shopping, choice of shopping area and amount spent on groceries per week. For each case you have assigned a participant identification number.

## Defining variables

The process of defining variables has seven optional steps. The primary step is naming your variable and the other steps cover labels (variable and value), missing values, variable type, column format and measurement level.

 Naming a variable

Variable names must comply with certain rules:

- Must begin with a letter. The remaining characters can be a letter, any digit, a full stop or the symbols @, #, _ or $.
- Cannot end with a full stop or underscore.
- Blanks and special characters cannot be used (for example, !, ?, ', and *).
- Must be unique; duplication is not allowed.
- The length of the name cannot exceed 64 bytes (typically 64 characters in single-byte languages e.g. English, German, French, Spanish etc.).
- Reserved keywords cannot be used as variable names e.g. ALL, AND, BY, EQ, GE, GT, LE, LT, NE, NOT, OR, TO, WITH.
- Names are not case sensitive, i.e. can be written in upper or lower case.
- Long variable names need to wrap to multiple lines in the output, so SPSS attempts to break lines at underscores, periods, and a change from lower to upper case.

*SPSS version 13.0 for Windows: Analysis without Anguish*, Sheridan J Coakes, Lyndall Steed, Peta Dzidic. ISBN-10 0-470-80914-0, ISBN-13 978-0-470-80914-3 ©2006 Sheridan J Coakes, Lyndall Steed, Peta Dzidic.

In the case of the variable *age*, the variable name can be *age* because this name complies with all of the rules listed. The variable *choice of shopping area* can be labelled *area*, and the other variables on the questionnaire could be *id*, *gender*, *allday* and *cost*.

## Variable labels

••••••••••••••••••••••••••••••••••••••••••••••••••••••••••••••••••••••••••••••••••••••••••••••••••

The variable label is the full description of the variable name and is an optional means of improving the interpretability of the output. For example, the first variable you will name in the data file is *id* and the label for this variable is 'participant identification number'. Suggested variable labels for the other variables appear in the following table.

| Variable name | Label |
|---|---|
| gender | optional |
| age | optional |
| allday | desire for 24-hour shopping facilities |
| area | choice of shopping area |
| cost | amount spent on groceries per week |

You will notice that the gender and age variables do not require variable labels because the variable names are self-explanatory.

## Value labels

••••••••••••••••••••••••••••••••••••••••••••••••••••••••••••••••••••••••••••••••••••••••••••••••••

It is possible to use alphanumeric codes for the variables; however, you may also wish to use a numeric code. For example, for gender you could assign a code of 1 for female and 2 for male. This type of variable is categorical because it has discrete categories. The variables *allday* and *area* are also categorical. When variables are measured using interval or ratio scales, then coding is not relevant unless categorisation is required.

Value codes and labels for the above variables are illustrated in the following table.

| Variable name | Label |
|---|---|
| id | not applicable |
| gender | 1 = female<br>2 = male |
| age | not applicable |
| allday | 1 = would use 24-hour shopping<br>2 = would not use 24-hour shopping |
| area | 1 = shop in suburb where living<br>2 = travel to next suburb<br>3 = travel further to shop |
| cost | not applicable |

## Missing values

••••••••••••••••••••••••••••••••••••••••••••••••••••••••••••••••••••••••••••••••••••••••••••••••••

It is rare to obtain complete data sets for all cases. When dealing with missing data you may leave the cell blank or assign missing value codes. If you choose the latter, then a number of rules apply:

• Missing value codes must be of the same data type as the data they represent. For example, for missing numeric data, missing value codes must also be numeric.

• Missing value codes cannot occur as data in the data set.

• By convention, the choice of digit is usually 9.

## Variable type

By default, SPSS assumes that all new variables are numeric with two decimal places. However, it is possible to select other variable types (such as date, currency, string) and vary the number of decimal places.

## Column format

It is possible to adjust the width of the Data Editor columns or change the alignment of data in the column (left, centre or right).

## Measurement level

You can specify the level of measurement as scale (interval or ratio), ordinal or nominal.

 **To define a variable**

1   Working in the Untitled — SPSS Data Editor window, double-click a variable name at the top of the column in the Data View or click the **Variable View** tab.

2   In the first blank cell of the **Name** column, type the first variable name (i.e. *id*) and press Enter.

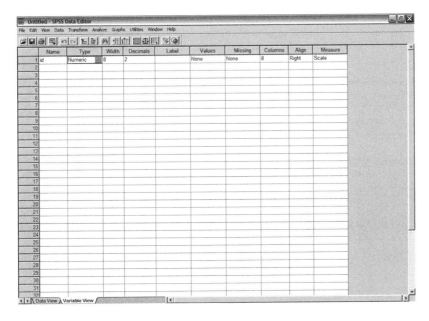

3   In the first blank cell of the **Label** column, type the label for the variable, i.e. *Identification Number*. You will notice that the width of the column automatically increases to accommodate the long label.

For the variable *id*, there are no value labels or missing values, and the other properties are appropriate so you can move on to the second variable.

If you return to the Data View, by clicking the **Data View** tab you will notice that the variable name *id* has appeared in the first column as a heading.

 To repeat this process for the second variable, gender

1      Working in the Variable View, in the second blank cell of the **Name** column, type the second variable name, i.e. *gender*, and press Enter.

Again, SPSS automatically supplies other properties such as type, width, values, etc. Since gender requires no further explanation a label will not be typed in. However, values are assigned.

2      Click on the second cell of the **Values** column and then on the button on the right to open the **Value Labels** box. In the **Value:** box, type the first value code for the variable (i.e. *1*) then tab. In the **Value Label:** box, type the label for this value, i.e. *female*.

3      Click on **Add**. You will notice that the value and its label have moved into the box below.

4      Repeat this process for the second value.

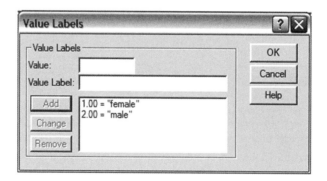

5      Click on **OK**. You will notice that there is now information in the cell.

CHAPTER 2 • *Preparation of data files*    **23**

To create a missing value

**1**    Click on the second cell of the **Missing** column and then on the button on the right to open the **Missing Values** dialogue box.

**2**    Select the **Discrete missing values** radio button.

**3**    In the first box, type the missing value code, i.e. *9.*

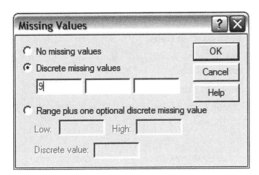

**4**    Click on **OK**. You will notice that the missing value has been recorded.

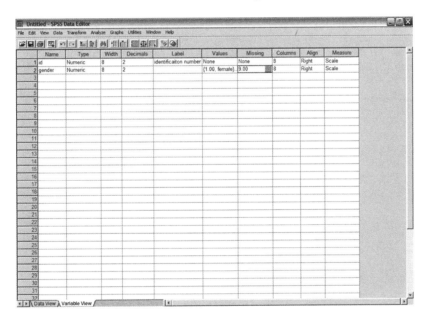

The previous process is then repeated for each variable you wish to define in your data file. As highlighted earlier in this chapter, other options such as **Type**, **Column Width** and **Measurement Level** are also available if you are dealing with different types of variable that require special conditions. For the variable *gender*, you may wish to select the nominal scale of measurement.

## Applying variable definition attributes to other variables
••••••••••••••••••••••••••••••••••••••••••••••••••••••••••••••••••••••••••••••

Once you have nominated variable definition attributes for a variable, you can copy one or more attributes and apply them to one or more variables. Basic copy and paste operations are used to apply variable definition attributes. For example, you may have several variables with a Likert scale response format. That is, you may have several variables that use the same response scale, where 1 = strongly disagree, 2 = disagree, 3 = neutral, 4 = agree and 5 = strongly agree. Having defined these value labels for one variable you can then copy them to other variables.

 **To apply variable definition attributes to other variables**

1   In the Variable View, select the attribute cell(s) you want to apply to other variables.

2   From the **Edit** menu click on **Copy**.

3   Select the attribute cell(s) to which you want to apply the attribute(s). You can select multiple target variables.

4   From the **Edit** menu click on **Paste**.

If you copy attributes to blank rows, then new variables are created with default attributes for all but the selected attributes.

## Entering data

  To enter the following two cases

| id | gender | age | allday | area | cost |
|---|---|---|---|---|---|
| 1 | male | 27 | 1 | 1 | 4 |
| 2 | female | 34 | 2 | 3 | 7 |

1   In the Data View click on the first cell in the **Untitled — SPSS Data Editor** window. You will notice that a heavy border appears around the cell, indicating that the cell is now active.

2   Type in the first value for *id*, i.e. *1*. This value is displayed in the cell editor at the top of the **Data Editor** window and also in the cell itself.

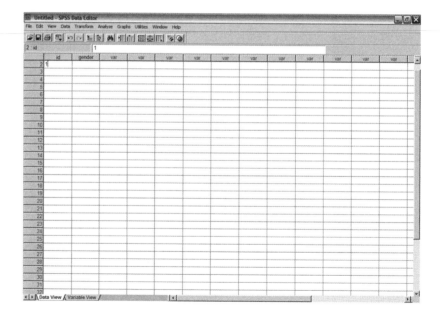

CHAPTER 2 • *Preparation of data files*   **25**

**3** Press Enter or move to another cell by using the arrow keys or mouse. Data values are not recorded until you press Enter or select another cell. Remember that it is more efficient to code gender numerically.

**4** To move around your data file quickly, you can hold down the Control key with an arrow key to take you to the limit of the file in that direction.

Having entered data for the first two cases, your **Data View** window will look like this:

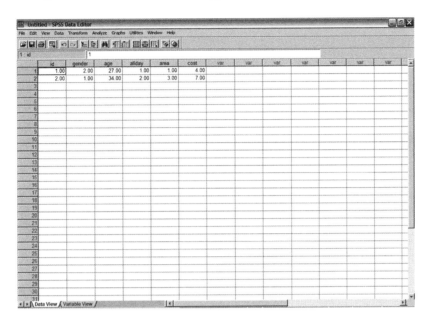

## Inserting and deleting cases and variables

Often you may need to insert or delete extra cases (rows) and variables (columns) in the existing data file. You can achieve this by using the menus as described below or by using the appropriate tools from the toolbar.

 **To insert a new case between existing cases**

**1** Select any cell in the case (row) below the position where you want to insert the new case.

**2** Select the **Data** menu and click on **Insert Case** or click on the **Insert Case** tool. A new case (row) will be inserted.

 **To insert a new variable between existing variables**

**1** Select any cell in the variable (column) to the right of the position where you want to insert a new variable.

**2** Select the **Data** menu and click on **Insert Variable** or click on the **Insert Variable** tool. A new variable (column) will be inserted.

**To delete a case (row)**

1    Click on the case number on the left side of the row if you wish to delete the entire case or select any cell in the row that you wish to delete.

2    Select the **Edit** menu and click on **Clear**. Alternatively, you can use the Delete button on the keyboard.

 **To delete a variable (column)**

1    Click on the variable name at the top of the column if you wish to delete the entire variable, or select any cell within the column that you wish to remove.

2    Select the **Edit** menu and click on **Clear**. Again, you can use the Delete button if you wish.

## Moving variables

 You may wish to change the sequence of variables in the **Data View** window. If you want to position the variable between two existing variables, then insert a new variable in the position where you want to move the variable.

 **To move a variable**

1    For the variable you want to move, click the variable name at the top of the column in the Data View or the row number in the Variable View. The entire variable is highlighted.

2    Select the **Edit** menu and click on **Cut**.

3    Click the variable name in the Data View or the row number in the Variable View where you want to move the variable to. The entire variable is highlighted.

4    Select the **Edit** menu and click on **Paste**.

## Saving data files

  **To save a data file for the first time**

1    First ensure that you are in the **Data View** window.

2    Click on the **File Save** tool.

3    You will be asked to give the file a name.

or

1    Select the **File** menu and click on **Save As...** to open the **Save Data As** dialogue box.

2    In the box for **File Name:** type in the file name of your choice. SPSS will append the extension .sav automatically. If you are saving data to a floppy disk, then remember to change to the appropriate drive.

3    Click on **Save**.

 **To save an existing data file**

1    First ensure that you are in the **Data Editor** window.

2    Click on the **File Save** tool.

or

1    Select the **File** menu and click on **Save Data**. Your changes will be saved to the existing file.

---

## Opening an existing data file

Once a data file has been saved in SPSS, it can be accessed in subsequent sessions. Furthermore, files that have been created in other software packages can be imported into SPSS.

 **To open an existing SPSS data file**

1 Select the **File** menu.

2 Click on **Open** and **Data...** to open the **Open File** dialogue box.

3 Select the file from the file list.

4 Click on **Open**.

 **To read a text data file**

1 Select the **File** menu.

2 Click on **Read Text Data** to open the **Open File** dialogue box.

3 Select the file from the file list.

4 Click on **Open**.

### Handy Hints

- It is more efficient to code gender numerically.
- Remember, basic copy and paste operations can be applied to variable definition attributes.

# Descriptive statistics

Descriptive statistics are used to explore the data collected, as shown in chapter 3; and to summarise and describe those data.

Descriptive statistics may be particularly useful if one just wants to make some general observations about the data collected, for example number of male and females, the age range and average (mean) age, the average length of residence in a community etc. Other statistics such as standard deviation and variance give more information about the distribution of each variable.

## Frequency distributions

A frequency distribution is a display of the frequency of occurrence of each score value. The frequency distribution can be represented in tabular form or, with more visual clarity, in graphical form. For continuous variables, measured on ratio or interval scales, histograms or frequency polygons are appropriate. For categorical variables, measured on nominal or ordinal scales, bar charts are suitable.

## Measures of central tendency and variability

The three main measures of central tendency are mode, median and mean. The measures of variability include range, interquartile range, standard deviation and variance. All of these measures of variability are more appropriate for interval or ratio data. You can also examine the normality of the distribution through the **Frequencies** procedure.

## Working example

One hundred tennis players participated in a serving competition. Gender and number of aces were recorded for each player. The data file can be found in Work4.sav on the website that accompanies this title and is shown in the following figure.

| | gender | aces | var | var | var | var | var | var | var | var | var | var | var |
|---|---|---|---|---|---|---|---|---|---|---|---|---|---|
| 1 | 1.00 | 5.00 | | | | | | | | | | | |
| 2 | 2.00 | 2.00 | | | | | | | | | | | |
| 3 | 1.00 | 4.00 | | | | | | | | | | | |
| 4 | 2.00 | 8.00 | | | | | | | | | | | |
| 5 | 1.00 | 8.00 | | | | | | | | | | | |
| 6 | 2.00 | 5.00 | | | | | | | | | | | |
| 7 | 1.00 | 5.00 | | | | | | | | | | | |
| 8 | 2.00 | 9.00 | | | | | | | | | | | |
| 9 | 1.00 | 9.00 | | | | | | | | | | | |
| 10 | 2.00 | 6.00 | | | | | | | | | | | |
| 11 | 1.00 | 5.00 | | | | | | | | | | | |

*SPSS version 13.0 for Windows: Analysis without Anguish*, Sheridan J Coakes, Lyndall Steed, Peta Dzidic. ISBN-10  0-470-80914-0, ISBN-13  978-0-470-80914-3 ©2006 Sheridan J Coakes, Lyndall Steed, Peta Dzidic.

**To obtain a frequency table, measures of central tendency and variability**

1   Select the **Analyze** menu.

2   Click on **Descriptive Statistics** and then on **Frequencies...** to open the **Frequencies** dialogue box.

3   Select the variable(s) you require (i.e. aces) and click on the ▶ button to move the variable into the **Variable(s):** box.

4   Click on the **Statistics...** command pushbutton to open the **Frequencies: Statistics** sub-dialogue box.

5   In the **Percentile Values** box, select the **Quartiles** check box.

6   In the **Central Tendency** box, select the **Mean**, **Median** and **Mode** check boxes.

7   In the **Dispersion** box, select the **Std. deviation**, **Variance**, **Range**, **Minimum** and **Maximum** check boxes.

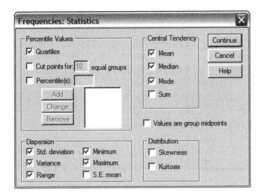

8   Click on **Continue**.

9   Click on the **Charts...** command pushbutton to open the **Frequencies: Charts** sub-dialogue box.

10  Click on the **Histogram(s)** radio button. You will notice that you can also obtain a normal curve overlay, so click on the **With normal curve** check box.

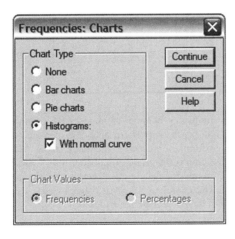

11  Click on **Continue** and then **OK**.

---

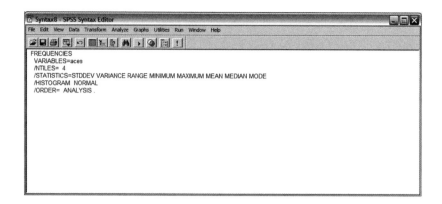

**Statistics**

aces

| N | Valid | 100 |
|---|---|---|
| | Missing | 0 |
| Mean | | 5.1100 |
| Median | | 5.0000 |
| Mode | | 5.00 |
| Std. Deviation | | 1.83620 |
| Variance | | 3.372 |
| Range | | 9.00 |
| Minimum | | 1.00 |
| Maximum | | 10.00 |
| Percentiles | 25 | 4.0000 |
| | 50 | 5.0000 |
| | 75 | 6.0000 |

**aces**

| | | Frequency | Percent | Valid Percent | Cumulative Percent |
|---|---|---|---|---|---|
| Valid | 1.00 | 3 | 3.0 | 3.0 | 3.0 |
| | 2.00 | 6 | 6.0 | 6.0 | 9.0 |
| | 3.00 | 7 | 7.0 | 7.0 | 16.0 |
| | 4.00 | 15 | 15.0 | 15.0 | 31.0 |
| | 5.00 | 35 | 35.0 | 35.0 | 66.0 |
| | 6.00 | 15 | 15.0 | 15.0 | 81.0 |
| | 7.00 | 8 | 8.0 | 8.0 | 89.0 |
| | 8.00 | 6 | 6.0 | 6.0 | 95.0 |
| | 9.00 | 4 | 4.0 | 4.0 | 99.0 |
| | 10.00 | 1 | 1.0 | 1.0 | 100.0 |
| | Total | 100 | 100.0 | 100.0 | |

In the frequency table, the frequency column summarises the total number of aces served. For example, only one person served ten aces. The percent column displays this frequency in percentage form for *all* cases, including those cases that may be missing. The valid percent column is the proportion of scores only for those cases that are valid. Because you have no missing data in this example, the percent and valid percent columns are identical. The cumulative percent column is the summation of the percentage for that score with the percentage for all lesser scores.

By obtaining the 25th and 75th percentiles for the distribution, the interquartile range can be calculated by subtracting one from the other. Therefore, in this example, the interquartile range is equal to $6 - 4 = 2$.

Histogram

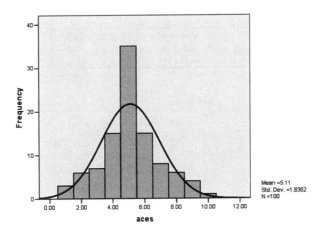

Mean =5.11
Std. Dev. =1.8362
N =100

  To obtain the appropriate output for a categorical variable

1   Select the **Analyze** menu.

2   Click on **Descriptive Statistics** and then on **Frequencies…** to open the **Frequencies** dialogue box.

3   Select the variable(s) you require (i.e. *gender*) and click on the ▶ button to move the variable into the **Variable(s):** box.

4   Click on the **Statistics…** command pushbutton to open the **Frequencies: Statistics** sub-dialogue box.

5   In the **Central Tendency** box, click on the **Mode** check box.

6   Click on **Continue**.

7   Click on the **Charts…** command pushbutton to open the **Frequencies: Charts** sub-dialogue box.

8   Select the **Bar chart(s)** radio button.

9   Click on **Continue** and then **OK**.

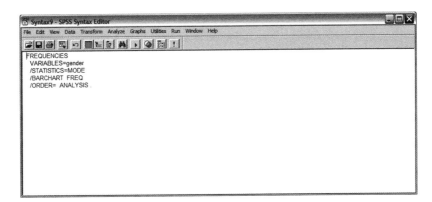

**gender**

| | | Frequency | Percent | Valid Percent | Cumulative Percent |
|---|---|---|---|---|---|
| Valid | 1.00 | 50 | 50.0 | 50.0 | 50.0 |
| | 2.00 | 50 | 50.0 | 50.0 | 100.0 |
| | Total | 100 | 100.0 | 100.0 | |

**gender**

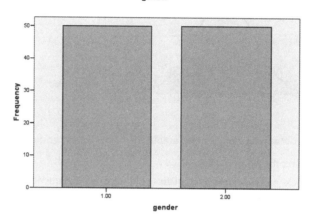

gender

# Descriptives command

It is also possible to obtain certain measures of central tendency and variability through the **Descriptives** command. This command also allows you to save standardised values as variables. These standardised or Z-scores are useful for further analysis (e.g. interaction terms in multiple regression) or in comparing samples from different populations. Furthermore, inspection of Z-scores will allow identification of outlying cases, which is useful in data screening. Z-scores greater than +3 and less than −3 are considered to be outliers.

**To obtain descriptive statistics and Z-scores**

1    Select the **Analyze** menu.

2    Click on **Descriptive Statistics** and then **Descriptives...** to open the **Descriptives** dialogue box.

3    Select the variable(s) you require (i.e. aces) and click on the ▶ button to move the variable into the **Variable(s):** box.

4    Select the **Save standardized values as variables** check box.

5    Click on the **Options** command pushbutton.

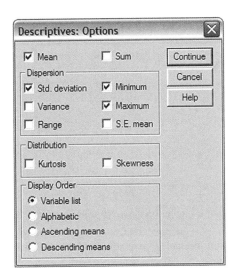

6    Note that the **Mean**, **Std. deviation**, **Minimum** and **Maximum** check boxes are automatically selected. If you wish to obtain additional descriptive statistics, select the appropriate check boxes.

7    Click on **Continue** and then **OK**.

```
DESCRIPTIVES
    VARIABLES=aces/SAVE
    /STATISTICS=MEAN STDDEV MIN MAX.
```

**Descriptive Statistics**

|  | N | Minimum | Maximum | Mean | Std. Deviation |
|---|---|---|---|---|---|
| aces | 100 | 1.00 | 10.00 | 5.1100 | 1.83620 |
| Valid N (listwise) | 100 |  |  |  |  |

If you switch back to the Data Editor window, you will notice that the Z-scores have been saved as another variable: *Zaces*.

## Handy Hint

- If unwanted check boxes are selected, click on them to deselect them.

# Correlation

Correlation looks at the relationship between two variables in a linear fashion.

A *Pearson product-moment correlation* coefficient describes the relationship between two continous variables and is available through the **Analyze** and **Correlate** menus.

A correlation between two dichotomous or categorical variables is called a *Phi coefficient* and is available through the **Crosstabs** option from the **Analyze** and **Descriptive Statistics** menus.

A correlation between a continuous and a categorical variable is called a *point-biserial correlation*. This option is not available in the SPSS for Windows package. However, you can use a Pearson product-moment correlation to correlate a dichotomous and a continuous variable. However, the proportion of each category of the dichotomous variable must be approximately equal and variables must be coded as 0 and 1.

When the assumptions underlying correlation cannot be met adequately, a nonparametric alternative is *Spearman's rank-order correlation*.

In this chapter, you will address bivariate and partial correlations using Pearson's product-moment correlation.

Simple bivariate correlation, also referred to as zero-order correlation, refers to the correlation between two continuous variables and is the most common measure of linear relationship. This coefficient has a range of possible values from −1 to +1. The value indicates the strength of the relationship, while the sign (+ or −) indicates the direction.

Partial correlation provides us with a single measure of linear association between two variables while adjusting for the effects of one or more additional variables.

## Assumption testing

Correlational analysis has a number of underlying assumptions:

1    **Related pairs** — data must be collected from related pairs: that is, if you obtain a score on an X variable, there must also be a score on the Y variable from the same participant.

2    **Scale of measurement** — data should be interval or ratio in nature.

3    **Normality** — the scores for each variable should be normally distributed.

4    **Linearity** — the relationship between the two variables must be linear.

5    **Homoscedasticity** — the variability in scores for one variable is roughly the same at all values of the other variable. That is, it is concerned with how the scores cluster uniformly about the regression line.

Assumptions 1 and 2 are a matter of research design. Assumption 3 can be tested using the procedures outlined in chapters 3 and 4. Assumptions 4 and 5 can be tested by examining scatterdots of the variables.

**CHAPTER 5 • *Correlation*** 57

*SPSS version 13.0 for Windows: Analysis without Anguish*, Sheridan J Coakes, Lyndall Steed, Peta Dzidic. ISBN-10  0-470-80914-0, ISBN-13  978-0-470-80914-3 ©2006 Sheridan J Coakes, Lyndall Steed, Peta Dzidic.

# Working example

Twenty students wishing to enter university were given an intelligence test (IQ) and their tertiary entrance examination scores (TEE) were recorded. You suspect that a positive relationship exists between these two variables and wish to test this directional hypothesis (one-tailed).

At the end of the academic year, the course averages for the same twenty students were obtained. You also wish to determine whether the relationship between TEE scores and course average is significant when IQ is controlled in the analysis.

The data can be found in Work5.sav on the website that accompanies this title and are shown in the following figure.

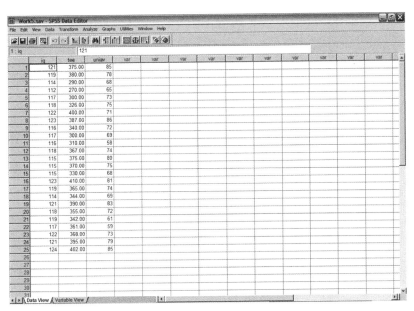

## To obtain a scatterdot

1    Select the **Graphs** menu.

2    Click on **Scatter/dot...** to open the **Scatter/dot** dialogue box.

3    Ensure that the **Simple Scatter** option is selected.

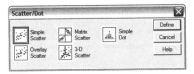

4    Click on the **Define** command pushbutton to open the **Simple Scatter** sub-dialogue box.

5    Select the first variable (i.e. *tee*) and click on the  button to move the variable into the **Y Axis:** box.

**6** Select the second variable (i.e. *iq*) and click on the ▶ button to move the variable into the **X Axis:** box.

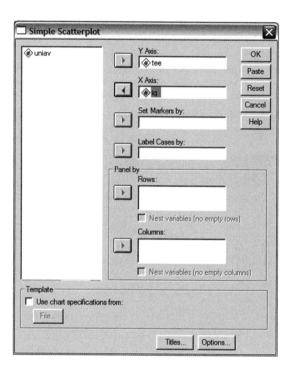

**7** Click on **OK**.

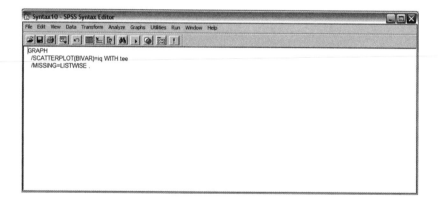

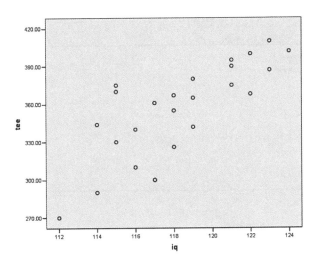

As you can see from the scatterdot, there is a linear relationship between IQ and TEE scores. Given that the scores cluster uniformly around the regression line, the assumption of homoscedasticity has not been violated.

Similarly, the scatterdot was obtained for TEE scores and course average, indicating that assumptions of linearity and homoscedasticity were not violated. The output of this plot is not displayed.

 **To obtain a bivariate Pearson product-moment correlation**

1  Select the **Analyze** menu.

2  Click on **Correlate** and then **Bivariate...** to open the **Bivariate Correlations** dialogue box.

3  Select the variables you require (i.e. *iq* and *tee*) and click on the ▶ button to move the variables into the **Variables:** box.

4  Ensure that the **Pearson** correlation option has been selected.

5  In the **Test of Significance** box, select the **One-tailed** radio button.

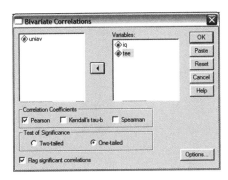

6  Click on **OK**.

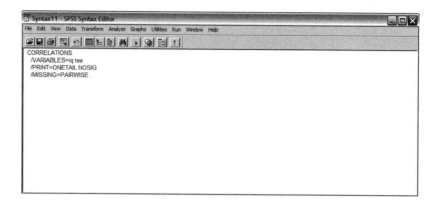

**Correlations**

| | | iq | tee |
|---|---|---|---|
| iq | Pearson Correlation | 1 | .767** |
| | Sig. (1-tailed) | | .000 |
| | N | 25 | 25 |
| tee | Pearson Correlation | .767** | 1 |
| | Sig. (1-tailed) | .000 | |
| | N | 25 | 25 |

**. Correlation is significant at the 0.01 level

To interpret the correlation coefficient, you examine the coefficient and its associated significance value (p). The output confirms the results of the scatterdot in that a significant positive relationship exists between IQ and TEE (r = .767, p < .05). Therefore, higher intelligence scores are associated with higher TEE scores.

A bivariate correlation was undertaken between students' intelligence scores and their tertiary entrance examination scores. It was hypothesised that a positive relationship would exist between these two variables. Results of the correlation indicate that higher intelligence scores are associated with higher TEE scores (r = .767, p < .05).

## Handy Hint

• Remember the assumptions for correlation can be examined using different procedures in SPSS. These procedures have been outlined in chapters 3, 4 and 5.

# CHAPTER 6

# T-tests

A t-test is used to determine whether there is a significant difference between two sets of scores. Three main types of t-test may be applied:

- one-sample
- independent groups
- repeated measures.

## Assumption testing

Each statistical test has certain assumptions that must be met before analysis. These assumptions need to be evaluated because the accuracy of test interpretation depends on whether assumptions are violated. Some of these assumptions are generic to all types of t-test but others are more specific.

The generic assumptions underlying all types of t-test are:

1  **Scale of measurement** — the data should be at the interval or ratio level of measurement.

2  **Random sampling** — the scores should be randomly sampled from the population of interest.

3  **Normality** — the scores should be normally distributed in the population.

Clearly, assumptions 1 and 2 are a matter of research design and not statistical analysis. Assumption 3 can be tested in a number of different ways, as outlined in chapter 3.

## Working example

A major oil company developed a petrol additive that was supposed to increase engine efficiency. Twenty-two cars were test driven both with and without the additive and the number of kilometres per litre was recorded. Whether the car was automatic or manual was also recorded and coded as 1 = manual and 2 = automatic.

During an earlier trial twenty-two cars were test driven using the additive. The mean number of kilometres per litre was 10.5.

You are interested in answering the following questions:

1  Are the cars in the present trial running more efficiently than those in the earlier trial? The one-sample t-test will help answer this question.

2  Does engine efficiency improve when the additive is used? This is a repeated measures t-test design.

3  Does engine efficiency with and without the additive differ between manual and automatic cars? This is an independent groups t-test.

*SPSS version 13.0 for Windows: Analysis without Anguish*, Sheridan J Coakes, Lyndall Steed, Peta Dzidic. ISBN-10  0-470-80914-0, ISBN-13  978-0-470-80914-3 ©2006 Sheridan J Coakes, Lyndall Steed, Peta Dzidic.

The data can be found in Work6.sav on the website that accompanies this title and are shown in the following figure.

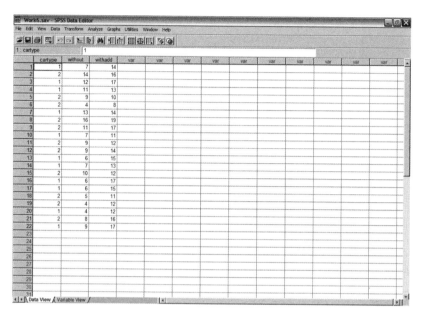

## The one-sample t-test

The one-sample t-test is used when you have data from a single sample of participants and you wish to know whether the mean of the population from which the sample is drawn is the same as the hypothesised mean.

 **To conduct a one-sample t-test**

1    Select the **Analyze** menu.

2    Click on **Compare Means** and then **One-Sample T Test...** to open the **One-Sample T Test** dialogue box.

3    Select the variable you require (i.e. *withadd*) and click on the ▶ button to move the variable into the **Test Variable(s):** box.

4    In the **Test Value:** box type the mean score (i.e. *10.5*).

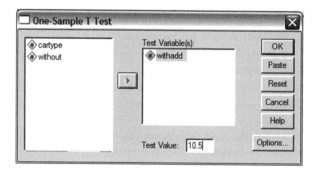

5    Click on **OK**.

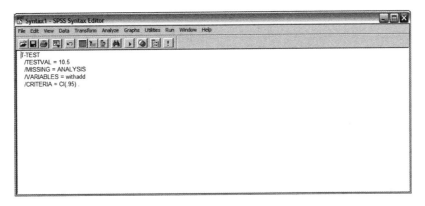

It is possible to determine whether a difference exists between the sample mean and the hypothesised mean by consulting the t-value, degree of freedom (df) and two-tail significance. If the value for two-tail significance is less than .05 (p < .05), then the difference between the means is significant.

The output indicates that there is a significant difference in engine efficiency between the present trial and the earlier trial. That is, the cars in the present trial appear to have greater engine efficiency than that of those in the earlier trial — t (21) = 5.74, p < .05.

### One-Sample Statistics

|  | N | Mean | Std. Deviation | Std. Error Mean |
|---|---|---|---|---|
| withadd | 22 | 13.86 | 2.748 | .586 |

### One-Sample Test

|  | Test Value = 10.5 | | | | | |
|---|---|---|---|---|---|---|
|  |  |  |  | Mean Difference | 95% Confidence Interval of the Difference | |
|  | t | df | Sig. (2-tailed) | | Lower | Upper |
| withadd | 5.741 | 21 | .000 | 3.364 | 2.15 | 4.58 |

# T-tests with more than one sample

In the last section, a one-sample t-test was used to determine whether a single sample of scores was likely to have been drawn from a hypothesised population. This section will extend the understanding of sampling distributions to ask whether two sets of scores are random samples from the same or different populations. If they are random samples from the same population, then any differences across conditions or groups can be attributed to random sampling variability. However, if the two sets of scores are random samples from different populations, then you can attribute any difference between means across conditions to the independent variable or the treatment effect.

## Repeated measures t-test

••••••••••••••••••••••••••••••••••••••••••••••••••••••••••••••••••••

The repeated measures t-test, also referred to as the dependent-samples or paired t-test, is used when you have data from only one group of participants. In other words, an individual obtains two scores under different levels of the independent variable. Data that are collected from the same group of participants are also referred to as within-subjects, because the same subject performs in both conditions. Studies which employ a pretest–posttest design are commonly analysed using repeated measures t-tests. In this form of design, the same participant obtains a score on the pretest and, after some intervention or manipulation, a score on the posttest. You wish to determine whether the difference between means for the two sets of scores is the same or different.

Before you attempt to answer this question, you must ensure that the assumptions of repeated measures t-test are met. You will remember from the section on assumption testing that a number of assumptions are generic to all types of t-test. The repeated measures t-test has one additional assumption:

1   **Normality of population difference scores** — the difference between the scores for each participant should be normally distributed. Providing the sample size is not too small (30+), violations of this assumption are of little concern.

Testing this assumption involves the same procedures as used for the single-sample t-test. Because you have two dependent variables, you will need to test the normality of each variable separately, which will allow you to assume that the difference scores are normally distributed. Having evaluated the assumption of normality for both pretest and posttest measures, you are ready to conduct a repeated measures t-test.

 **To conduct a repeated measures t-test**

1   Select the **Analyze** menu.

2   Click on **Compare Means** and then **Paired-Samples T Test...** to open the **Paired-Sample T Test** dialogue box.

3   Select the variables you require (i.e. *without* and *withadd*) and press the ▶ button to move the variables into the **Paired Variables:** box.

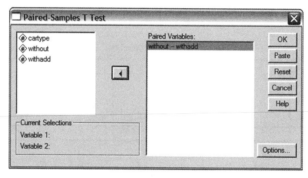

4   Click on **OK**.

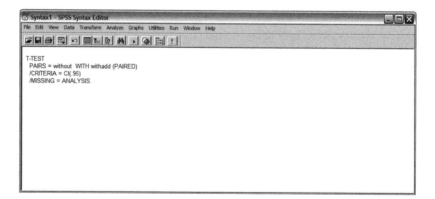

**Paired Samples Statistics**

| | | Mean | N | Std. Deviation | Std. Error Mean |
|---|---|---|---|---|---|
| Pair 1 | without | 8.50 | 22 | 3.335 | .711 |
| | withadd | 13.86 | 22 | 2.748 | .586 |

**Paired Samples Correlations**

| | | N | Correlation | Sig. |
|---|---|---|---|---|
| Pair 1 | without & withadd | 22 | .559 | .007 |

**Paired Samples Test**

| | | Paired Differences | | | | | t | df | Sig. (2-tailed) |
|---|---|---|---|---|---|---|---|---|---|
| | | | | | 95% Confidence Interval of the Difference | | | | |
| | | Mean | Std. Deviation | Std. Error Mean | Lower | Upper | | | |
| Pair 1 | without - withadd | -5.364 | 2.904 | .619 | -6.651 | -4.076 | -8.663 | 21 | .000 |

By looking at the t-value, df and two-tail significance, you can determine whether the groups come from the same or different populations. The correct way to determine significance is to consult the critical t-tables that are available at the back of most statistical textbooks, using the dfs. However, significance can also be determined by looking at the probability level (p) specified under the heading 'two-tail significance'. If the probability value is less than the specified alpha value, then the observed t-value is significant. The 95 per cent confidence interval indicates that 95 per cent of the time the interval specified will contain the true difference between the population means.

As can be seen from the output, a significant difference exists between engine efficiency with and without the additive. The additive significantly improves the number of kilometres to the litre, $\underline{t}$ (21) = 8.66, p < .05.

## Independent groups t-test

An independent groups t-test is appropriate when different participants have performed in each of the different conditions, in other words, when the participants in one condition are different from the participants in the other condition. This is commonly referred to as a between-subjects design. Again, you wish to determine whether the difference between means for the two sets of scores is significant. The independent groups t-test has two additional assumptions.

1    **Independence of groups** — participants should appear in only one group and these groups are unrelated.

2    **Homogeneity of variance** — the groups should come from populations with equal variances. To test for homogeneity of variance, SPSS uses the Levene test for equality of variances. If this test is significant (p < .05), then you reject the null hypothesis and accept the alternative hypothesis that the variances are unequal. In this instance the unequal variance estimates are consulted. If the test is not significant (p > .05), then you accept the null hypothesis that there are no significant differences between the variances of the groups. In this case, you would consult the equal variance estimates. This explanation will make more sense when you consult the output of the independent groups t-test.

66    *SPSS: Analysis without Anguish*

Assumption 1 is a matter of research design while assumption 2 is tested in the independent groups analysis. Before proceeding you need to check the normality of the data. Because you have different participants in each condition, you need to check the normality of each set of scores separately. This is achieved through the **Explore** dialogue box using the **Factor List** option.

 **To screen for normality**

1    Select the **Analyze** menu.

2    Click on **Descriptive Statistics** and then **Explore...** to open the **Explore** dialogue box.

3    Select the dependent variable(s) (i.e. *without* and *withadd*) and click on the ▶ button to move the variables into the **Dependent List:** box.

4    Select the grouping variable (i.e. *cartype*) and click on the ▶ button to move this variable into the **Factor List:** box.

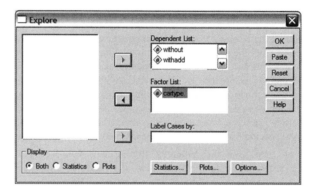

5    Click on **OK**.

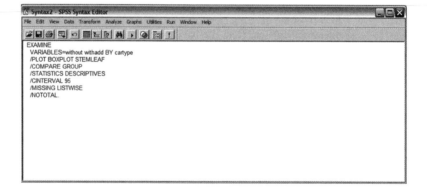

**Descriptives**

| | cartype | | | | Statistic | Std. Error |
|---|---|---|---|---|---|---|
| without | manual | Mean | | | 8.00 | .863 |
| | | 95% Confidence | Lower Bound | | 6.08 | |
| | | Interval for Mean | Upper Bound | | 9.92 | |
| | | 5% Trimmed Mean | | | 7.94 | |
| | | Median | | | 7.00 | |
| | | Variance | | | 8.200 | |
| | | Std. Deviation | | | 2.864 | |
| | | Minimum | | | 4 | |
| | | Maximum | | | 13 | |
| | | Range | | | 9 | |
| | | Interquartile Range | | | 5 | |
| | | Skewness | | | .656 | .661 |
| | | Kurtosis | | | -.704 | 1.279 |
| | automatic | Mean | | | 9.00 | 1.152 |
| | | 95% Confidence | Lower Bound | | 6.43 | |
| | | Interval for Mean | Upper Bound | | 11.57 | |
| | | 5% Trimmed Mean | | | 8.89 | |
| | | Median | | | 9.00 | |
| | | Variance | | | 14.600 | |
| | | Std. Deviation | | | 3.821 | |
| | | Minimum | | | 4 | |
| | | Maximum | | | 16 | |
| | | Range | | | 12 | |
| | | Interquartile Range | | | 6 | |
| | | Skewness | | | .355 | .661 |
| | | Kurtosis | | | -.253 | 1.279 |
| withadd | manual | Mean | | | 14.36 | .622 |
| | | 95% Confidence | Lower Bound | | 12.98 | |
| | | Interval for Mean | Upper Bound | | 15.75 | |
| | | 5% Trimmed Mean | | | 14.40 | |
| | | Median | | | 14.00 | |
| | | Variance | | | 4.255 | |
| | | Std. Deviation | | | 2.063 | |
| | | Minimum | | | 11 | |
| | | Maximum | | | 17 | |
| | | Range | | | 6 | |
| | | Interquartile Range | | | 4 | |
| | | Skewness | | | -.013 | .661 |
| | | Kurtosis | | | -1.012 | 1.279 |
| | automatic | Mean | | | 13.36 | 1.002 |
| | | 95% Confidence | Lower Bound | | 11.13 | |
| | | Interval for Mean | Upper Bound | | 15.60 | |
| | | 5% Trimmed Mean | | | 13.35 | |
| | | Median | | | 12.00 | |
| | | Variance | | | 11.055 | |
| | | Std. Deviation | | | 3.325 | |
| | | Minimum | | | 8 | |
| | | Maximum | | | 19 | |
| | | Range | | | 11 | |
| | | Interquartile Range | | | 5 | |
| | | Skewness | | | .169 | .661 |
| | | Kurtosis | | | -.749 | 1.279 |

In reviewing the descriptive statistics and the other output such as stem-and-leaf plots and boxplots (not shown), it is clear that there is minimal violation to the assumption of normality.

**To conduct an independent groups t-test**

**1**     Select the **Analyze** menu.

**2**     Click on **Compare Means** and then **Independent-Samples T Test...** to open the **Independent Samples T Test** dialogue box.

**3**     Select the test variable(s) (i.e. *without*) and then click on the ▶ button to move the variables into the **Test Variable(s):** box.

**4**     Select the grouping variable (i.e. *cartype*) and click on the ▶ button to move the variable into the **Grouping Variable:** box.

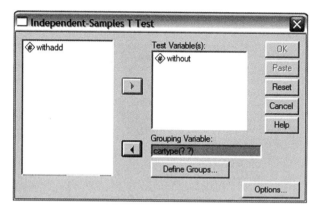

**5**     Click on the **Define Groups...** command pushbutton to open the **Define Groups** sub-dialogue box.

**6**     In the **Group 1:** box, type the lowest value for the variable (i.e. *1*), then tab. Enter the second value for the variable (i.e. *2*) in the **Group 2:** box.

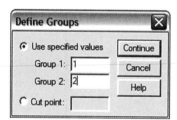

**7**     Click on **Continue** and then **OK**.

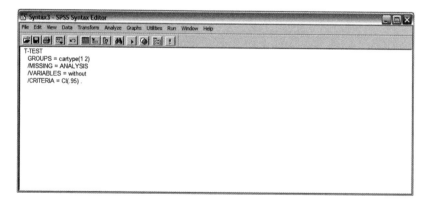

CHAPTER 6 • *T-tests* **69**

186    Managing Information with Technology

You will notice that the syntax for the independent groups t-test is different from that of the repeated measures t-test. In the case of the independent groups t-test, you have a grouping variable so you can distinguish between groups 1 and 2 when comparing engine efficiency.

**Group Statistics**

| | cartype | N | Mean | Std. Deviation | Std. Error Mean |
|---|---|---|---|---|---|
| without | manual | 11 | 8.00 | 2.864 | .863 |
| | automatic | 11 | 9.00 | 3.821 | 1.152 |

**Independent Samples Test**

| | | Levene's Test for Equality of Variances | | t-test for Equality of Means | | | | | | |
|---|---|---|---|---|---|---|---|---|---|---|
| | | | | | | | | | 95% Confidence Interval of the Difference | |
| | | F | Sig. | t | df | Sig. (2-tailed) | Mean Difference | Std. Error Difference | Lower | Upper |
| without | Equal variances assumed | .172 | .683 | -.695 | 20 | .495 | -1.000 | 1.440 | -4.003 | 2.003 |
| | Equal variances not assumed | | | -.695 | 18.539 | .496 | -1.000 | 1.440 | -4.018 | 2.018 |

Given that Levene's test has a probability greater than .05, you can assume that the population variances are relatively equal. Therefore, you can use the t-value, df and two-tail significance for the equal variance estimates to determine whether car type differences exist. The two-tail significance for *without* additive indicates that $p > .05$ and, therefore, is not significant. You therefore accept the null hypothesis and reject the alternative hypothesis. The two groups must come from the same population because no significant differences exist — $t$ (20) = .695, $p > .05$.

Although it is possible to perform two t-tests with the one command, for the sake of clarity two separate procedures are shown.

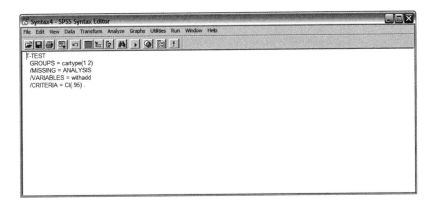

**Group Statistics**

| | cartype | N | Mean | Std. Deviation | Std. Error Mean |
|---|---|---|---|---|---|
| withadd | manual | 11 | 14.36 | 2.063 | .622 |
| | automatic | 11 | 13.36 | 3.325 | 1.002 |

| | Levene's Test for Equality of Variances | | t-test for Equality of Means | | | | | | |
| | F | Sig. | t | df | Sig. (2-tailed) | Mean Difference | Std. Error Difference | 95% Confidence Interval of the Difference | |
| | | | | | | | | Lower | Upper |
|---|---|---|---|---|---|---|---|---|---|
| withadd  Equal variances assumed | 3.390 | .080 | .848 | 20 | .407 | 1.000 | 1.180 | -1.461 | 3.461 |
| Equal variances not assumed | | | .848 | 16.704 | .409 | 1.000 | 1.180 | -1.492 | 3.492 |

In relation to *withadd*, Levene's test was not significant and so the equal variance estimates are interpreted. Consulting the t-value, df and two-tail significance, again no significant differences are apparent (p > .05). That is, there is no significant difference in engine efficiency between manual and automatic cars either with or without the additive — t (20) = .848, p > .05.

## Handy Hints

- Remember to meet assumptions before analysis. Scale of measurement and random sampling are a matter of research design. Normality, however, can be tested in various ways as outlined in chapter 3. For repeated measures designs, there is the additional assumption of normality of population difference scores. For independent groups t-tests there are the additional assumptions of independence of groups and homogeneity of variance.

- Conduct a one-sample t-test when you have data from a single population and are interested in determining whether the sample population mean is the same as the hypothesised mean. You are determining whether a single sample of scores was likely to have been drawn from the hypothesised population.

- Conduct a repeated measures t-test (also called a dependent sampled, paired t-test or within–subject) when considering data sourced from one group of participants, where each participant has two scores under different levels of the independent variable. You are considering whether two sets of random scores are from the same or different population. If you observe that they are from the same population, differences can be attributed to random sampling variability. Alternatively, if observed from the same population, differences are due to the independent variable or treatment effect.

- Conduct an independent groups t-test (also called a between-subjects design) when different participants have performed in each of the conditions.

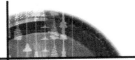

# Index